C:

Power User's Guide

C: Power User's Guide

Herbert Schildt

Osborne **McGraw-Hill**
Berkeley, California

Osborne **McGraw-Hill**
2600 Tenth Street
Berkeley, California 94710
U.S.A.

For information on translations and book distributors outside of the U.S.A., please write
to Osborne **McGraw-Hill** at the above address.

A complete list of trademarks appears on page 375.

C: Power User's Guide

1234567890 DODO 8987

ISBN 0-07-881307-7

Contents

Preface

If you want to create world-class programs written in C then this book is for you!

My name is Herb Schildt. I am a veteran programmer of numerous campaigns who has been programming in C for over ten years. Before I began writing this book I looked at a number of successful software products trying to determine what common feature or features they had that less successful programs did not. I wanted to know what it was that made one product so much more successful than another, similar one. After a while, a connecting thread appeared. The successful products were designed by someone who not only had a firm grasp of the specific application but also had *complete mastery of the entire computer environment*, including the operating system and the hardware itself. Only a programmer who has total control of these things can produce programs with snappy user interfaces that execute efficiently and offer users the greatest flexibility.

This book unlocks many of the secrets used by master programmers to achieve professional results. In it, you will explore the techniques and methods that make programs sizzle. After you have finished, you will be able to write programs that demand the attention they deserve. Among the topics covered are

- Direct video RAM accessing for lightning-fast screen displays

- Pop-up and pull-down menus

- Pop-up window routines

- Terminate and stay resident programs

- Mouse interfacing

- Graphics functions including object rotations

- Language interpreters

- File transfers via the serial port

This book is for any and every C programmer from novice to professional. Even if you are a beginner, you will be able to use the functions and programs in this book without having to understand all the subtle details of their operation. More advanced readers can use the routines as a basis for their own applications.

The code in this book conforms to the proposed ANSI standard except where some PC-specific functions are employed. Thus, all the routines should compile on any compiler that supports the ANSI standard. For development, I used both Turbo C and Microsoft C.

Some of the many useful and interesting functions and programs contained in this book are quite long. If you're like me, you would probably like to use them, but dread typing them into the computer and then searching for the inevitable typos that stop a program in its tracks. For this reason, I offer the source code for all the functions and programs contained in this book on diskette. The cost is $24.95. Just fill in the order form on the next page and mail it, along with your payment, to the address given. Or, if you're in a hurry, call my consulting office at (217) 586-4021 to place your order. (Visa and Mastercard are accepted.)

Please send me _____ copies, at $24.95 each, of the programs in *C: Power User's Guide*. Foreign orders, please add $5 shipping and handling.

Preferred disk size (check one): ☐ 5 1/4-inch ☐ 3 1/2-inch

Name _____

Address _____

City _____ State _____ ZIP _____

Telephone _____

Method of payment: check _____ Visa _____ MC _____

Credit card number: _____

Expiration date: _____

Signature: _____

Send to:

Herbert Schildt
RR 1, Box 130
Mahomet, Il 61853
or phone: (217) 586-4021

This is solely the offer of Herbert Schildt. Osborne/McGraw-Hill assumes no responsibility for fulfillment of this offer.

1: Pop-up and Pull-down Menus

One of the most obvious trademarks of a professionally written program is the use of pop-up or pull-down menus. When correctly implemented, these menus give programs the snappy feel that users have come to expect. Although conceptually simple, pop-up and pull-down menus present some substantial programming challenges.

Creating pop-up and pull-down menus requires direct control of the screen. Although the actual menu routines are quite portable, the routines to access the screen are intrinsically hardware- and operating system-dependent and must bypass C's normal console I/O functions. The video access routines developed here work with any computer that uses DOS and has an IBM compatible ROM-BIOS for its operating system. DOS-BIOS was chosen because it is the operating system in widest use, but you can generalize the basic concept to other systems.

Even if you are not interested in pop-up or pull-down menus at this time, you should still read the parts of this chapter that discuss video adapters; knowledge of many of the basic concepts is needed for understanding later chapters.

WHAT ARE POP-UP AND PULL-DOWN MENUS?

It is important to understand what pop-up and pull-down menus are and how they differ from standard menus. When a standard menu is used, the screen is either cleared or scrolled and the menu is presented. When a selection is made, the screen is again cleared or scrolled and the program continues. The selection is made using either the number or the first letter of each option.

When a pop-up or pull-down menu is activated, it overwrites what is currently on the screen. After the selection is made, the screen is restored to its previous state. You select an option from a pop-up and pull-down menu in one of two ways: (1) by pressing a *hot key*, which is a letter or number associated with one of the various menu options or (2) by using the arrow keys to move a highlight to the option you want and then pressing ENTER. Generally, the highlighted option is shown in reverse video.

The key difference between standard menus and pop-up or pull-down menus is that activating a standard menu stops the program. A pop-up or pull-down menu, on the other hand, appears to "suspend" the current activity of the program. From a user's point of view, a standard menu can cause a break in concentration, while pop-up or pull-down menus are simply slight interruptions; the user's concentration is not impaired.

The difference between pop-up and pull-down menus is simple. Only one pop-up menu may be on the screen at any one time. It is used when the menu is only one level deep, that is, when the selections in the menu have no subselections. On the other hand, several pull-down menus may be active simultaneously. They are used when a selection from one menu may require the use of another menu to determine certain options. For example, you might use pull-down menus if you are designing a program that orders fruit. If the user selects "apple," the next menu prompts for the color of the apple, and a third menu displays apples that meet the previously determined specifications.

You can think of a pop-up menu as simply a pull-down menu that doesn't have any submenus, but developing separate routines for these two types of menus has certain advantages because the pull-down menus require much more overhead in a program than the simple pop-up menu.

Although there are many ways to structure a menu on the screen, the functions developed in this chapter use the most common form. This method places each menu item on a new line with the first item at the top. This is the approach illustrated in Figure 1-1 for a simple mailing list menu.

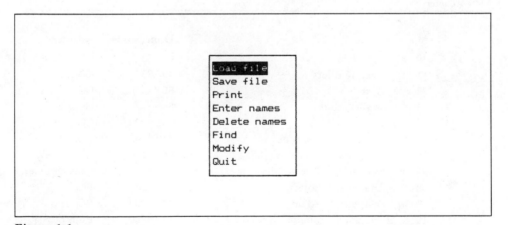

Figure 1-1.

A simple mailing list menu

UNDERSTANDING THE VIDEO ADAPTERS

Because the creation of pop-up and pull-down menus requires direct control of the screen, it is important to understand the video display adapters. The three most common types of adapters are the monochrome adapter, the color/graphics adapter (CGA), and the enhanced graphics adapter (EGA). The CGA and the EGA may have several modes of operation, including 40- or 80-column text or graphics operation. These modes are shown in Table 1-1. The menu routines developed in this chapter are designed to be used in 80-column text mode, which is by far the most common mode of operation for general-purpose applications. This means that the video mode of the system must be either 2, 3, or 7. No matter what mode is used, the upper left-hand corner is 0,0.

Table 1-1.

Screen Modes Available for Various
Video Adapters

Mode	Type	Dimensions	Adapters
0	text, b/w	40×25	CGA, EGA
1	text, 16 colors	40×25	CGA, EGA
2	text, b/w	80×25	CGA, EGA
3	text, 16 colors	80×25	CGA, EGA
4	graphics, 4 colors	320×200	CGA, EGA
5	graphics, 4 grey tones	320×200	CGA, EGA
6	graphics, b/w	640×200	CGA, EGA
7	text, b/w	80×25	monochrome
8	graphics, 16 colors	160×200	PCjr
9	graphics, 16 colors	320×200	PCjr
10	graphics, 4 colors PCjr, 16 colors EGA	640×200	PCjr, EGA
13	graphics, 16 colors	320×200	EGA
14	graphics, 16 colors	640×200	EGA
15	graphics, 4 colors	640×350	EGA

The characters displayed on the screen are held in some reserved RAM on the display adapters. The location of the monochrome memory is B0000000H and the CGA and EGA video RAM starts at B8000000H. (They are different in order to allow a separate graphics and text screen to be used—but this is seldom done in practice.) Although the CGA and EGA function differently in some modes, they are the same in modes 2 or 3.

Each character displayed on the screen requires two bytes of video memory. The first byte holds the actual character, the second holds its *screen attribute.* For color adapters the attribute byte is interpreted as shown in Table 1-2. If you have a CGA or EGA, the default mode is 3, and the characters are displayed with an attribute byte value of 7. This turns the three foreground colors on, producing white. To produce reverse video, the foreground bits are turned off and the three background bits are turned on, producing a value of 70H.

The monochrome adapter recognizes the blinking and intensity bits. Fortunately, it is designed to interpret an attribute of 7 as normal text (white on black) and 70H as reverse video. Also, a value of 1 produces underlined characters.

Each adapter actually has four times as much memory as it needs to display text in 80-column mode. There are two reasons for this. First,

Table 1-2.

The Video Attribute Byte

Bit	Binary Value	Meaning When Set
0	1	blue foreground
1	2	green foreground
2	4	red foreground
3	8	low intensity
4	16	blue background
5	32	green background
6	64	red background
7	128	blinking character

the extra memory is needed for graphics (except in the monochrome adapter, of course). The second is to allow multiple screens to be held in RAM and then simply switched in when needed. Each region of memory is called a *video page* and the effect of switching the active video page is quite dramatic. By default, page 0 is used when DOS initializes, and virtually all applications use page 0. For this reason it will be used in the routines in this chapter. However, you can use other pages if you desire.

There are three ways to access the video adapter. The first is through DOS calls, which is far too slow for pop-up or pull-down menus. The second is through ROM-BIOS routines, which is quicker and may be fast enough on faster machines, like the AT or PS/2 line, if the menus are small. The third way is by reading and writing the video RAM directly, which is very fast, but requires more work on your part. This chapter develops two separate sets of video routines. One uses the ROM-BIOS and the other accesses the video RAM directly.

ACCESSING THE SCREEN THROUGH BIOS

Because pop-up and pull-down menu functions must save what is on their portion of the screen and restore it after the selection has been made, you must have routines that save and load a portion of the screen. The method of saving and restoring a portion of the screen developed in this section relies on calls to two built-in ROM-BIOS functions that read and write characters on the screen.

As you may know, calls into the ROM-BIOS can be quite slow. However, they are (more or less) guaranteed to work on any computer that has an IBM-compatible ROM-BIOS even if the actual screen hardware is different. Later in this chapter, you will see how to access directly the video RAM of an IBM PC or 100%-compatible machine in order to increase performance. However, using direct video RAM accessing reduces portability to some extent because it requires the computer to be 100% hardware-compatible with the IBM PC standard. Therefore, the

ROM-BIOS menu routines should be used in applications that require the widest portability.

Using int86( )

Calls are made to the ROM-BIOS using software interrupts. The ROM-BIOS has several different interrupts for varying purposes. The one we will use to access the screen is interrupt 16 (10H), which is used to access the video display. (If you are not familiar with accessing the ROM-BIOS, you will find a good discussion of the subject in my book *C: The Complete Reference* [Berkeley: Osborne/McGraw-Hill, 1987].) Like many ROM-BIOS interrupts, interrupt 16 has several options that are selected based on the value of the AH register. If the function returns a value it is generally returned in AL. However, sometimes other registers are used if several values are returned. To access the ROM-BIOS interrupts, you will need to use a C function called **int86( )**. (Some compilers may call this function by a different name, but both Microsoft C and Turbo C call it **int86( )**. The following discussion applies specifically to these compilers, but you should be able to generalize.)

The **int86( )** function takes this general form:

```
int int86(num, inregs, outregs)
int num; /* the interrupt number */
union REGS *inregs; /* the input register values */
union REGS *outregs; /* the output register values */
```

The return value of **int86( )** is the value of the AX register. The type REGS is supplied in the header DOS.H. The type REGS shown here is defined by Turbo C*; however, it is similar to those defined by Microsoft C and other compilers.

---

*Copyright © 1987, Borland International, Inc. Printed with permission from the header file of DOS.H in the Turbo C compiler. All rights reserved.

```
struct WORDREGS
       {
       unsigned int     ax, bx, cx, dx, si, di, cflag;
       };

struct BYTEREGS
       {
       unsigned char    al, ah, bl, bh, cl, ch, dl, dh;
       };

union  REGS    {
       struct  WORDREGS x;
       struct  BYTEREGS h;
       };
```

As you can see, **REGS** is a union of two structures. Using the
WORDREGS structure allows you to access the registers of the CPU as
16-bit quantities. **BYTEREGS** gives you access to the individual 8-bit
registers. For example, to access interrupt number 16, function number
5, you would use this code sequence.

```
union REGS in, out;

in.h.ah = 5;
int86(16, &in, &out);
```

Saving a Portion of the Screen

To save what is on the screen, the current value at each screen location
must be read and stored. To read a character from a specific screen
location, use interrupt 16, function number 8, which returns the character and its associated attribute that is at the current position of the
cursor. Therefore, to read characters from a specific portion of the
screen you must have a way of positioning the cursor. Although some C
compilers supply such a function, many do not. Therefore, the one
shown here, called **goto_xy( )**, can be used. It uses the interrupt 16,
function 2 with the column coordinate in DL and the row coordinate in
DH. The video page is specified in BH (using the default page 0).

```
/* send the cursor to x,y */
void goto_xy(x,y)
int x,y;
{
  union REGS r;

  r.h.ah=2; /* cursor addressing function */
  r.h.dl=y; /* column coordinate */
  r.h.dh=x; /* row coordinate */
  r.h.bh=0; /* video page */
  int86(0x10, &r, &r);
}
```

Interrupt 16, function 8 returns the character at the current cursor position in AL and its attribute in AH. The function **save_video( )**, shown here, reads a portion of the screen, saves the information into a buffer, and clears that portion of the screen.

```
/* save a portion of the screen */
void save_video(startx, endx, starty, endy, buf_ptr)
int startx, endx, starty, endy;
unsigned int *buf_ptr; /* buffer where screen will be stored */
{
  union REGS r;
  register int i,j;
  for(i=starty; i<endy; i++)
    for(j=startx; j<endx; j++) {
      goto_xy(j, i);
      r.h.ah = 8; /* read character function */
      r.h.bh = 0; /* assume active display page is 0 */
      *buf_ptr++ = int86(0x10, &r, &r);
      putchar(' '); /* clear the screen */
    }
}
```

The first four parameters of **save_video** specify that the X,Y coordinates of the upper-left and lower-right corners of the region be saved. The parameter **buf_ptr** is an integer pointer to the region of memory that will hold the information. It must be large enough to hold the amount of information being read from the screen.

The programs in this chapter allocate the buffer dynamically, but you could use some other scheme if it makes more sense for your own specific application. Remember, however, that the buffer must remain in existence until the screen is restored to its previous condition. The function also clears the specified region by writing spaces to each location.

Restoring the Screen

Restoring the screen once the menu selection has been made is simply a matter of writing the previously stored information back into the video RAM. To do this, use interrupt 16, function 9, which requires the character to be in AL, its attribute in BL, the video page in BH, and the number of times to write the character in CX (1, in this case). The function shown here, **restore__video( )**, puts the information in the buffer pointed to by **buf__ptr** on the screen, given the beginning and ending X,Y coordinates.

```
/* restore a portion of the screen */
void restore_video(startx, endx, starty, endy, buf_ptr)
int startx, endx, starty, endy;
unsigned char *buf_ptr; /* buffer containing screen info */
{
  union REGS r;
  register int i,j;

  for(i=starty; i<endy; i++)
    for(j=startx; j<endx; j++) {
      goto_xy(j, i);
      r.h.ah = 9; /* write character function */
      r.h.bh = 0; /* assume active display page is 0 */
      r.x.cx = 1; /* number of times to write the character */
      r.h.al = *buf_ptr++; /* character */
      r.h.bl = *buf_ptr++; /* attribute */
      int86(0x10, &r, &r);
    }
}
```

CREATING POP-UP MENUS

Several pieces of information must be passed to a function that creates a pop-up menu. The first is a list of the menu options. Since the menu entries are strings to be displayed, the easiest way to pass a list of strings to a function is to put the strings in a two-dimensional array and pass a pointer to that array. As stated earlier, a menu item may be selected by either moving the highlight to the desired entry and pressing ENTER or by pressing the key indicated for that entry. For the function to know which keys are "hot" and what they mean, the names of these keys must be passed to it. The best way to do this is to pass a string that contains the hot key characters in the same order as the menu strings.

The **pop-up**( ) function must also know how many items are in the menu, so this number must be passed to it. The **pop-up**( ) function also needs to know where to put the menu, so the X,Y coordinates are needed. Finally, it may be desirable to place a border around the menu in some situations but not in others. Therefore, a border on/off value has to be passed. To begin development of the **popup**( ) function, we need this declaration:

```
/* display a pop-up menu and return selection */
int popup(menu, keys, count, x, y, border)
char *menu[];     /* menu text */
char *keys;       /* hot keys */
int count;        /* number of menu items */
int x, y;         /* X,Y coordinates of left hand corner */
int border;       /* no border if 0 */
```

The **popup**( ) function must do the following:

- Save the part of the screen used by the menu

- Display the border if requested

- Display the menu

- Input the user's response

- Restore the screen to its original condition

Two of these goals are accomplished by the **save_video**( ) and **restore_video**( ) functions discussed in the previous section. Let's see how to achieve the other three now.

Displaying the Menu

The key to displaying the menu is to keep in mind that **popup**( ) is passed a pointer to an array of string pointers. To display the individual strings, you simply index the pointer like an array. Each entry in the array is a pointer to the corresponding menu entry. The following function, called **display__menu**( ), displays each menu item using this method.

```
/* display the menu in its proper location */
void display_menu(menu, x, y, count)
char *menu[];
int x, y, count;
{
  register int i;

  for(i=0; i<count; i++, x++) {
    goto_xy(x, y);
    printf(menu[i]);
  }
}
```

As you can see, it is passed a pointer to the array of strings to be displayed, the X,Y coordinates at which to begin displaying them, and the number of entries in the menu.

By far the easiest way to create the two-dimensional array that holds the menu selection strings is to create variables using this general form:

```
char *<menu-name>[ ] = {
"first selection",
"second selection",
.
.
.
"Nth selection"
}
```

This declaration automatically causes the C compiler to place the strings in its runtime string table. The variable then points to the first character of the first string in the table. For example, this declaration creates a variable called **fruit** that points to the "A" in "Apple."

```
char *fruit[]= {
  "Apple",
  "Orange",
  "Pear",
  "Grape",
  "Raspberry",
  "Strawberry"
};
```

Displaying the Border

If a border is requested, this routine can be used to put a border around a menu given the coordinates of the upper-left and lower-right corners. It uses the line characters that are part of the standard character set on a PC or compatible. You may substitute others if you like.

```
void draw_border(startx, starty, endx, endy)
int startx, starty, endx, endy;
{
  register int i;

  for(i=startx+1; i<endx; i++) {
    goto_xy(i, starty);
    putchar(179);
    goto_xy(i, endy);
    putchar(179);
  }

  for(i=starty+1; i<endy; i++) {
    goto_xy(startx, i);
    putchar(196);
    goto_xy(endx, i);
    putchar(196);
  }
  goto_xy(startx, starty); putchar(218);
  goto_xy(startx, endy); putchar(191);
  goto_xy(endx, starty); putchar(192);
  goto_xy(endx, endy); putchar(217);

}
```

Inputting the User's Response

As stated, the user may enter a response in one of two ways. First, the UP ARROW and DOWN ARROW keys can be used to move the highlight to the desired item and then ENTER is pressed to actually select it. (The highlighted item in the menus in this book are displayed in reverse video — a common practice.) The SPACE BAR may also be used to move the highlight. The second way an item can be selected is by pressing the hot key associated with it. The function **get—resp( )**, shown here, accomplishes these goals.

```
/* input user's selection */
get_resp(x, y, count, menu, keys)
int x, y, count;
char *menu[];
char *keys;
{
  union inkey {
    char ch[2];
    int i;
  } c;
  int arrow_choice=0, key_choice;

  y++;

  /* highlight the first selection */
  goto_xy(x, y);
  write_video(x, y, menu[0], REV_VID); /* reverse video */

  for(;;) {
    while(!bioskey(1)) ; /* wait for key stroke */
    c.i = bioskey(0);    /* read the key */

    /* reset the selection to normal video */
    goto_xy(x+arrow_choice, y);
    write_video(x+arrow_choice, y,
      menu[arrow_choice], NORM_VID); /* redisplay */

    if(c.ch[0]) { /* is normal key */
      /* see if it is a hot key */
      key_choice = is_in(keys, tolower(c.ch[0]));
      if(key_choice) return key_choice-1;
      /* check for ENTER or space bar */
      switch(c.ch[0]) {
        case '\r': return arrow_choice;
        case ' ' : arrow_choice++;
          break;
        case ESC : return -1; /* cancel */
      }
    }
```

```
else {   /* is special key */
  switch(c.ch[1]) {
    case 72: arrow_choice--; /* up arrow */
      break;
    case 80: arrow_choice++; /* down arrow */
      break;
  }
}
if(arrow_choice==count) arrow_choice=0;
if(arrow_choice<0) arrow_choice=count-1;
    /* highlight the next selection */
    goto_xy(x+arrow_choice, y);
    write_video(x+arrow_choice, y, menu[arrow_choice], REV_VID);
  }
}
```

When **get_resp( )** begins execution, the first menu item is highlighted.
The macro **REV_VID** is defined elsewhere as 70H and **NORM_VID** as 7. The ESCAPE key is used to abort from a menu. The value of
ESC is 27. Then the routine enters the loop that waits for the user's
response. It uses **bioskey( )** first to wait until a key is pressed, and then
to read the key. The **bioskey( )** function is specific to Turbo C. If you
have a different C compiler, you can use the following version of the
function.

```
/* emulate part of the Turbo C bioskey() function */
bioskey(c)
int c;
{
  switch(c) {
    case 0: return get_key();
    case 1: return kbhit();
  }
}

/* read the 16-bit scan code of a key */
get_key()
{
  union REGS r;

  r.h.ah = 0;
  return int86(0x16, &r, &r);
}
```

The reason you must use **bioskey( )** instead of **getchar( )**, for example, is
that the routine must be able to read the full 16-bit scan code generated
by striking a key. If the key pressed is a character key, the character is

returned in the low-order eight bits and the high-order eight bits are 0. However, if a special key is pressed, such as an arrow key, the low-order byte is 0 and the high-order byte contains that key's position code. The position codes for the UP ARROW and DOWN ARROW keys are 72 and 80. Functions like **getchar( )** only return the character code, so it is necessary to bypass them and read the scan code directly.

Each time an arrow key is pressed, the item that is currently highlighted is redisplayed in normal video and the next one is highlighted. Pressing the DOWN ARROW key when the highlight is already at the bottom of the screen causes it to wrap around to the first item. The same thing applies in reverse when the UP ARROW key is pressed when the first item is already highlighted.

The function **write__video** is used by **get__resp( )** to write a string to the video display at the specified X,Y position using the specified attribute. **Write__video( )**, shown here, is used to display a menu entry in reverse video when highlighted or to return it to normal video when not highlighted.

```
/* display a string with specified attribute */
void write_video(x, y, p, attrib)
int x, y;
char *p;
int attrib;
{
  union REGS r;
  register int i,j;

  for(i=y; *p; i++) {
      goto_xy(x, i);
      r.h.ah = 9; /* write character function */
      r.h.bh = 0; /* assume active display page is 0 */
      r.x.cx = 1; /* number of times to write the character */
      r.h.al = *p++; /* character */
      r.h.bl = attrib; /* attribute */
      int86(0x10, &r, &r);
  }
}
```

The function **is__in( )** returns the position of the hot key in the string. If the user pressed a non-hot key, **is__in( )** returns 0.

```
is_in(s, c)
char *s, c;
{
  register int i;

  for(i=0; *s; i++) if(*s++==c) return i+1;
  return 0;
}
```

The popup ( ) Function

Now that all the pieces have been created, the **popup**( ) function can be
assembled as shown here.

```
/* display a pop-up menu and return selection
   returns -2 if menu cannot be constructed
   returns -1 if user hits escape key
   otherwise the item number is returned starting
   with 0 as the first (top most) entry
*/
int popup(menu, keys, count, x, y, border)
char *menu[];    /* menu text */
char *keys;      /* hot keys */
int count;       /* number of menu items */
int x, y;        /* X,Y coordinates of left hand corner */
int border;      /* no border if 0 */
{
  register int i, len;
  int endx, endy, choice;
  unsigned int *p;

  if((x>24) || (x<0) || (y>79) || (y<0)) {
    printf("range error");
    return -2;
  }

  /* compute the dimensions */
  len = 0;
  for(i=0; i<count; i++)
   if(strlen(menu[i]) > len) len = strlen(menu[i]);
  endy = len + 2 + y;
  endx = count + 1 + x;
  if((endx+1>24) || (endy+1>79)) {
    printf("menu won't fit");
    return -2;
  }

  /* allocate enough memory for video buffer*/
  p = (unsigned int *) malloc((endx-x+1) * (endy-y+1));
  if(!p) exit(1);  /* install your own error handler here */
```

```
    /* save the current screen data */
    save_video(x, endx+1, y, endy+1, p);

    if(border) draw_border(x, y, endx, endy);

    /* display the menu */
    display_menu(menu, x+1, y+1, count);

    /* get the user's response */
    choice = get_resp(x+1, y, count, menu, keys);

    /* restore the original screen */
    restore_video(x, endx+1, y, endy+1, (char *) p);
    free(p);
    return choice;
}
```

As you can see, **popup( )** checks for an out-of-range location and for an
oversized menu. It returns −2 if one of these situations exists. Because
get_resp( ) returns a −1 when the user presses the ESCAPE key, a
return value of −1 by **popup( )** should be considered as a "cancel menu"
request. If the user makes a selection, the return value will be in the
range 0 through **count** −1 with the first menu entry corresponding to 0.
As written, **popup( )** uses C's dynamic allocation routines to provide
temporary storage for the screen information. This is usually the best
approach but feel free to change it if it makes sense for your specific
application.

Putting It All Together

The sample program shown here uses all the routines developed to
display three pop-up menus. The only function you haven't seen is called
cls( ), which clears the screen. Some C compilers do not include a
function to do this, so if your compiler doesn't you can use the one shown
in the program.

```
/* Pop-up menu routines for text mode operation. */

#include "stdio.h"
#include "dos.h"
#include "stdlib.h"
```

```
#define BORDER 1
#define ESC 27
#define REV_VID 0x70
#define NORM_VID 7

void save_video(), restore_video();
void goto_xy(), cls(), write_video();
void display_menu(), draw_border();

char *fruit[]= {
  "Apple",
  "Orange",
  "Pear",
  "Grape",
  "Raspberry",
  "Strawberry"
};

char *color[]= {
  "Red",
  "Yellow",
  "Orange",
  "Green",
};

char *apple_type[]= {
  "Red delicious",
  "Jonathan",
  "Winesap",
  "Rome"
};

main()
{
  int i;

  cls();
  goto_xy(0,0);
  for(i=0; i<25; i++)
    printf("This is a test of the pop-up window routines.\n");
  popup(fruit, "aopgrs", 6, 1, 3, BORDER);
  popup(color, "ryog", 4, 5, 10, BORDER);
  popup(apple_type, "rjwr", 4, 10, 18, BORDER);
}

/* display a pop-up menu and return selection
   returns -2 if menu cannot be constructed
   returns -1 if user hits escape key
   otherwise the item number is returned starting
   with 0 as the first (top most) entry
*/
int popup(menu, keys, count, x, y, border)
char *menu[];    /* menu text */
char *keys;      /* hot keys */
int count;       /* number of menu items */
int x, y;        /* X,Y coordinates of left hand corner */
int border;      /* no border if 0 */
{
```

```
register int i, len;
int endx, endy, choice;
unsigned int *p;

if((x>24) || (x<0) || (y>79) || (y<0)) {
  printf("range error");
  return -2;
}

/* compute the dimensions */
len = 0;
for(i=0; i<count; i++)
 if(strlen(menu[i]) > len) len = strlen(menu[i]);
endy = len + 2 + y;
endx = count + 1 + x;
if((endx+1>24) || (endy+1>79)) {
  printf("menu won't fit");
  return -2;
}

/* allocate enough memory for it */
p = (unsigned int *) malloc((endx-x+1) * (endy-y+1));
if(!p) exit(1);  /* install your own error handler here */

/* save the current screen data */
save_video(x, endx+1, y, endy+1, p);

if(border) draw_border(x, y, endx, endy);

/* display the menu */
display_menu(menu, x+1, y+1, count);

/* get the user's response */
choice = get_resp(x+1, y, count, menu, keys);

/* restore the original screen */
restore_video(x, endx+1, y, endy+1, (char *) p);
free(p);
return choice;
}


/* display the menu in its proper location */
void display_menu(menu, x, y, count)
char *menu[];
int x, y, count;
{
  register int i;

  for(i=0; i<count; i++, x++) {
    goto_xy(x, y);
    printf(menu[i]);
  }
}

void draw_border(startx, starty, endx, endy)
int startx, starty, endx, endy;
{
  register int i;
```

```c
       for(i=startx+1; i<endx; i++) {
          goto_xy(i, starty);
          putchar(179);
          goto_xy(i, endy);
          putchar(179);
       }

       for(i=starty+1; i<endy; i++) {
          goto_xy(startx, i);
          putchar(196);
          goto_xy(endx, i);
          putchar(196);
       }
       goto_xy(startx, starty); putchar(218);
       goto_xy(startx, endy); putchar(191);
       goto_xy(endx, starty); putchar(192);
       goto_xy(endx, endy); putchar(217);

}

/* input user's selection */
get_resp(x, y, count, menu, keys)
int x, y, count;
char *menu[];
char *keys;
{
   union inkey {
      char ch[2];
      int i;
   } c;
   int arrow_choice=0, key_choice;

   y++;

   /* highlight the first selection */
   goto_xy(x, y);
   write_video(x, y, menu[0], REV_VID); /* reverse video */

   for(;;) {
      while(!bioskey(1)) ; /* wait for key stroke */
      c.i = bioskey(0);     /* read the key */

      /* reset the selection to normal video */
      goto_xy(x+arrow_choice, y);
      write_video(x+arrow_choice, y,
        menu[arrow_choice], NORM_VID); /* redisplay */

      if(c.ch[0]) { /* is normal key */
        /* see if it is a hot key */
        key_choice = is_in(keys, tolower(c.ch[0]));
        if(key_choice) return key_choice-1;
        /* check for ENTER or space bar */
        switch(c.ch[0]) {
          case '\r': return arrow_choice;
          case ' ' : arrow_choice++;
             break;
          case ESC : return -1; /* cancel */
        }
      }
```

```
      else {   /* is special key */
        switch(c.ch[1]) {
          case 72: arrow_choice--; /* up arrow */
            break;
          case 80: arrow_choice++; /* down arrow */
            break;
        }
      }
      if(arrow_choice==count) arrow_choice=0;
      if(arrow_choice<0) arrow_choice=count-1;

      /* highlight the next selection */
      goto_xy(x+arrow_choice, y);
      write_video(x+arrow_choice, y, menu[arrow_choice], REV_VID);
    }
}

/* display a string with specified attribute */
void write_video(x, y, p, attrib)
int x, y;
char *p;
int attrib;
{
  union REGS r;
  register int i,j;

  for(i=y; *p; i++) {
      goto_xy(x, i);
      r.h.ah = 9; /* write character function */
      r.h.bh = 0; /* assume active display page is 0 */
      r.x.cx = 1; /* number of times to write the character */
      r.h.al = *p++; /* character */
      r.h.bl = attrib; /* attribute */
      int86(0x10, &r, &r);
  }
}


/* save a portion of the screen */
void save_video(startx, endx, starty, endy, buf_ptr)
int startx, endx, starty, endy;
unsigned int *buf_ptr;
{
  union REGS r;
  register int i,j;
  for(i=starty; i<endy; i++)
    for(j=startx; j<endx; j++) {
      goto_xy(j, i);
      r.h.ah = 8; /* read character function */
      r.h.bh = 0; /* assume active display page is 0 */
      *buf_ptr++ = int86(0x10, &r, &r);
      putchar(' '); /* clear the screen */
    }
}

/* restore a portion of the screen */
void restore_video(startx, endx, starty, endy, buf_ptr)
int startx, endx, starty, endy;
unsigned char *buf_ptr;
{
```

```
    union REGS r;
    register int i,j;

    for(i=starty; i<endy; i++)
      for(j=startx; j<endx; j++) {
        goto_xy(j, i);
        r.h.ah = 9; /* write character function */
        r.h.bh = 0; /* assume active display page is 0 */
        r.x.cx = 1; /* number of times to write the character */
        r.h.al = *buf_ptr++; /* character */
        r.h.bl = *buf_ptr++; /* attribute */
        int86(0x10, &r, &r);
      }
}


/* clear the screen */
void cls()
{
  union REGS r;

  r.h.ah=6; /* screen scroll code */
  r.h.al=0; /* clear screen code */
  r.h.ch=0; /* start row */
  r.h.cl=0; /* start column */
  r.h.dh=24; /* end row */
  r.h.dl=79; /* end column */
  r.h.bh=7;  /* blank line is blank */
  int86(0x10, &r, &r);
}

/* send the cursor to x,y */
void goto_xy(x,y)
int x,y;
{
  union REGS r;

  r.h.ah=2; /* cursor addressing function */
  r.h.dl=y; /* column coordinate */
  r.h.dh=x; /* row coordinate */
  r.h.bh=0; /* video page */
  int86(0x10, &r, &r);
}

is_in(s, c)
char *s, c;
{
  register int i;

  for(i=0; *s; i++) if(*s++==c) return i+1;
  return 0;
}
```

You should enter this program into your computer and try it. As it
runs, each menu is displayed in turn. (In this program the responses are
discarded, but a real application would, of course, process them.) A
series of the screens produced is shown in Figure 1-2. Unless you have a

```
This is a test of the pop-up menu routines.
Thi┌───────────┐f the pop-up menu routines.
Thi│Apple      │f the pop-up menu routines.
Thi│Orange     │f the pop-up menu routines.
Thi│Pear       │f the pop-up menu routines.
Thi│Grape      │f the pop-up menu routines.
Thi│Raspberry  │f the pop-up menu routines.
Thi│Strawberry │f the pop-up menu routines.
Thi└───────────┘f the pop-up menu routines.
This is a test of the pop-up menu routines.
This is a test of the pop-up menu routines.
This is a test of the pop-up menu routines.
This is a test of the pop-up menu routines.
This is a test of the pop-up menu routines.
This is a test of the pop-up menu routines.
This is a test of the pop-up menu routines.
This is a test of the pop-up menu routines.
This is a test of the pop-up menu routines.
This is a test of the pop-up menu routines.
This is a test of the pop-up menu routines.
This is a test of the pop-up menu routines.
This is a test of the pop-up menu routines.
This is a test of the pop-up menu routines.
```

Figure 1-2. (a)

Sample output of the pop-up menu
program

very fast computer, you will probably notice that the pop-up action is somewhat sluggish. The only way to solve this problem is to read and write characters directly to and from the video RAM, which is the subject of the next section. Again, the only important advantage of using the ROM-BIOS approach is that the pop-up menu routines work on any computer that supports BIOS-level compatibility with the IBM BIOS even if the computer is not 100% hardware-compatible.

```
This is a test of the pop-up menu routines.
This is a test of the pop-up menu routines.
This is a test of the pop-up menu routines.
This is a test of the pop-up menu routines.
This is a test of the pop-up menu routines.
This is a         he pop-up menu routines.
This is a  Red    he pop-up menu routines.
This is a  Yellow he pop-up menu routines.
This is a  Orange he pop-up menu routines.
This is a  Green  he pop-up menu routines.
This is a         he pop-up menu routines.
This is a test of the pop-up menu routines.
This is a test of the pop-up menu routines.
This is a test of the pop-up menu routines.
This is a test of the pop-up menu routines.
This is a test of the pop-up menu routines.
This is a test of the pop-up menu routines.
This is a test of the pop-up menu routines.
This is a test of the pop-up menu routines.
This is a test of the pop-up menu routines.
This is a test of the pop-up menu routines.
This is a test of the pop-up menu routines.
This is a test of the pop-up menu routines.
```

Figure 1-2. (b)

Sample output of the pop-up menu
program

ACCESSING THE VIDEO RAM DIRECTLY

To create menus that really "pop" up, you must bypass the ROM-BIOS
function calls and directly access the video RAM. Doing this allows
characters to be displayed on the screen blindingly fast. By directly
reading and writing from and to the video RAM, you can turn the rather
sluggish pop-up menus into real speedsters!

```
This is a test of the pop-up menu routines.
This is a test of the pop-up menu routines.
This is a test of the pop-up menu routines.
This is a test of the pop-up menu routines.
This is a test of the pop-up menu routines.
This is a test of the pop-up menu routines.
This is a test of the pop-up menu routines.
This is a test of the pop-up menu routines.
This is a test of the pop-up menu routines.
This is a test of the pop-up menu routines.
This is a test of           ┌─────────────┐ routines.
This is a test of           │Red delicious│ routines.
This is a test of           │Jonathan     │ routines.
This is a test of           │Winesap      │ routines.
This is a test of           │Rome         │ routines.
This is a test of           └─────────────┘ routines.
This is a test of the pop-up menu routines.
This is a test of the pop-up menu routines.
This is a test of the pop-up menu routines.
This is a test of the pop-up menu routines.
This is a test of the pop-up menu routines.
This is a test of the pop-up menu routines.
This is a test of the pop-up menu routines.
```

Figure 1-2. (c)

Sample output of the pop-up menu
program

Reading and writing the video RAM requires the use of FAR
pointers. If your C compiler does not support FAR pointers, you cannot
directly access the video RAM. FAR pointers can be supported in one of
two ways by a C compiler. First, the common **far** keyword extension is
used by a great many compilers. It allows a pointer to be declared as
FAR. The other way is to use a large memory model compiler in which
all pointers are FAR by default. The routines used in this chapter use the
far type modifier. If you desire, you can remove it and simply compile the
code using a large memory model compiler.

Determining the Location
of the Video RAM

The monochrome adapter has its video RAM at B0000000H while the others are located at B8000000H. For the menu routines to operate correctly for each adapter, they need to know which adapter is in the system. Fortunately, there is an easy way to do this. The ROM-BIOS interrupt 16, function 15 returns the current video mode. As mentioned earlier, the routines developed in this chapter require that the mode be either 2, 3, or 7. The CGA and EGA adapters can use modes 2 and 3 but not mode 7; only the monochrome adapter can use this mode. Therefore, if the current video mode is 7, a monochrome adapter is in use; otherwise, it is either a CGA or EGA. For our purposes, the CGA and the EGA function the same in text mode so it doesn't matter which is in the system. Therefore, the **popup( )** function must see which adapter is in the system and set a global pointer variable to the proper address. This fragment of code accomplishes just that.

```
vmode = video_mode();
if((vmode!=2) && (vmode!=3) && (vmode!=7)) {
  printf("video must be in 80 column text mode");
  exit(1);
}
/* set proper address of video RAM */
if(vmode==7) vid_mem = (char far *) 0xB0000000;
else vid_mem = (char far *) 0xB8000000;
```

The function **video_mode( )** returns the current video mode, and the variable **vid_mem** is declared as a global **char far** elsewhere.

Converting save_video( ) and restore_video( )

Once the variable **vid_mem** has been given the proper address, it is a simple matter to use it to read or write characters to or from the video RAM. Remember, the video memory requires two bytes for each character, one for the character itself and one for its attribute. Because the character byte is first and the attribute is second, it takes 160 bytes for each line on the screen. Hence, to find the address of a specific character position, you must use this formula:

address $=$ address of adapter $+$ X$*$160 $+$ Y$*$2

The functions **save_video( )** and **restore_video( )** look like the one shown here when direct video RAM accessing is used.

```
/* save a portion of the screen using direct
   video RAM accessing
*/
void save_video(startx, endx, starty, endy, buf_ptr)
int startx, endx, starty, endy;
unsigned char *buf_ptr;
{
  register int i,j;
  char far *v, far *t;

  v = vid_mem;
  for(i=starty; i<endy; i++)
    for(j=startx; j<endx; j++) {
      t = v + (j*160) + i*2; /* compute the address */
      *buf_ptr++ = *t++; /* read the character */
      *buf_ptr++ = *t;   /* read the attribute */
      *(t-1) = ' ';  /* clear the window */
    }
}


/* restore a portion of the screen using direct
   video RAM accessing
*/
void restore_video(startx, endx, starty, endy, buf_ptr)
int startx, endx, starty, endy;
unsigned char *buf_ptr;
{
  register int i,j;
  char far *v, far *t;

  v = vid_mem;
  t = v;
  for(i=starty; i<endy; i++)
    for(j=startx; j<endx; j++) {
      v = t;
      v += (j*160) + i*2; /* compute the address */
      *v++ = *buf_ptr++;  /* write the character */
      *v = *buf_ptr++;    /* write the attribute */
    }
}
```

As you can see, the characters and attributes to be written or read are accessed through the use of pointers to the video memory. The other functions that read and write characters are converted in the same way.

One new function (shown here) is required if all accesses to the video display are to be done directly. Called **write_char**( ), it writes one character to the specified screen location with the specified attribute.

```c
/* write character with specified attribute */
void write_char(x, y, ch, attrib)
int x, y;
char ch;
int attrib;
{
  register int i;
  char far *v;

  v = vid_mem;
  v += (x*160) + y*2; /* compute the address */
  *v++ = ch;  /* write the character */
  *v = attrib;    /* write the attribute */
}
```

The complete direct memory access version of the pop-up menu functions are shown here along with the same sample test program. You should enter it into your computer and compare its performance to that of the ROM-BIOS version. As you will see, the difference is quite dramatic. The menus seem to appear and disappear instantaneously.

```c
/* Pop-up menu routines for text mode operation
   using direct video RAM reads and writes. */

#include "stdio.h"
#include "dos.h"
#include "stdlib.h"

#define BORDER 1
#define ESC 27
#define REV_VID 0x70
#define NORM_VID 7

void save_video(), restore_video();
void goto_xy(), cls(), write_string(), write_char();
void display_menu(), draw_border();
char far *vid_mem;
```

```c
char *fruit[]= {
  "Apple",
  "Orange",
  "Pear",
  "Grape",
  "Raspberry",
  "Strawberry"
};

char *color[]= {
  "Red",
  "Yellow",
  "Orange",
  "Green",
};

char *apple_type[]= {
  "Red delicious",
  "Jonathan",
  "Winesap",
  "Rome"
};

main()
{
  int i;

  cls();
  goto_xy(0,0);
  for(i=0; i<25; i++)
    printf("This is a test of the pop-up window routines.\n");

  popup(fruit, "aopgrs", 6, 1, 3, BORDER);
  popup(color, "ryog", 4, 5, 10, BORDER);
  popup(apple_type, "rjwr", 4, 10, 18, BORDER);
}

/* display a pop-up menu and return selection
   returns -2 if menu cannot be constructed
   returns -1 if user hits escape key
   otherwise the item number is returned starting
   with 0 as the first (top most) entry
*/
int popup(menu, keys, count, x, y, border)
char *menu[];    /* menu text */
char *keys;      /* hot keys */
int count;       /* number of menu items */
int x, y;        /* X,Y coordinates of left hand corner */
int border;      /* no border if 0 */
{
  register int i, len;
  int endx, endy, choice, vmode;
  unsigned char *p;

  if((x>24) || (x<0) || (y>79) || (y<0)) {
    printf("range error");
    return -2;
  }
```

```
    vmode = video_mode();
    if((vmode!=2) && (vmode!=3) && (vmode!=7)) {
      printf("video must be in 80 column text mode");
      exit(1);
    }
    /* set proper address of video RAM */
    if(vmode==7) vid_mem = (char far *) 0xB0000000;
    else vid_mem = (char far *) 0xB8000000;

    /* compute the dimensions */
    len = 0;
    for(i=0; i<count; i++)
      if(strlen(menu[i]) > len) len = strlen(menu[i]);
    endy = len + 2 + y;
    endx = count + 1 + x;
    if((endx+1>24) || (endy+1>79)) {
      printf("menu won't fit");
      return -2;
    }

    /* allocate enough memory to hold video buffer*/
    p = (unsigned char *) malloc(2 * (endx-x+1) * (endy-y+1));
    if(!p) exit(1); /* put your own error handler here */

    /* save the current screen data */
    save_video(x, endx+1, y, endy+1, p);

    if(border) draw_border(x, y, endx, endy);

    /* display the menu */
    display_menu(menu, x+1, y+1, count);

    /* get the user's response */
    choice = get_resp(x+1, y, count, menu, keys);

    /* restore the original screen */
    restore_video(x, endx+1, y, endy+1,  p);
    free(p);
    return choice;
}


/* display the menu in its proper location */
void display_menu(menu, x, y, count)
char *menu[];
int x, y, count;
{
  register int i;

  for(i=0; i<count; i++, x++)
    write_string(x, y, menu[i], NORM_VID);
}

void draw_border(startx, starty, endx, endy)
int startx, starty, endx, endy;
{
  register int i;
  char far *v, far *t;
```

```
        v = vid_mem;
        t = v;
        for(i=startx+1; i<endx; i++) {
            v += (i*160) + starty*2;
            *v++ = 179;
            *v = NORM_VID;
            v = t;
            v += (i*160) + endy*2;
            *v++ = 179;
            *v = NORM_VID;
            v = t;
        }
        for(i=starty+1; i<endy; i++) {
            v += (startx*160) + i*2;
            *v++ = 196;
            *v = NORM_VID;
            v = t;
            v += (endx*160) + i*2;
            *v++ = 196;
            *v = NORM_VID;
            v = t;
        }
        write_char(startx, starty, 218, NORM_VID);
        write_char(startx, endy, 191, NORM_VID);
        write_char(endx, starty, 192, NORM_VID);
        write_char(endx, endy, 217, NORM_VID);
}

/* input user's selection */
get_resp(x, y, count, menu, keys)
int x, y, count;
char *menu[];
char *keys;
{
    union inkey {
        char ch[2];
        int i;
    } c;
    int arrow_choice=0, key_choice;

    y++;

    /* highlight the first selection */
    goto_xy(x, y);
    write_string(x, y, menu[0], REV_VID); /* reverse video */

    for(;;) {
        while(!bioskey(1)) ; /* wait for key stroke */
        c.i = bioskey(0);    /* read the key */

        /* reset the selection to normal video */
        goto_xy(x+arrow_choice, y);
        write_string(x+arrow_choice, y,
            menu[arrow_choice], NORM_VID); /* redisplay */

        if(c.ch[0]) { /* is normal key */
            /* see if it is a hot key */
            key_choice = is_in(keys, tolower(c.ch[0]));
            if(key_choice) return key_choice-1;
```

```
      /* check for ENTER or space bar */
      switch(c.ch[0]) {
        case '\r': return arrow_choice;
        case ' ' : arrow_choice++;
          break;
        case ESC : return -1;  /* cancel */
      }
    }
    else {  /* is special key */
      switch(c.ch[1]) {
        case 72: arrow_choice--; /* up arrow */
          break;
        case 80: arrow_choice++; /* down arrow */
          break;
      }
    }

      if(arrow_choice==count) arrow_choice=0;
      if(arrow_choice<0) arrow_choice=count-1;

      /* highlight the next selection */
      goto_xy(x+arrow_choice, y);
      write_string(x+arrow_choice, y, menu[arrow_choice], REV_VID);
    }
  }

/* display a string with specified attribute */
void write_string(x, y, p, attrib)
int x, y;
char *p;
int attrib;
{
  register int i;
  char far *v;

  v = vid_mem;
  v += (x*160) + y*2;  /* compute the address */
  for(i=y; *p; i++) {
    *v++ = *p++;  /* write the character */
    *v++ = attrib;    /* write the attribute */
   }
}

/* write character with specified attribute */
void write_char(x, y, ch, attrib)
int x, y;
char ch;
int attrib;
{
  register int i;
  char far *v;

  v = vid_mem;
  v += (x*160) + y*2; /* compute the address */
  *v++ = ch;  /* write the character */
  *v = attrib;     /* write the attribute */
}

/* save a portion of the screen using direct
   video RAM accessing
```

```
*/
void save_video(startx, endx, starty, endy, buf_ptr)
int startx, endx, starty, endy;
unsigned char *buf_ptr;
{
  register int i,j;
  char far *v, far *t;

  v = vid_mem;
  for(i=starty; i<endy; i++)
    for(j=startx; j<endx; j++) {
      t = v + (j*160) + i*2; /* compute the address */
      *buf_ptr++ = *t++; /* read the character */
      *buf_ptr++ = *t;   /* read the attribute */
      *(t-1) = ' ';  /* clear the window */
    }
}

/* restore a portion of the screen using direct
   video RAM accessing
*/
void restore_video(startx, endx, starty, endy, buf_ptr)
int startx, endx, starty, endy;
unsigned char *buf_ptr;
{
  register int i,j;
  char far *v, far *t;

  v = vid_mem;
  t = v;
  for(i=starty; i<endy; i++)
    for(j=startx; j<endx; j++) {
      v = t;
      v += (j*160) + i*2; /* compute the address */
      *v++ = *buf_ptr++; /* write the character */
      *v = *buf_ptr++;    /* write the attribute */
    }
}


/* clear the screen */
void cls()
{
  union REGS r;

  r.h.ah=6; /* screen scroll code */
  r.h.al=0; /* clear screen code */
  r.h.ch=0; /* start row */
  r.h.cl=0; /* start column */
  r.h.dh=24; /* end row */
  r.h.dl=79; /* end column */
  r.h.bh=7;  /* blank line is blank */
  int86(0x10, &r, &r);
}

/* send the cursor to x,y */
void goto_xy(x,y)
int x,y;
{
  union REGS r;
```

```
    r.h.ah=2; /* cursor addressing function */
    r.h.dl=y; /* column coordinate */
    r.h.dh=x; /* row coordinate */
    r.h.bh=0; /* video page */
    int86(0x10, &r, &r);
}

/* returns the current video mode */
video_mode()
{
  union REGS r;

  r.h.ah = 15;   /* get video mode */
  return int86(0x10, &r, &r) & 255;
}

is_in(s, c)
char *s, c;
{
  register int i;

  for(i=0; *s; i++) if(*s++==c) return i+1;
  return 0;
}
```

CREATING PULL-DOWN WINDOWS

Pull-down windows are fundamentally different from simple pop-up menus in that two or more pull-down menus may appear to be active at any one time. Generally, pull-down menus allow the user to select options within options and are used to support a system of menus. Unlike the **popup( )** function that saved the screen, displayed the menu, and then restored the screen, the **pulldown( )** function developed in this section only saves the screen (if necessary), displays the menu, and returns the user's selection. The restoration of the screen is handled as a separate task elsewhere in the program. Before you can create pull-down menus, you must change the way you think about the menu.

Menu Frames

Central to the creation of pull-down, multilevel menus is the *menu frame*. In essence, the pull-down menu routines require that each menu have its frame of reference defined the entire time the program that is using the menus is running. Each menu is activated by its frame number and the necessary information is loaded as needed by the various menu support functions.

The best way to support the menu frame approach is to create an array of structures that will hold all information relevant to a menu. The structure is defined as shown here:

```
struct menu_frame {
  int startx, endx, starty, endy;
  unsigned char *p; /* pointer to screen info */
  char **menu; /* pointer to menu strings */
  char *keys;  /* pointer to hot keys */
  int border;  /* border on/off */
  int count;   /* number of selections */
  int active;  /* is menu already active */
} frame[MAX_FRAME];
```

where **MAX_FRAME** is a macro that determines how many menus you can have. The only additional information required by the pull-down routines that are not needed by the pop-up functions is the **active** flag. It is used to signal when a menu is already on the screen and to prevent the original screen information from being overwritten.

Creating a Menu Frame

Before a menu can be used, a frame must be created for it. The function **make_menu( )**, shown here, creates this frame.

```
/* construct a pull-down menu frame
   1 is returned if menu frame can be constructed;
   otherwise 0 is returned.
*/
make_menu(num, menu, keys, count, x, y, border)
int num;         /* menu number */
char *menu[];    /* menu text */
char *keys;      /* hot keys */
int count;       /* number of menu items */
int x, y;        /* X,Y coordinates of left hand corner */
int border;      /* no border if 0 */
{
   register int i, len;
```

```
  int endx, endy, choice, vmode;
  unsigned char *p;

  if(num>MAX_FRAME) {
    printf("Too many menus\n");
    return 0;
  }

  if((x>24) || (x<0) || (y>79) || (y<0)) {
    printf("range error");
    return 0;
  }

  /* compute the size */
  len = 0;
  for(i=0; i<count; i++)
   if(strlen(menu[i]) > len) len = strlen(menu[i]);
  endy = len + 2 + y;
  endx = count + 1 + x;
  if((endx+1>24) || (endy+1>79)) {
    printf("menu won't fit");
    return 0;
  }

  /* allocate enough memory to hold video buffer*/
  p = (unsigned char *) malloc(2 * (endx-x+1) * (endy-y+1));
  if(!p) exit(1); /* put your own error handler here */

  /* construct the frame */
  frame[num].startx = x; frame[num].endx = endx;
  frame[num].starty = y; frame[num].endy = endy;
  frame[num].p = p;
  frame[num].menu = (char **) menu;
  frame[num].border = border;
  frame[num].keys = keys;
  frame[num].count = count;
  frame[num].active = 0;
  return 1;
}
```

You call **make—menu**( ) with the same arguments as were used with **popup**( ) except that the number of the menu must be specified in the first argument. This number is used to identify the menu.

The pulldown( ) Function

The **pulldown**( ) function is shown here:

```
/* Display a pull-down menu and return selection.
   Returns -1 if user presses the escape key;
   otherwise the number of the selection is
   returned beginning with 0.
*/
```

```
int pulldown(num)
int num; /* frame number */
{
  int  vmode, choice;

  vmode = video_mode();
  if((vmode!=2) && (vmode!=3) && (vmode!=7)) {
    printf("video must be in 80 column text mode");
    exit(1);
  }
  /* set proper address of video RAM */
  if(vmode==7) vid_mem = (char far *) 0xB0000000;
  else vid_mem = (char far *) 0xB8000000;

  /* get active window */
  if(!frame[num].active) { /* not currently in use */
    save_video(num);       /* save the current screen */
    frame[num].active = 1; /* set active flag */
  }

  if(frame[num].border) draw_border(num);

  display_menu(num);       /* display the menu */
  return get_resp(num); /* return response */
}
```

To use **pulldown( )**, simply pass it the number of the menu you want displayed. However, you must remember to restore the screen using **restore_video( )** elsewhere in your program. Remember, the point of pull-down menus is to allow two or more menus to remain on the screen, and potentially active, as the user selects various options. Therefore, you do not want to restore the screen until the entire selection process is complete.

Notice that the portion of the screen used by the menu is saved only if the **active** flag is 0. Since a pull-down menu must be able to be re-entered, the screen must not be saved multiple times. (Otherwise, the menu itself would be saved, thus overwriting the original contents of the screen, which were already saved.)

Restoring the Screen

Like the other menu support functions, the modified **restore_video( )** function shown here has been converted to work with frames.

As such, only the menu number is now passed to **restore—video( )**, which makes for a clean interface.

```
/* restore a portion of the screen */
void restore_video(num)
int num;
{
  register int i,j;
  char far *v, far *t;
  char *buf_ptr;

  buf_ptr = frame[num].p;
  v = vid_mem;
  t = v;
  for(i=frame[num].starty; i<frame[num].endy+1; i++)
    for(j=frame[num].startx; j<frame[num].endx+1; j++) {
      v = t;
      v += (j*160) + i*2; /* compute the address */
      *v++ = *buf_ptr++;  /* write the character */
      *v = *buf_ptr++;    /* write the attribute */
    }
  frame[num].active = 0; /* deactivate */
}
```

A Sample Program Using
the Pull-Down Routines

All the pull-down menu functions along with a simple sample program are shown here and should be entered into your computer.

```
/* Pull-down menu routines for text mode operation and
    short sample program.
*/

#include "stdio.h"
#include "dos.h"
#include "stdlib.h"

#define BORDER 1
#define ESC 27
#define MAX_FRAME 10
#define REV_VID 0x70
#define NORM_VID 7

void save_video(), restore_video(), pd_driver();
void goto_xy(), cls(), write_string(), write_char();
void display_menu(), draw_border();
char far *vid_mem;
```

```c
struct menu_frame {
  int startx, endx, starty, endy;
  unsigned char *p;
  char **menu;
  char *keys;
  int border, count;
  int active;
} frame[MAX_FRAME], i;

char *fruit[]= {
  "Apple",
  "Orange",
  "Pear",
  "Grape",
  "Raspberry",
  "Strawberry"
};

char *color[]= {
  "Red",
  "Yellow",
  "Orange",
  "Green",
};

char *apple_type[]= {
  "Red delicious",
  "Jonathan",
  "Winesap",
  "Rome"
};

char *grape_type[]= {
  "Concord",
  "cAnadice",
  "Thompson",
  "Red flame"
};

main()
{
  int i;

  cls();
  goto_xy(0,0);

  /* first, create the menu frames */
  make_menu(0, fruit, "aopgrs", 6, 5, 20, BORDER);
  make_menu(1, color, "ryog", 4, 9, 28, BORDER);
  make_menu(2, apple_type, "rjwr", 4, 12, 32, BORDER);
  make_menu(3, grape_type, "catr", 4, 9, 10, BORDER);

  printf("Select your fruit:");

  pd_driver(); /* activate the menu system */
}

void pd_driver()
{
  int choice1, choice2, selection;
```

```
/* now, activate as needed */
while((choice1=pulldown(0)) != -1) {
  switch(choice1) {
    case 0:  /* wants an apple */
      while((choice2=pulldown(1)) != -1) {
        if(choice2==0) selection = pulldown(2); /* red apple */
        restore_video(2);
      }
      restore_video(1);
      break;
    case 1:
    case 2: goto_xy(1,0);
      printf("out of that selection");
      break;
    case 3:  /* wants a grape */
      selection = pulldown(3);
      restore_video(3);
      break;
    case 4:
    case 5: goto_xy(1,0);
      printf("out of that selection");
      break;
  }
}

  restore_video(0);
}

/* display a pull-down menu and return selection */
int pulldown(num)
int num; /* menu number */
{
  int  vmode, choice;

  vmode = video_mode();
  if((vmode!=2) && (vmode!=3) && (vmode!=7)) {
    printf("video must be in 80 column text mode");
    exit(1);
  }
  /* set proper address of video RAM */
  if(vmode==7) vid_mem = (char far *) 0xB0000000;
  else vid_mem = (char far *) 0xB8000000;

  /* get active window */
  if(!frame[num].active) { /* not currently in use */
    save_video(num);        /* save the current screen */
    frame[num].active = 1; /* set active flag */
  }

  if(frame[num].border) draw_border(num);

  display_menu(num);      /* display the menu */
  return get_resp(num); /* return response */
}


/* construct a pull down menu frame
   1 is returned if menu frame can be constructed
   otherwise 0 is returned.
*/
```

```
make_menu(num, menu, keys, count, x, y, border)
int num;          /* menu number */
char *menu[];     /* menu text */
char *keys;       /* hot keys */
int count;        /* number of menu items */
int x, y;         /* X,Y coordinates of left hand corner */
int border;       /* no border if 0 */
{
  register int i, len;
  int endx, endy, choice, vmode;
  unsigned char *p;

  if(num>MAX_FRAME) {
    printf("Too many menus\n");
    return 0;
  }

  if((x>24) || (x<0) || (y>79) || (y<0)) {
    printf("range error");
    return 0;
  }

  /* compute the size */
  len = 0;
  for(i=0; i<count; i++)
   if(strlen(menu[i]) > len) len = strlen(menu[i]);
  endy = len + 2 + y;
  endx = count + 1 + x;
  if((endx+1>24) || (endy+1>79)) {
    printf("menu won't fit");
    return 0;
  }

  /* allocate enough memory to hold it */
  p = (unsigned char *) malloc(2 * (endx-x+1) * (endy-y+1));
  if(!p) exit(1); /* put your own error handler here */

  /* construct the frame */
  frame[num].startx = x; frame[num].endx = endx;
  frame[num].starty = y; frame[num].endy = endy;
  frame[num].p = p;
  frame[num].menu = (char **) menu;
  frame[num].border = border;
  frame[num].keys = keys;
  frame[num].count = count;
  frame[num].active = 0;
  return 1;
}

/* display the menu in its proper location */
void display_menu(num)
int num;
{
  register int i, x;
  char **m;

  x = frame[num].startx+1;
  m = frame[num].menu;

  for(i=0; i<frame[num].count; i++, x++)
    write_string(x, frame[num].starty+1,
               m[i], NORM_VID);
```

```
}

void draw_border(num)
int num;
{
  register int i;
  char far *v, far *t;

v = vid_mem;
t = v;
for(i=frame[num].startx+1; i<frame[num].endx; i++) {
    v += (i*160) + frame[num].starty*2;
    *v++ = 179;
    *v = NORM_VID;
    v = t;
    v += (i*160) + frame[num].endy*2;
    *v++ = 179;
    *v = NORM_VID;
    v = t;
}
for(i=frame[num].starty+1; i<frame[num].endy; i++) {
    v += (frame[num].startx*160) + i*2;
    *v++ = 196;
    *v = NORM_VID;
    v = t;
    v += (frame[num].endx*160) + i*2;
    *v++ = 196;
    *v = NORM_VID;
    v = t;
}
  write_char(frame[num].startx, frame[num].starty, 218, NORM_VID);
  write_char(frame[num].startx, frame[num].endy, 191, NORM_VID);
  write_char(frame[num].endx, frame[num].starty, 192, NORM_VID);
  write_char(frame[num].endx, frame[num].endy, 217, NORM_VID);
}

/* input user's selection */
get_resp(num)
int num;
{
  union inkey {
    char ch[2];
    int i;
  } c;
  int arrow_choice=0, key_choice;
  int x, y;

  x = frame[num].startx+1;
  y = frame[num].starty+1;

  /* highlight the first selection */
  goto_xy(x, y);
  write_string(x, y, frame[num].menu[0], REV_VID);

  for(;;) {
    while(!bioskey(1)) ; /* wait for key stroke */
    c.i = bioskey(0);    /* read the key */

    /* reset the selection to normal video */
    goto_xy(x+arrow_choice, y);
    write_string(x+arrow_choice, y,
      frame[num].menu[arrow_choice], NORM_VID); /* redisplay */
```

```
      if(c.ch[0]) { /* is normal key */
        /* see if it is a hot key */
        key_choice = is_in(frame[num].keys, tolower(c.ch[0]));
        if(key_choice) return key_choice-1;
        /* check for ENTER or space bar */
        switch(c.ch[0]) {
          case '\r': return arrow_choice;
          case ' ' : arrow_choice++;
            break;
          case ESC : return -1; /* cancel */
        }
      }
      else {  /* is special key */
        switch(c.ch[1]) {
          case 72: arrow_choice--; /* up arrow */
            break;
          case 80: arrow_choice++; /* down arrow */
            break;
        }
      }
      if(arrow_choice==frame[num].count) arrow_choice=0;
      if(arrow_choice<0) arrow_choice = frame[num].count-1;

      /* highlight the next selection */
      goto_xy(x+arrow_choice, y);
      write_string(x+arrow_choice, y,
        frame[num].menu[arrow_choice], REV_VID);
  }
}

/* display a string with specified attribute */
void write_string(x, y, p, attrib)
int x, y;
char *p;
int attrib;
{
  register int i;
  char far *v;

  v = vid_mem;
  v += (x*160) + y*2; /* compute the address */
  for(i=y; *p; i++) {
    *v++ = *p++;  /* write the character */
    *v++ = attrib;    /* write the attribute */
   }
}

/* write character with specified attribute */
void write_char(x, y, ch, attrib)
int x, y;
char ch;
int attrib;
{
  register int i;
  char far *v;

  v = vid_mem;
  v += (x*160) + y*2; /* compute the address */
  *v++ = ch;  /* write the character */
  *v = attrib;    /* write the attribute */
}
```

```c
/* save a portion of the screen */
void save_video(num)
int num;
{
  register int i,j;
  char *buf_ptr;
  char far *v, far *t;

  buf_ptr = frame[num].p;
  v = vid_mem;
  for(i=frame[num].starty; i<frame[num].endy+1; i++)
    for(j=frame[num].startx; j<frame[num].endx+1; j++) {
      t = (v + (j*160) + i*2);
      *buf_ptr++ = *t++;
      *buf_ptr++ = *t;
      *(t-1) = ' ';  /* clear the window */
    }
}

/* restore a portion of the screen */
void restore_video(num)
int num;
{
  register int i,j;
  char far *v, far *t;
  char *buf_ptr;

  buf_ptr = frame[num].p;
  v = vid_mem;
  t = v;
  for(i=frame[num].starty; i<frame[num].endy+1; i++)
    for(j=frame[num].startx; j<frame[num].endx+1; j++) {
      v = t;
      v += (j*160) + i*2; /* compute the address */
      *v++ = *buf_ptr++; /* write the character */
      *v = *buf_ptr++;    /* write the attribute */
    }
  frame[num].active = 0; /* deactivate */
}


/* clear the screen */
void cls()
{
  union REGS r;

  r.h.ah=6; /* screen scroll code */
  r.h.al=0; /* clear screen code */
  r.h.ch=0; /* start row */
  r.h.cl=0; /* start column */
  r.h.dh=24; /* end row */
  r.h.dl=79; /* end column */
  r.h.bh=7;  /* blank line is black */
  int86(0x10, &r, &r);
}

/* send the cursor to x,y */
void goto_xy(x,y)
int x,y;
{
  union REGS r;
```

```
   r.h.ah=2; /* cursor addressing function */
   r.h.dl=y; /* column coordinate */
   r.h.dh=x; /* row coordinate */
   r.h.bh=0; /* video page */
   int86(0x10, &r, &r);
}

/* returns the current video mode */
video_mode()
{
   union REGS r;

   r.h.ah = 15;  /* get video mode */
   return int86(0x10, &r, &r) & 255;
}

is_in(s, c)
char *s, c;
{
   register int i;

   for(i=0; *s; i++) if(*s++==c) return i+1;
   return 0;
}
```

In this example, if the user selects "Apple," he or she is prompted for the color of the apple; if "Red" is chosen, the list of red apples is displayed. However, if "Grape" is selected, the user is prompted for the type of grape desired. The Apple selection menus are shown in Figure 1-3.

Look closely at the **pd__driver**( ) function that follows **main**( ). When using pull-down menus, you must create a custom function that drives the menu system. The basic strategy of the driver function will be much like **pd__driver**( ) in this example. Remember, this sample program only illustrates how to activate the menus. Your real application program will have to process the selections in a meaningful way. Keep in mind that the following sequence must be performed for a pull-down menu to be used:

1. Create the menu using **make__menu**( ).

2. Activate the menu using **pulldown**( ).

3. Restore the screen using **restore__video**( ) as each menu is exited.

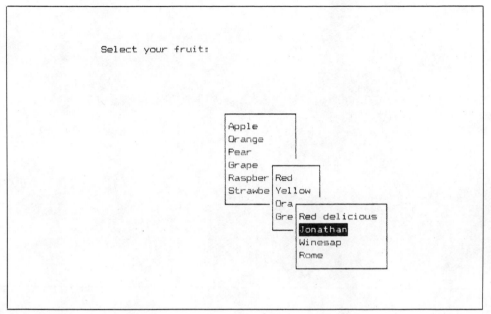

Figure 1-3.

The Apple menus from the pull-
down menu sample program

ADDING OPTIONS

The menu routines developed in this chapter fit the needs of many situations. However, you might want to try adding some of these options:

- Allow a menu title to be displayed

- Allow line menus (all options on one line)

- Use different colors for different menus

- Allow different types of borders to be specified

2: Pop-up
Windows

Pop-up windows can give your programs a professional look and feel that cannot be achieved by other means. Pop-up windows leave the impression that you, the programmer, have mastery over the screen. Since the user generally judges a program by its user interface, this positive impression is generalized to the program as a whole.

This chapter develops a complete set of pop-up window functions that enable you to create and use multiple windows. The window routines make use of the direct video RAM accessing functions developed in Chapter 1. Because windows tend, in general, to be much larger in size than menus, the ROM-BIOS video functions simply cannot be used—even on the fastest computers. For pop-up windows to be effective they must come and go instantly.

Before developing window functions, it is important to understand exactly what a pop-up window is and how it is used.

POP-UP WINDOW THEORY

A pop-up window is a portion of the screen that is used for a specific purpose. When the window appears, what is currently on the screen is saved and the window is displayed. When the application using that window is finished, the window is removed and the original contents of the screen are restored. (This is similar to the pop-up menu process.) It is possible to have several windows on the screen at the same time.

Although not strictly necessary, all good window implementations allow the dimensions and screen position of a window to be changed interactively. Hence, the window functions cannot assume that a window will always be in the same place or of the same size.

Window routines are difficult to develop because the application using the window must not be allowed to write past the boundaries of the window. Because the size of the window may change without the application's knowledge, it is the job of the window routines — not the application — to prevent overwriting. Therefore, all of C's normal console I/O routines, such as **printf( )** or **gets( )**, cannot be used, and alternative window-specific I/O functions must be substituted. In fact, developing these window-specific I/O functions is the hardest part of creating window routines.

The theory behind using windows is quite simple. Each separate task of a program uses its own window. When the task is begun, its window is activated. When the task completes, its window is removed. If a task is interrupted, it is suspended but its own window is not removed, and the interrupting task simply activates its own window on top of the other window. (Without the use of windows, each task generally clears the screen. This causes the user to break concentration. However, when windows are used, the interrupting task is viewed as a temporary pause.)

To understand how windows might be used effectively, imagine that you have written a text editor that includes some extra features, including a note pad, a four-function calculator, and a decimal to hexadecimal converter. Because these functions are not actually directly related to the act of text editing, it makes sense to use a pop-up window whenever one of them is activated. Therefore, when one of the extra features is used, the main task of editing is simply suspended; it is not completely disrupted.

WINDOW FRAMES

Implementing pop-up windows correctly requires that all attributes required for their frame of reference be available to all of the window functions at any time. To accomplish this, we will use the frame concept, similar to that used by the pull-down menu routines. However, a window frame (no pun intended) contains some different information. To hold the frames, the array of structures shown here is used.

```
struct window_frame {
  int startx, endx, starty, endy; /* window position */
  int curx, cury; /* current cursor position in window */
  unsigned char *p; /* buffer pointer */
  char *header; /* header message */
  int border; /* border on/off */
  int active; /* on screen yes/no */
} frame[MAX_FRAME];
```

The variables **startx**, **starty**, **endx**, and **endy** hold the coordinates of the upper-left corner and the lower-right corner of the window. The current position of the cursor inside the window is found in **curx** and **cury**. These values are stored because the cursor must be manually manipulated and maintained by the window routines. The pointer **p** points to the region of memory that holds what was previously on the portion of the screen overwritten by the window. Often, a window has a header that is a message identifying what the window is. This message is pointed to by **header**. The variable **border** is used to specify whether the window will have a border around it. The **active** variable is set to "1" if the window is currently on the screen and "0" otherwise.

From a programming point of view, using windows is quite easy. First, you create a window frame. Then, when you need the window, you activate it and use the special window-specific I/O functions to write to it. When the window is no longer needed, you deactivate it.

CREATING THE WINDOW FRAME

The function used to create a window frame is called **make_window( )**, shown here.

```
/* Construct a pull down window frame.
   1 is returned if window frame can be constructed;
   otherwise 0 is returned.
*/
make_window(num, header, startx, starty, endx, endy, border)
int num;        /* window number */
char *header;   /* header text */
int startx, starty; /* X,Y coordinates of upper left corner */
int endx, endy; /* X,Y coordinates of lower right corner */
int border;     /* no border if 0 */
{
  unsigned char *p;

  if(num>MAX_FRAME) {
    printf("Too many windows\n");
    return 0;
  }

  if((startx>24) || (startx<0) || (starty>78) || (starty<0)) {
    printf("range error");
    return 0;
  }

  if((endx>24) || (endy>79)) {
    printf("window won't fit");
    return 0;
  }

  /* allocate enough memory to hold it */
  p = (unsigned char *) malloc(2*(endx-startx+1)*(endy-starty+1));
  if(!p) exit(1); /* put your own error handler here */

  /* construct the frame */
  frame[num].startx = startx; frame[num].endx = endx;
  frame[num].starty = starty; frame[num].endy = endy;
  frame[num].p = p;
  frame[num].header = header;
  frame[num].border = border;
  frame[num].active = 0;
  frame[num].curx = 0; frame[num].cury = 0;
  return 1;
}
```

As you can see by looking at the function's declaration, it requires that you pass it the number of the window you wish to create a frame for and all other relevant information. For example, this call to **make_window( )** creates a frame for window 0 that has the header "Editor

[Esc to exit]", has the upper-left corner at 0,0 and the lower-right corner at 24,78, and uses a border.

```
make_window(0, " Editor [Esc to exit] ", 0, 0, 24, 78, BORDER);
```

Notice that the cursor position variables **curx** and **cury** are initialized to 0. This means that when the window is first activated, the cursor will be in the upper-left corner. The function also makes sure that the window fits on the screen.

ACTIVATING AND DEACTIVATING A WINDOW

To activate a window, use the **window( )** function shown here where **num** will contain the frame number of the window you want to use.

```
/* Display a pull-down window. */
void window(num)
int num; /* window number */
{
  int  vmode, choice;
  int x, y;

  vmode = video_mode();
  if((vmode!=2) && (vmode!=3) && (vmode!=7)) {
    printf("video must be in 80 column text mode");
    exit(1);
  }
  /* set proper address of video RAM */
  if(vmode==7) vid_mem = (char far *) 0xB0000000;
  else vid_mem = (char far *) 0xB8000000;

  /* get active window */
  if(!frame[num].active) { /* not currently in use */
    save_video(num);        /* save the current screen */
    frame[num].active = 1; /* set active flag */
  }

  if(frame[num].border) draw_border(num);
  display_header(num); /* display the window */

  x = frame[num].startx + frame[num].curx + 1;
  y = frame[num].starty + frame[num].cury + 1;
  goto_xy(x, y);
}
```

As you can see, it is very similar to the **menu( )** function developed in the previous chapter. The **vid_mem** variable is a global **char far** pointer that is defined elsewhere.

The function **display_header( )**, shown here, is used to display a header message at the top-center of the window. If the message does not fit, it will not be displayed.

```
/* Display the header message in its proper location. */
void display_header(num)
int num;
{
  register int y, len;

  y = frame[num].starty;

  /* Calculate the correct starting position to center
     the header message - if negative, message won't
     fit.
  */
  len = strlen(frame[num].header);
  len = (frame[num].endy - y - len) / 2;
  if(len<0) return; /* don't display it */
  y = y +len;

  write_string(frame[num].startx, y,
           frame[num].header, NORM_VID);
}
```

If you want the message displayed in reverse video, substitute **REV_VID** (defined as 70H) for **NORM_VID** (defined as 7).

To deactivate a window, use the **deactivate( )** function shown here, passing it the number of the window to remove.

```
/* Deactivate a window and remove it from the screen. */
deactivate(num)
int num;
{
  /* reset the cursor postion to upper left corner */
  frame[num].curx = 0;
  frame[num].cury = 0;
  restore_video(num);
}
```

As shown, the function resets the cursor position to 0,0. However, since you may encounter some situations in which it is more desirable not to reset the cursor variables, feel free to change this feature if you like.

WINDOW I/O FUNCTIONS

Before a window can be used it is necessary to develop a large number of window-specific console I/O functions. To understand why so many functions are needed, simply think about how many console I/O functions are in C's standard library. The functions developed in this chapter actually represent just a minimal set necessary to use windows. Although they do not include window-specific versions of all C's console I/O functions they still entail a lot of code. As you will see, even the simplest operation, such as reading a character from the keyboard or putting a character on the screen, requires quite a bit of code because it must manually keep track of the current cursor position and not allow boundaries to be overwritten. Remember, none of the automatic features provided by DOS are available to manipulate the screen. For example, when a carriage return is needed, it must be done manually, inside the routine; it is not possible to simply use a DOS call to output a carriage return linefeed sequence.

All of the window I/O functions begin with the word *window* for easy identification. Also, all the window I/O functions take as their first argument the number of the window being accessed.

The Window Cursor Positioning Function

It may seem like an unusual place to start, but the first function that is needed is a window equivalent of the **goto__xy( )** function. The reason for this is simple. Since the window-specific I/O routines must manually maintain the cursor, there must be some way to put the cursor where it is supposed to be. The function, **window__xy( )**, shown here, does just that. (In the window routines developed here, location 0,0 is the upper-left corner of the window.)

```
/* Position cursor in a window at specified location.
   Returns 0 if out of range;
   non-zero otherwise.
```

```
*/
window_xy(num, x, y)
int num, x, y;
{
  if(x<0 || x+frame[num].startx>=frame[num].endx-1)
    return 0;
  if(y<0 || y+frame[num].starty>=frame[num].endy-1)
    return 0;
  frame[num].curx = x;
  frame[num].cury = y;
  goto_xy(frame[num].startx+x+1, frame[num].starty+y+1);
  return 1;
}
```

The key to understanding **window_xy( )** is remembering that a specific X,Y coordinate is always in the same position inside the specified window no matter where the window is on the screen; that is, the X,Y location is relative to the window, not to the screen. Stated a different way, if you request the cursor to be at window location 2,2, it will be placed two lines down and two characters over from the upper-left corner no matter where that window is actually positioned on the screen. Physically placing the cursor at that relative position means translating it into actual screen coordinates. That is what is done by **window_xy( )**. In addition, **window_xy( )** does not allow the cursor to be positioned outside the specified window.

The window_getche( ) Function

With windows you cannot use **getche( )**, which reads a key stroke and echoes it to the screen, because it allows a window to be overrun, so an alternative function called **window_getche( )** must be developed. This function reads a character from the current cursor position in the specified window.

```
/* Input keystrokes inside a window.
   Returns full 16 bit scan code.
*/
window_getche(num)
int num;
{
  union inkey {
    char ch[2];
    int i;
  } c;

  if(!frame[num].active) return 0; /* window not active */
```

```
window_xy(num, frame[num].curx, frame[num].cury);

c.i = bioskey(0);       /* read the key */

if(c.ch[0]) {
  switch(c.ch[0]) {
    case '\r': /* the ENTER key is pressed */
      break;
    case BKSP: /* back space */
      break;
    default:
      if(frame[num].cury+frame[num].starty < frame[num].endy-1) {
        write_char(frame[num].startx + frame[num].curx+1,
          frame[num].starty+frame[num].cury+1, c.ch[0], NORM_VID);
        frame[num].cury++;
      }
  }
  if(frame[num].curx < 0) frame[num].curx = 0;
  if(frame[num].curx+frame[num].startx > frame[num].endx-2)
    frame[num].curx--;
  window_xy(num, frame[num].curx, frame[num].cury);
}
return c.i;
}
```

Unlike **getche( )**, **window__getche( )** returns the full 16-bit scan code. This means that you will have access to the standard character codes in the lower eight bits, as well as the position code in the upper eight bits. If you want to ignore the position code, simply assign the return value of **window__getche( )** to a character.

The function operates like this. First, if the frame is not active (that is, if it is not on the screen) the function returns "0." Since it is not possible to generate a 0 from the keyboard, your routines could check for this possible error. Next, the cursor is positioned to its current position in the window and the key is read. If it is a normal key and is not a RETURN or BACKSPACE key, the current Y cursor variable for that frame is incremented and the key is echoed. If the cursor is at a boundary, the Y value is decremented. The final call to **window__xy( )** is used to advance the cursor on the screen to the next position.

The **window__getche( )** function does not let you type past a window boundary. Keep in mind that all windows have borders, even if some are not explicitly displayed with lines. When the border is not displayed, blank space is used. The reason for this is that the window must be distinguished from the background. Even if the border is not drawn, characters may not be written outside the window.

As stated in Chapter 1, the **bioskey( )** function is specific to Turbo C. If you are using another C compiler, you can use the version of **bioskey( )** shown in Chapter 1.

The window_gets( ) Function

To read a string from within a window, use the **window_gets( )** function shown here. It is not as sophisticated as most **gets( )** functions, but it works for most applications. You can always add functionality if you desire.

```
/* Read a string from a window. */
void window_gets(num, s)
int num;
char *s;
{
  char ch, *temp;

  temp = s;
  for(;;) {
    ch = window_getche(num);
    switch(ch) {
      case '\r':  /* the ENTER key is pressed */
        *s='\0';
        return;
      case BKSP: /* backspace */
        if(s>temp) {
          s--;
          frame[num].cury--;
          if(frame[num].cury<0) frame[num].cury = 0;
          window_xy(num, frame[num].curx, frame[num].cury);
          write_char(frame[num].startx+ frame[num].curx+1,
            frame[num].starty+frame[num].cury+1, ' ', NORM_VID);
        }
        break;
      default: *s = ch;
        s++;
    }
  }
}
```

When the BACKSPACE key is pressed, it is necessary to back up the cursor manually, erase what is there, and write a space.

The window__putchar( ) Function

Writing a character to a window involves checking that the window is active and that the character will not cross the window boundary. After the character is written, the cursor position must be advanced. The function **window__putchar( )**, shown here, accomplishes these tasks.

```
/* Write a character at the current cursor position
   in the specified window.
   Returns 0 if window not active;
   1 otherwise.
*/
window_putchar(num, ch)
int num;
char ch;
{
  register int x, y;
  char far *v;

  /* make sure window is active */
  if(!frame[num].active) return 0;

  x = frame[num].curx + frame[num].startx + 1;
  y = frame[num].cury + frame[num].starty + 1;

  v = vid_mem;
  v += (x*160) + y*2; /* compute the address */
  if(y>=frame[num].endy) {
    return 1;
  }
  if(x>=frame[num].endx) {
    return 1;
  }

  if(ch=='\n') { /* newline char */
    x++;
    y = frame[num].startx+1;
    v = vid_mem;
    v += (x*160) + y*2; /* compute the address */
    frame[num].curx++;  /* increment X */
    frame[num].cury = 0; /* reset Y */
  }
  else {
    frame[num].cury++;
    *v++ = ch;  /* write the character */
    *v++ = NORM_VID;    /* normal video attribute */
  }
  window_xy(num, frame[num].curx, frame[num].cury);
  return 1;
}
```

This function does not consider it an error condition if the character cannot be written because a window boundary would be crossed. The reason for this is that the size of a window can be dynamically changed, meaning that messages that previously fit may not fit at a later time. The function simply does not display a character that is outside the window.

Notice that a carriage return requires the cursor to be manually positioned down one line, if possible, and on the left side of the window.

The window_puts( ) Function

The **window_puts( )** function writes the specified string to the indicated window using **window_putchar( )**.

```
/* Write a string at the current cursor position
   in the specified window.
   Returns 0 if window not active;
   1 otherwise.
*/
window_puts(num, str)
int num;
char *str;
{
    /* make sure window is active */
    if(!frame[num].active) return 0;

    for( ; *str;  str++)
      window_putchar(num, *str);
    return 1;
}
```

Miscellaneous Screen-Handling Functions

The window package also includes these screen functions:

Function	Purpose
window_cls( )	clears a window
window_cleol( )	clears from current cursor position to end of line
window_upline( )	moves the cursor up one line
window_downline( )	moves the cursor down one line
window_bksp( )	moves the cursor back one space

These functions are shown here. You can create other, custom screen
functions following the same general format used by these routines.

```
/* Clear a window. */
void window_cls(num)
int num;
{
  register int i,j;
  char far *v, far *t;

  v = vid_mem;
  t = v;
  for(i=frame[num].starty+1; i<frame[num].endy; i++)
    for(j=frame[num].startx+1; j<frame[num].endx; j++) {
      v = t;
      v += (j*160) + i*2;
      *v++ = ' ';  /* write a space */
      *v = NORM_VID;    /* normal */
    }
  frame[num].curx = 0;
  frame[num].cury = 0;
}

/* Clear to end of line. */
void window_cleol(num)
int num;
{
  register int i, x, y;

  x = frame[num].curx;
  y = frame[num].cury;
  window_xy(num, frame[num].curx, frame[num].cury);

  for(i=frame[num].cury; i<frame[num].endy-1; i++)
    window_putchar(num,' ');
  window_xy(num, x, y);
}

/* Move cursor up one line.
   Returns non-zero if successful;
   0 otherwise.
*/
window_upline(num)
int num;
{
  if(frame[num].curx>0) {
    frame[num].curx--;
    window_xy(num, frame[num].curx, frame[num].cury);
    return 1;
  }
  return 0;
}

/* Move cursor down one line.
   Returns non-zero if successful;
   0 otherwise.
```

```
*/
window_downline(num)
int num;
{
  if(frame[num].curx<frame[num].endx-frame[num].startx-1) {
    frame[num].curx++;
    window_xy(num, frame[num].curx, frame[num].cury);
    return 1;
  }
  return 1;
}

/* back up one character. */
window_bksp(num)
int num;
{
  if(frame[num].cury>0) {
    frame[num].cury--;
    window_xy(num, frame[num].curx, frame[num].cury);
    window_putchar(num, ' ');
    frame[num].cury--;
    window_xy(num, frame[num].curx, frame[num].cury);
  }
}
```

CHANGING THE SIZE AND POSITION
OF A WINDOW AT RUNTIME

Although you use **make__window**( ) to define the initial size and
position of the window, these parameters can be dynamically altered at
runtime. The basic theory behind altering a window is to change one or
more of the frame parameters based on instructions from the user, erase
the current window, and redraw it with the new parameters. The
routines called **size**( ) and **move**( ), shown here, are used to resize or
reposition a specified window. The arrow keys as well as the HOME, END,
PGDN, and PGUP keys are used to manipulate the shape or position of
the window.

```
/* Interactively change the size of a window.
*/
void size(num)
int num;
{
  char ch;
  int x, y, startx, starty;

  /* activate if necessary */
  if(!frame[num].active) window(num);
```

```
       startx = x = frame[num].startx;
       starty = y = frame[num].starty;
       window_xy(num, 0, 0);

       do {
         ch = get_special();
         switch(ch) {
           case 75: /* left */
             starty--;
             break;
           case 77: /* right */
             starty++;
             break;
           case 72: /* up */
             startx--;
             break;
           case 80: /* down */
             startx++;
             break;
           case 71: /* up left */
             startx--; starty--;
             break;
           case 73: /* up right */
             startx--; starty++;
             break;
           case 79: /* down left*/
             startx++; starty--;
             break;
           case 81: /* down right */
             startx++; starty++;
             break;
           case 60: /* F2: cancel and use original size */
             startx = x;
             starty = y;
             ch = 59;
         }
         /* see if out-of-range */
         if(startx<0) startx++;
         if(startx>=frame[num].endx) startx--;
         if(starty<0) starty++;
         if(starty>=frame[num].endy) starty--;
         deactivate(num); /* erase old size */
         frame[num].startx = startx;
         frame[num].starty = starty;
         window(num); /* display new size */
       } while(ch!=59); /* F1 to accept change */
       deactivate(num);
     }

     /* Interactively move a window
     */
     void move(num)
     int num;
     {
       char ch;
       int x, y, ex, ey, startx, starty, endx, endy;

       /* activate if necessary */
       if(!frame[num].active) window(num);

       startx = x = frame[num].startx;
       starty = y = frame[num].starty;
```

```
            endx = ex = frame[num].endx;
            endy = ey = frame[num].endy;
            window_xy(num, 0, 0);

            do {
              ch = get_special();
              switch(ch) {
                case 75: /* left */
                  starty--;
                  endy--;
                  break;
                case 77: /* right */
                  starty++;
                  endy++;
                  break;
                case 72: /* up */
                  startx--;
                  endx--;
                  break;
                case 80: /* down */
                  startx++;
                  endx++;
                  break;
                case 71: /* up left */
                  startx--; starty--;
                  endx--; endy--;
                  break;
                case 73: /* up right */
                  startx--; starty++;
                  endx--; endy++;
                  break;
                case 79: /* down left*/
                  startx++; starty--;
                  endx++; endy--;
                  break;
                case 81: /* down right */
                  startx++; starty++;
                  endx++; endy++;
                  break;
                case 60: /* F2: cancel and use original size */
                  startx = x;
                  starty = y;
                  endx = ex;
                  endy = ey;
                  ch = 59;
              }

              /* see if out-of-range */
              if(startx<0) {
                startx++;
                endx++;
              }
              if(endx>=25) {
                startx--;
                endx--;
              }
              if(starty<0) {
                starty++;
                endy++;
              }
              if(endy>=79) {
                starty--;
                endy--;
```

```
        }
        deactivate(num); /* erase at old position */
        frame[num].startx = startx;
        frame[num].starty = starty;
        frame[num].endx = endx;
        frame[num].endy = endy;
        window(num); /* display at new position */
        } while(ch!=59); /* F1 to accept change */
    deactivate(num);
}
```

For both the **size**( ) and **move**( ) functions, when you have finished altering the window, press the F1 key. The new size or position of the window will be used whenever that window is activated unless you change it again. To abort either function press the F2 key; the window returns to its former size or position. These routines assume that the window that is being resized or moved is not already active since any existing contents of the window will be overwritten.

CREATING APPLICATIONS THAT USE POP-UP WINDOWS

The single most important thing to remember about using windows is to always use the window-specific I/O routines. Employing any of the standard C functions invites trouble by creating the possibility that the window boundary will be overwritten. Since no window equivalent of the **printf**( ) function was developed (you may want to develop one on your own, however), the easiest way to output data types other than characters and strings is to use C's standard **sprintf**( ) to transform whatever data type(s) you have into a formatted string and then use **window__puts**( ) to write the string to the window. The same method applies to inputting information other than characters and strings. Use **window__gets**( ) to read numbers and convert them into the desired data type using C's standard **sscanf**( ) function, which takes a string as input instead of input from the keyboard.

The window frame is generally created by another part of the program, not by the actual function or functions that comprise the window-based application. The creation of the window frames is generally performed inside either **main( )** or an initialization function called once at the start of the program. Let's look at three simple window-based applications.

Decimal to Hexadecimal Converter

Examine the code to the decimal to hexadecimal converter shown here.

```
/* Decimal to hexadecimal converter. */
void dectohex()
{
  char in[80], out[80];
  int n;

  window(1);
  do {
    window_xy(1, 0, 0);  /* go to first line */
    window_cleol(1); /* clear the line */
    window_puts(1, "dec: "); /* prompt */
    window_gets(1, in); /* read the number */
    window_putchar(1, '\n'); /* go to next line */
    window_cleol(1); /* clear it */
    sscanf(in,"%d", &n); /* convert to internal format */
    sprintf(out, "%s%X", "hex: ",n); /* convert to hex */
    window_puts(1, out); /* output hex */
  } while(*in);
  deactivate(1);
}
```

This function activates its window and then loops, inputting decimal numbers and outputting their hexadecimal equivalents, until the user presses ENTER when prompted for the decimal number. The window is deactivated before the function returns.

Four-Function Calculator

A very useful and popular pop-up window application is a calculator. The one developed here is "stack-based," which means that you enter the operands first and then the operator (like postfix notation). The operands are placed on a stack. Each time an operator is encountered the top two operands are removed and the operation is applied to them. The answer is printed and the result is pushed on the stack. For example, to find the answer to (10+5)/5 you would first enter 10, then 5, then the +.

This will result in the number 15 being displayed and also being put on the top of the stack. Next, enter 5 followed by the /. The answer 3 is displayed. The stack is 100 elements deep, which means that you can enter several operands before entering the operator.

The **calc**( ) function plus the **push**( ) and **pop**( ) stack routines are shown here. Although this version works only with integers, you can easily change it to work with real numbers.

```
#define MAX 100

int *p;   /* pointer into the stack */
int *tos; /* points to top of stack */
int *bos; /* points to bottom of stack */

/* Stack based, postfix notation four-function calculator */
void calc()
{
  char in[80], out[80];
  int answer, stack[MAX];
  int a,b;

  p = stack;
  tos = p;
  bos = p+MAX-1;

  window(2);
  do {
    window_xy(2, 0, 0);
    window_cleol(2);
    window_puts(2, ": "); /* calc prompt */
    window_gets(2, in);
    window_puts(2, "\n ");
    window_cleol(2);
    switch(*in) {
      case '+':
        a = pop();
        b = pop();
        answer = a+b;
        push(a+b);
        break;
      case '-':
        a = pop();
        b = pop();
        answer = b-a;
        push(b-a);
        break;
      case '*':
        a = pop();
        b = pop();
        answer = b*a;
        push(b*a);
        break;
      case '/':
        a = pop();
        b=pop();
        if(a==0) {
            window_puts("divide by 0\n");
```

```
            break;
        }
        answer = b/a;
        push(b/a);
        break;
      default:
        push(atoi(in));
        continue;
    }
    sprintf(out, "%d", answer);
    window_puts(2, out);
  } while(*in);
  deactivate(2);
}

/* Place a number on the stack.
   Returns 1 if successful;
   0 if stack is full.
*/
push(i)
int i;
{
  if(p>bos) return 0;

  *p=i;
  p++;
  return 1;
}

/* Retrieve top element from the stack.
   Returns 0 on stack underflows.
*/
pop()
{
  p--;
  if(p<tos) {
    p++;
    return 0;
  }
  return *p;
}
```

Pop-up Notepad

Another very useful pop-up application is the notepad. Often when
using a program, you may want to insert a note. When a pop-up notepad
is available, all you have to do is activate it, enter the note, and then
return to whatever you were doing. A very simple notepad function is
shown here.

```
#include "ctype.h"

/* Pop-up note pad. */
#define MAX_NOTE 10
#define BKSP 8
char notes[MAX_NOTE][80];

void notepad()
{
  static first=1;
  register int i, j;
  union inkey {
    char ch[2];
    int i;
  } c;
  char ch;

  /* initialize notes array if necessary */
  if(first) {
    for(i=0; i<MAX_NOTE; i++)
      *notes[i] = '\0';
    first = !first;
  }

  window(3);
  /* display the existing notes */
  for(i=0; i<MAX_NOTE; i++) {
    if(*notes[i]) window_puts(3, notes[i]);
    window_putchar(3, '\n');
  }

  i=0;
  window_xy(3, 0, 0);

  for(;;) {
    c.i = window_getche(3);        /* read the key */
    if(tolower(c.ch[1])==59) { /* F1 to quit */
      deactivate(3);
      break;
    }

    /* if normal key read in the note */
    if(isprint(c.ch[0]) || c.ch[0]==BKSP) {
      window_cleol(3);
      notes[i][0] = c.ch[0];
      j = 1;
      window_putchar(3, notes[i][0]);
      do {
        ch = window_getche(3);
        if(ch==BKSP) {
          if(j>0) {
            j--;
            window_bksp(3);
          }
        }
        else {
          notes[i][j] = ch;
          j++;
        }
```

```
    } while(notes[i][j-1]!='\r');
    notes[i][j-1] = '\0';
    i++;
    window_putchar(3, '\n');
  }
  else {  /* is special key */
    switch(c.ch[1]) {
      case 72:  /* up arrow */
        if(i>0) {
          i--;
          window_upline(3);
        }
        break;
      case 80:  /* down arrow */
        if(i<MAX_NOTE-1) {
          i++;
          window_downline(3);
        }
        break;
    }
  }
}
}
```

The **notepad( )** functions allows up to ten lines to be entered. You use the UP ARROW and DOWN ARROW keys to go to the line of your choice. If the line previously held a message, the line is erased. The F1 function key is used to exit the notepad.

PUTTING IT ALL TOGETHER

The sample program shown in this section includes all the window routines, the video support functions developed in Chapter 1, and the three window applications. It simulates an editor, and allows you to use the function keys to activate the various window applications or to demonstrate different features of the window system. You should enter it into your computer at this time.

```
/* Window routines with simple demostration program.
   An editor is simulated.  Three special pop-up window
   utilities illustrate both the power and magic of
   windowing software and also serve as examples of
   window programming.  The pop-up window routines
   are a four-function calculator, a decimal to hex
   converter, and a pop-up note pad.
*/
```

```c
#include "stdio.h"
#include "dos.h"
#include "stdlib.h"

#define BORDER 1
#define ESC 27
#define MAX_FRAME 10
#define REV_VID 0x70
#define NORM_VID 7
#define BKSP 8

void save_video(), restore_video(), pd_driver();
void goto_xy(), cls(), write_string(), write_char();
void display_header(), draw_border();
void window_gets(), size(), move(), window_cls();
void window_cleol(), window();
void dectohex(), notepad(), calc();

char far *vid_mem;

struct window_frame {
  int startx, endx, starty, endy;
  int curx, cury; /* current cursor position in window */
  unsigned char *p; /* pointer to buffer */
  char *header; /* header message */
  int border; /* border on/off */
  int active; /* on screen yes/no */
} frame[MAX_FRAME];

main()
{
  union inkey {
    char ch[2];
    int i;
  } c;
  int i;
  char ch;

  cls();
  goto_xy(0,0);

  /* first, create the window frames */
  make_window(0, " Editor [Esc to exit] ", 0, 0, 24, 78, BORDER);
  make_window(1, " Decimal to Hex ", 7, 40, 10, 70, BORDER);
  make_window(2, " Calculator ", 8, 20, 12, 60, BORDER);
  make_window(3, " Notepad [F1 to exit] ", 5, 20, 17, 60, BORDER);

  /* use window() to activate the specified window */
  window(0);
  do {
    c.i = window_getche(0);
    ch = c.i; /* use only low-order byte */
    if(ch=='\r') /* must do explicit crlf */
        window_putchar(0, '\n');

    switch(c.ch[1]) { /* see if arrow or function key */
      case 59: /* F1 demonstrate the window_xy() function */
        window(1);
        for(i=0; i<10; i++)
          if(window_xy(1, i, i)) window_putchar(1,'X');
```

```
            getch();
            deactivate(1);
            break;
        case 60: /* F2 demonstrate sizing and moving a window */
            size(1);
            move(1);
            break;
        case 61: /* F3 invoke the calculator */
            calc();
            break;
        case 62: /* F4 invoke the dec to hex converter */
            dectohex();
            break;
        case 63: /* F5 invoke the note pad */
            notepad();
            break;
        case 72: /* up */
            window_upline(0);
            break;
        case 80: /* down */
            window_downline(0);
            break;
    }
  } while (ch!=ESC);
  deactivate(0); /* remove window */
}

/***********************************************************/
/* Window functions                                       */
/***********************************************************/

/* Display a pull-down window. */
void window(num)
int num; /* window number */
{
  int  vmode, choice;
  int x, y;

  vmode = video_mode();
  if((vmode!=2) && (vmode!=3) && (vmode!=7)) {
    printf("video must be in 80 column text mode");
    exit(1);
  }
  /* set proper address of video RAM */
  if(vmode==7) vid_mem = (char far *) 0xB0000000;
  else vid_mem = (char far *) 0xB8000000;

  /* get active window */
  if(!frame[num].active) { /* not currently in use */
    save_video(num);       /* save the current screen */
    frame[num].active = 1; /* set active flag */
  }

  if(frame[num].border) draw_border(num);
  display_header(num); /* display the window */

  x = frame[num].startx + frame[num].curx + 1;
  y = frame[num].starty + frame[num].cury + 1;
  goto_xy(x, y);
}
```

```
/* Construct a pull down window frame
   1 is returned if window frame can be constructed;
   otherwise 0 is returned.
*/
make_window(num, header, startx, starty, endx, endy, border)
int num;          /* window number */
char *header;     /* header text */
int startx, starty; /* X,Y coordinates of upper left corner */
int endx, endy; /* X,Y coordinates of lower right corner */
int border;       /* no border if 0 */
{
  unsigned char *p;

  if(num>MAX_FRAME) {
    printf("Too many windows\n");
    return 0;
  }

  if((startx>24) || (startx<0) || (starty>78) || (starty<0)) {
    printf("range error");
    return 0;
  }

  if((endx>24) || (endy>79)) {
    printf("window won't fit");
    return 0;
  }

  /* allocate enough memory to hold it */
  p = (unsigned char *) malloc(2*(endx-startx+1)*(endy-starty+1));
  if(!p) exit(1); /* put your own error handler here */

  /* construct the frame */
  frame[num].startx = startx; frame[num].endx = endx;
  frame[num].starty = starty; frame[num].endy = endy;
  frame[num].p = p;
  frame[num].header = header;
  frame[num].border = border;
  frame[num].active = 0;
  frame[num].curx = 0; frame[num].cury = 0;
  return 1;
}

/* Deactivate a window and remove it from the screen. */
deactivate(num)
int num;
{
  /* reset the cursor postion to upper left corner */
  frame[num].curx = 0;
  frame[num].cury = 0;
  restore_video(num);
}

/* Interactively change the size of a window.
*/
void size(num)
int num;
{
  char ch;
  int x, y, startx, starty;
```

```
      /* activate if necessary */
      if(!frame[num].active) window(num);

      startx = x = frame[num].startx;
      starty = y = frame[num].starty;
      window_xy(num, 0, 0);

      do {
        ch = get_special();
        switch(ch) {
          case 75: /* left */
            starty--;
            break;
          case 77: /* right */
            starty++;
            break;
          case 72: /* up */
            startx--;
            break;
          case 80: /* down */
            startx++;
            break;
          case 71: /* up left */
            startx--; starty--;
            break;
          case 73: /* up right */
            startx--; starty++;
            break;
          case 79: /* down left*/
            startx++; starty--;
            break;
          case 81: /* down right */
            startx++; starty++;
            break;
          case 60: /* F2: cancel and use original size */
            startx = x;
            starty = y;
            ch = 59;
        }
        /* see if out-of-range */
        if(startx<0) startx++;
        if(startx>=frame[num].endx) startx--;
        if(starty<0) starty++;
        if(starty>=frame[num].endy) starty--;
        deactivate(num);
        frame[num].startx = startx;
        frame[num].starty = starty;
        window(num);
      } while(ch!=59);
      deactivate(num);
    }


    /* Interactively move a window
    */
    void move(num)
    int num;
    {
      char ch;
      int x, y, ex, ey, startx, starty, endx, endy;
```

```
/* activate if necessary */
if(!frame[num].active) window(num);

startx = x = frame[num].startx;
starty = y = frame[num].starty;
endx = ex = frame[num].endx;
endy = ey = frame[num].endy;
window_xy(num, 0, 0);

do {
  ch = get_special();
  switch(ch) {
    case 75: /* left */
      starty--;
      endy--;
      break;
    case 77: /* right */
      starty++;
      endy++;
      break;
    case 72: /* up */
      startx--;
      endx--;
      break;
    case 80: /* down */
      startx++;
      endx++;
      break;
    case 71: /* up left */
      startx--; starty--;
      endx--; endy--;
      break;
    case 73: /* up right */
      startx--; starty++;
      endx--; endy++;
      break;
    case 79: /* down left*/
      startx++; starty--;
      endx++; endy--;
      break;
    case 81: /* down right */
      startx++; starty++;
      endx++; endy++;
      break;
    case 60: /* F2: cancel and use original size */
      startx = x;
      starty = y;
      endx = ex;
      endy = ey;
      ch = 59;
  }

  /* see if out-of-range */
  if(startx<0) {
    startx++;
    endx++;
  }
  if(endx>=25) {
    startx--;
    endx--;
```

```
      }
      if(starty<0) {
        starty++;
        endy++;
      }
      if(endy>=79) {
        starty--;
        endy--;
      }
      deactivate(num);
      frame[num].startx = startx;
      frame[num].starty = starty;
      frame[num].endx = endx;
      frame[num].endy = endy;
      window(num);
  } while(ch!=59);
  deactivate(num);
}

/* Display the header message in its proper location. */
void display_header(num)
int num;
{
  register int y, len;

  y = frame[num].starty;

  /* Calculate the correct starting position to center
     the header message - if negative, message won't
     fit.
  */
  len = strlen(frame[num].header);
  len = (frame[num].endy - y - len) / 2;
  if(len<0) return; /* don't display it */
  y = y +len;

  write_string(frame[num].startx, y,
               frame[num].header, NORM_VID);
}

void draw_border(num)
int num;
{
  register int i;
  char far *v, far *t;

  v = vid_mem;
  t = v;
  for(i=frame[num].startx+1; i<frame[num].endx; i++) {
      v += (i*160) + frame[num].starty*2;
      *v++ = 179;
      *v = NORM_VID;
      v = t;
      v += (i*160) + frame[num].endy*2;
      *v++ = 179;
      *v = NORM_VID;
      v = t;
  }
  for(i=frame[num].starty+1; i<frame[num].endy; i++) {
      v += (frame[num].startx*160) + i*2;
      *v++ = 196;
```

```
      *v = NORM_VID;
      v = t;
      v += (frame[num].endx*160) + i*2;
      *v++ = 196;
      *v = NORM_VID;
      v = t;
   }
   write_char(frame[num].startx, frame[num].starty, 218, NORM_VID);
   write_char(frame[num].startx, frame[num].endy, 191, NORM_VID);
   write_char(frame[num].endx, frame[num].starty, 192, NORM_VID);
   write_char(frame[num].endx, frame[num].endy, 217, NORM_VID);
}

/**************************************************************/
/* Window I/O functions                                     */
/**************************************************************/

/* Write a string at the current cursor position
   in the specified window.
   Returns 0 if window not active;
   1 otherwise.
*/
window_puts(num, str)
int num;
char *str;
{
   /* make sure window is active */
   if(!frame[num].active) return 0;

   for( ; *str;  str++)
     window_putchar(num, *str);
   return 1;
}

/* Write a character at the current cursor position
   in the specified window.
   Returns 0 if window not active;
   1 otherwise.
*/
window_putchar(num, ch)
int num;
char ch;
{
   register int x, y;
   char far *v;

   /* make sure window is active */
   if(!frame[num].active) return 0;

   x = frame[num].curx + frame[num].startx + 1;
   y = frame[num].cury + frame[num].starty + 1;

   v = vid_mem;
   v += (x*160) + y*2; /* compute the address */
   if(y>=frame[num].endy) {
     return 1;
   }
   if(x>=frame[num].endx) {
     return 1;
   }
```

```
      if(ch=='\n') { /* newline char */
        x++;
        y = frame[num].startx+1;
        v = vid_mem;
        v += (x*160) + y*2; /* compute the address */
        frame[num].curx++;  /* increment X */
        frame[num].cury = 0; /* reset Y */
      }
      else {
        frame[num].cury++;
        *v++ = ch;  /* write the character */
        *v++ = NORM_VID;     /* normal video attribute */
      }
      window_xy(num, frame[num].curx, frame[num].cury);
      return 1;
    }


    /* Position cursor in a window at specified location.
       Returns 0 if out of range;
       non-zero otherwise.
    */
    window_xy(num, x, y)
    int num, x, y;
    {
      if(x<0 || x+frame[num].startx>=frame[num].endx-1)
        return 0;
      if(y<0 || y+frame[num].starty>=frame[num].endy-1)
        return 0;
      frame[num].curx = x;
      frame[num].cury = y;
      goto_xy(frame[num].startx+x+1, frame[num].starty+y+1);
      return 1;
    }


    /* Read a string from a window. */
    void window_gets(num, s)
    int num;
    char *s;
    {
      char ch, *temp;

      temp = s;
      for(;;) {
        ch = window_getche(num);
        switch(ch) {
          case '\r':  /* the ENTER key is pressed */
            *s='\0';
            return;
          case BKSP: /* backspace */
            if(s>temp) {
              s--;
              frame[num].cury--;
              if(frame[num].cury<0) frame[num].cury = 0;
                window_xy(num, frame[num].curx, frame[num].cury);
                  write_char(frame[num].startx+ frame[num].curx+1,
                  frame[num].starty+frame[num].cury+1, ' ', NORM_VID);
            }
            break;
          default: *s = ch;
            s++;
        }
      }
    }
```

```
/* Input keystrokes inside a window.
   Returns full 16 bit scan code.
*/
window_getche(num)
int num;
{
  union inkey {
    char ch[2];
    int i;
  } c;

  if(!frame[num].active) return 0; /* window not active */

  window_xy(num, frame[num].curx, frame[num].cury);

  c.i = bioskey(0);        /* read the key */

  if(c.ch[0]) {
    switch(c.ch[0]) {
      case '\r': /* the ENTER key is pressed */
        break;
      case BKSP: /* back space */
        break;
      default:
        if(frame[num].cury+frame[num].starty < frame[num].endy-1) {
        write_char(frame[num].startx+ frame[num].curx+1,
          frame[num].starty+frame[num].cury+1, c.ch[0], NORM_VID);
          frame[num].cury++;
        }
    }
    if(frame[num].curx < 0) frame[num].curx = 0;
    if(frame[num].curx+frame[num].startx > frame[num].endx-2)
      frame[num].curx--;
    window_xy(num, frame[num].curx, frame[num].cury);
  }
  return c.i;
}

/* Clear a window. */
void window_cls(num)
int num;
{
  register int i,j;
  char far *v, far *t;

  v = vid_mem;
  t = v;
  for(i=frame[num].starty+1; i<frame[num].endy; i++)
    for(j=frame[num].startx+1; j<frame[num].endx; j++) {
      v = t;
      v += (j*160) + i*2;
      *v++ = ' ';  /* write a space */
      *v = NORM_VID;    /* normal */
    }
  frame[num].curx = 0;
  frame[num].cury = 0;
}

/* Clear to end of line. */
void window_cleol(num)
int num;
{
```

```
    register int i, x, y;

    x = frame[num].curx;
    y = frame[num].cury;
    window_xy(num, frame[num].curx, frame[num].cury);

    for(i=frame[num].cury; i<frame[num].endy-1; i++)
      window_putchar(num,' ');
    window_xy(num, x, y);
}

/* Move cursor up one line.
   Returns non-zero if successful;
   0 otherwise.
*/
window_upline(num)
int num;
{
  if(frame[num].curx>0) {
    frame[num].curx--;
    window_xy(num, frame[num].curx, frame[num].cury);
    return 1;
  }
  return 0;
}

/* Move cursor down one line.
   Returns non-zero if successful;
   0 otherwise.
*/
window_downline(num)
int num;
{
  if(frame[num].curx<frame[num].endx-frame[num].startx-1) {
    frame[num].curx++;
    window_xy(num, frame[num].curx, frame[num].cury);
    return 1;
  }
  return 1;
}

/* back up one character. */
window_bksp(num)
int num;
{
  if(frame[num].cury>0) {
    frame[num].cury--;
    window_xy(num, frame[num].curx, frame[num].cury);
    window_putchar(num, ' ');
    frame[num].cury--;
    window_xy(num, frame[num].curx, frame[num].cury);
  }
}

/*****************************************************/
/* Misc. functions                                 */
/*****************************************************/

/* Display a string with specifed attribute. */
void write_string(x, y, p, attrib)
int x, y;
char *p;
```

```
  int attrib;
  {
    register int i;
    char far *v;

    v = vid_mem;
    v += (x*160) + y*2; /* compute the address */
    for(i=y; *p; i++) {
      *v++ = *p++;  /* write the character */
      *v++ = attrib;    /* write the attribute */
    }
  }

  /* Write character with specified attribute. */
  void write_char(x, y, ch, attrib)
  int x, y;
  char ch;
  int attrib;
  {
    register int i;
    char far *v;

    v = vid_mem;
    v += (x*160) + y*2;
    *v++ = ch;  /* write the character */
    *v = attrib;    /* write the attribute */
  }

  /* Save a portion of the screen. */
  void save_video(num)
  int num;
  {
    register int i,j;
    char *buf_ptr;
    char far *v, far *t;

    buf_ptr = frame[num].p;
    v = vid_mem;
    for(i=frame[num].starty; i<frame[num].endy+1; i++)
      for(j=frame[num].startx; j<frame[num].endx+1; j++) {
        t = (v + (j*160) + i*2);
        *buf_ptr++ = *t++;
        *buf_ptr++ = *t;
        *(t-1) = ' ';  /* clear the window */
      }
  }

  /* Restore a portion of the screen. */
  void restore_video(num)
  int num;
  {
    register int i,j;
    char far *v, far *t;
    char *buf_ptr;

    buf_ptr = frame[num].p;
    v = vid_mem;
    t = v;
    for(i=frame[num].starty; i<frame[num].endy+1; i++)
      for(j=frame[num].startx; j<frame[num].endx+1; j++) {
        v = t;
        v += (j*160) + i*2;
```

```
      *v++ = *buf_ptr++;   /* write the character */
      *v = *buf_ptr++;     /* write the attribute */
   }
   frame[num].active = 0; /* restore_video */
}

/* Clear the screen. */
void cls()
{
   union REGS r;

   r.h.ah=6; /* screen scroll code */
   r.h.al=0; /* clear screen code */
   r.h.ch=0; /* start row */
   r.h.cl=0; /* start column */
   r.h.dh=24; /* end row */
   r.h.dl=79; /* end column */
   r.h.bh=7;  /* blank line is black */
   int86(0x10, &r, &r);
}

/* Send the cursor to the specified X,Y position. */
void goto_xy(x,y)
int x,y;
{
   union REGS r;

   r.h.ah=2; /* cursor addressing function */
   r.h.dl=y; /* column coordinate */
   r.h.dh=x; /* row coordinate */
   r.h.bh=0; /* video page */
   int86(0x10, &r, &r);
}

/* Return the position code of arrow and function keys. */
get_special()
{
   union inkey {
      char ch[2];
      int i;
   } c;

 /* while(!bioskey(1)) ; /* wait for key stroke */
   c.i = bioskey(0);       /* read the key */

   return c.ch[1];
}

/* Returns the current video mode. */
video_mode()
{
   union REGS r;

   r.h.ah = 15;  /* get video mode */
   return int86(0x10, &r, &r) & 255;
}

is_in(s, c)
```

```
char *s, c;
{
  register int i;

  for(i=0; *s; i++) if(*s++==c) return i+1;
  return 0;
}

#include "ctype.h"
/*****************************************************/
/* pop-up window functions                        */
/*****************************************************/

#define MAX 100

int *p;    /* pointer into the stack */
int *tos;  /* points to top of stack */
int *bos;  /* points to bottom of stack */

/* Stack based, postfix notation four-function calculator */
void calc()
{
  char in[80], out[80];
  int answer, stack[MAX];
  int a,b;

  p = stack;
  tos = p;
  bos = p+MAX-1;

  window(2);
  do {
    window_xy(2, 0, 0);
    window_cleol(2);
    window_puts(2, ": "); /* calc prompt */
    window_gets(2, in);
    window_puts(2, "\n ");
    window_cleol(2);
    switch(*in) {
      case '+':
        a = pop();
        b = pop();
        answer = a+b;
        push(a+b);
        break;
      case '-':
        a = pop();
        b = pop();
        answer = b-a;
        push(b-a);
        break;
      case '*':
        a = pop();
        b = pop();
        answer = b*a;
        push(b*a);
        break;
```

```
    case '/':
      a = pop();
      b=pop();
      if(a==0) {
          window_puts("divide by 0\n");
          break;
      }
      answer = b/a;
      push(b/a);
      break;
    default:
      push(atoi(in));
      continue;
  }
  sprintf(out, "%d", answer);
  window_puts(2, out);
} while(*in);
deactivate(2);
}

/* Place a number on the stack.
   Returns 1 if successful;
   0 if stack is full.
*/
push(i)
int i;
{
  if(p>bos) return 0;

  *p=i;
  p++;
  return 1;
}

/* Retrieve top element from the stack.
   Returns 0 on stack underflows.
*/
pop()
{
  p--;
  if(p<tos) {
    p++;
    return 0;
  }
  return *p;
}


/*********************************************************/

/* Decimal to hexadecimal converter. */
void dectohex()
{
  char in[80], out[80];
  int n;

  window(1);
  do {
    window_xy(1, 0, 0);  /* go to first line */
    window_cleol(1); /* clear the line */
    window_puts(1, "dec: "); /* prompt */
    window_gets(1, in); /* read the number */
```

```
    window_putchar(1, '\n'); /* go to next line */
    window_cleol(1); /* clear it */
    sscanf(in,"%d", &n); /* convert to internal format */
    sprintf(out, "%s%X", "hex: ",n); /* convert to hex */
    window_puts(1, out); /* output hex */
  } while(*in);
  deactivate(1);
}

/*****************************************************/

/* Pop-up note pad. */
#define MAX_NOTE 10
#define BKSP 8
char notes[MAX_NOTE][80];

void notepad()
{
  static first=1;
  register int i, j;
  union inkey {
    char ch[2];
    int i;
  } c;
  char ch;

  /* initialize notes array if necessary */
  if(first) {
    for(i=0; i<MAX_NOTE; i++)
      *notes[i] = '\0';
    first = !first;
  }

  window(3);
  /* display the existing notes */
  for(i=0; i<MAX_NOTE; i++) {
    if(*notes[i]) window_puts(3, notes[i]);
    window_putchar(3, '\n');
  }

  i=0;
  window_xy(3, 0, 0);

  for(;;) {
    c.i = bioskey(0);      /* read the key */
    if(tolower(c.ch[1])==59) { /* F1 to quit */
      deactivate(3);
      break;
    }

    /* if normal key */
    if(isprint(c.ch[0]) || c.ch[0]==BKSP) {
      window_cleol(3);
      notes[i][0] = c.ch[0];
      j = 1;
      window_putchar(3, notes[i][0]);
      do {
        ch = window_getche(3);
        if(ch==BKSP) {
          if(j>0) {
            j--;
            window_bksp(3);
```

```
          }
        }
        else {
          notes[i][j] = ch;
          j++;
        }
      } while(notes[i][j-1]!='\r');
      notes[i][j-1] = '\0';
      i++;
      window_putchar(3, '\n');
    }
    else {   /* is special key */
      switch(c.ch[1]) {
        case 72:   /* up arrow */
          if(i>0) {
            i--;
            window_upline(3);
          }
          break;
        case 80:   /* down arrow */
          if(i<MAX_NOTE-1) {
            i++;
            window_downline(3);
          }
          break;
      }
    }
  }
}
```

The first five function keys do the following:

F1   demonstrates the **window__xy( )** function
F2   demonstrates sizing and moving a window
F3   invokes the calculator
F4   invokes the decimal to hexadecimal converter
F5   invokes the notepad

Figures 2-1, 2-2, and 2-3 illustrate the appearance of the pop-up menus on the screen. In Figure 2-4, the decimal to hexadecimal converter window has been enlarged and moved.

WINDOW MODIFICATIONS

With the window routines developed in this chapter, you must always specify the window to use. This approach gives you, the programmer, the greatest flexibility. Another way of handling windows is the stack-based method.

```
 ──────────────────── Editor [Esc to exit] ────────────────────
│                                                                │
│ To whom it may concern:                                        │
│                                                                │
│ This is to inform you that D. W. Porkbellies will no longer    │
│ be providing its customers with the following products:        │
│                                                                │
│                  ──────────── Calculator ───────────           │
│                 │                                   │          │
│                 │ :                                 │          │
│                 │                                   │          │
│                 │                                   │          │
│                  ───────────────────────────────────           │
│                                                                │
│                                                                │
│                                                                │
│                                                                │
│                                                                │
│                                                                │
│                                                                │
│                                                                │
│                                                                │
│                                                                │
 ────────────────────────────────────────────────────────────
```

Figure 2-1.

The calculator window

```
 ──────────────────── Editor [Esc to exit] ────────────────────
│                                                                │
│ To whom it may concern:                                        │
│                                                                │
│ This is to inform you that D. W. Porkbellies will no longer    │
│ be providing its customers with the following products:        │
│                                      ──── Decimal to Hex ────   │
│                 . meat and oats fak │ dec: 12                │  │
│                                     │ hex: C                 │  │
│                 . lime cola drink p  ────────────────────────   │
│                                                                │
│                 . syrup coated sizzle links                    │
│                                                                │
│                                                                │
│                                                                │
│                                                                │
│                                                                │
│                                                                │
│                                                                │
│                                                                │
│                                                                │
 ────────────────────────────────────────────────────────────
```

Figure 2-2.

The decimal to hexadecimal window

```
┌──────────────────── Editor [Esc to exit] ─────────────────────┐
│                                                                │
│ To whom it may concern:                                        │
│                                                                │
│ This is to inform you that D. W. Porkbellies will no longer    │
│ be providing its cu┌────────── Notepad [F1 to exit] ─────────┐ │
│                     │ call Sherry                             │ │
│                     │ go to the store                         │ │
│                     │                                         │ │
│                     │                                         │ │
│                     │                                         │ │
│                     │                                         │ │
│                     │                                         │ │
│                     │                                         │ │
│                     │                                         │ │
│                     │                                         │ │
│                     └─────────────────────────────────────────┘ │
│                                                                │
│                                                                │
│                                                                │
│                                                                │
│                                                                │
│                                                                │
└────────────────────────────────────────────────────────────────┘
```

Figure 2-3.

The notepad window

```
┌──────────────────── Editor [Esc to exit] ─────────────────────┐
│                                                                │
│ To whom it may concern:                                        │
│                                                                │
│ This is to inform you that D. W. Porkbellies will no longer    │
│ be providing its customers with the following products:        │
│                                                                │
│                                                                │
│                . meat and oats fake burgers                    │
│                                                                │
│                . lime cola drink pops                          │
│                                                                │
│              ┌──── Decimal to Hex ────┐le links                │
│              │                         │                        │
│              │                         │                        │
│              │                         │                        │
│              │                         │                        │
│              │                         │                        │
│              │                         │                        │
│              └─────────────────────────┘                       │
│                                                                │
└────────────────────────────────────────────────────────────────┘
```

Figure 2-4.

The decimal to hexadecimal window
resized and moved

In this approach, the window-specified I/O routines do not take the window number as an argument. Instead, the window numbers are pushed on a stack in the order in which they are activated. The window routines always use the window that is on top of the stack. When a window is deactivated, its number is popped off the stack. The advantage to this method is that you don't have to worry about which window number you are using. You might find it interesting to modify the window routines to work in this way.

Another variation is to allow a window to scroll when the cursor is at the bottom. As the routines are presently written, when the cursor is at the bottom of the window and RETURN is pressed, nothing happens. However, you can alter the routines so that the top line is scrolled off the screen and a blank one is brought up from the bottom.

Finally, for those readers who have color displays, using different color borders for different windows can, if applied correctly, add even more visual appeal to your application.

3: Terminate and Stay Resident Pop-up Programs

An apparently simple concept, creating terminate and stay resident (TSR) pop-up programs, is actually one of the most difficult programming tasks in the PC environment. For this chapter, you had better strap on your safety belt and put on your crash helmet, because TSR programming is fraught with peril! The risks, however, are balanced by the rewards—truly professional results of which any world-class programmer would be proud.

Because TSR programs must, by nature, work closely with the hardware and operating system, the material in this chapter is applicable only to the PC line of computers running DOS. Also, for reasons that will become apparent, the examples are specific to Turbo C; they can, however, be generalized to other compilers.

WARNING: Intrinsic to the development and use of a TSR program is the modification of the interrupt vector table. The program examples shown in this chapter were compiled using Turbo C version

1.0 and run correctly with no known side effects, but they may not work correctly with a different compiler. In addition, if you enter the code manually, you can easily create a small error. In either of these situations you must expect several system crashes. As you know, it is possible to destroy data on your hard disk, so make sure your backups are current. I am sure that I crashed my model 60 at least 100 times during the two-day period I worked on the basic skeleton of code. (Fortunately, I did not crash my hard disk.)

WHAT IS A TSR PROGRAM?

A TSR program exits via a call to DOS function 49, which causes the program to return to DOS, while the program itself is left in memory that is no longer usable by DOS. In this way, the program can be instantly activated without having to be loaded again. One of the many well-known examples of TSR programs is Borland's Sidekick.

Most TSR programs are activated through the use of an interrupt, which may be generated in several ways. The most common interrupts are the clock, keyboard, and print screen. For TSR pop-up programs either the key-press or the print screen interrupt is generally used because it allows the user to activate the TSR program with a single keystroke.

INTERRUPTS ON THE 8086 FAMILY
OF PROCESSORS

The 8086 family of processors supports 256 vectored interrupts. A *vectored interrupt* begins executing an interrupt service routine (ISR) at the location specified in the interrupt vector table. Although some older processors force an ISR to be in a special location in memory, a vectored interrupt allows you to specify the location of the ISR.

The vector table is 1024 bytes long and begins at location 0000:0000. Since the address of the ISR may be anywhere in memory, a 32-bit (4-byte) address is required. Therefore, each entry in the table is 4 bytes wide. The addresses are arranged such that interrupt 0 finds the address of its ISR at location 0000:0000, interrupt 1 finds the address of its ISR at 0000:0004, interrupt 2 finds its ISR's address at 0000:0008, and so on.

When an interrupt occurs, it causes all interrupts to be disabled. Your ISR must enable interrupts upon entry to avoid crashing the system. The ISR must also end with an IRET instruction.

INTERRUPTS VERSUS DOS AND BIOS: TROUBLE IN DOS-LAND

Programmers frequently complain that DOS is not *re-entrant*, that is, while being used by a program DOS may not be used by a second program. (This helps explain why DOS is not multitasking.) Thus, the ISR cannot use any DOS functions, and attempting to do so causes a system crash; you must provide code to control directly many functions for which you would normally have used DOS calls. Fortunately, for video output, we can use the direct video RAM routines from Chapters 1 and 2.

The BIOS allows some re-entrancy. For example, interrupt 16, keyboard input, is usable without side effects. Some other services, however, may not be safe to use. The only way to find out is through experimentation. If a function cannot be used, you will know because the computer will crash! For the examples in the chapter — and for many real world programs — interrupt 16 is all that is needed.

Because many of the C standard library functions use DOS or BIOS, they have to be recoded so that no DOS or unusable BIOS calls are made. Keep in mind that the I/O functions are not the only ones that use DOS or BIOS. For example, the memory allocation function **malloc( )** generally uses a DOS call to determine how much free memory is available in the system. Worse, what works with one compiler may not work with another. This is the main reason why TSR programs are so difficult to write and port to new environments and why so few TSR programs are created even though they are so popular.

Essentially, you must think of a TSR program as being a "renegade" program whose existence is not known to DOS. Further, to maintain its secrecy the TSR program must avoid all interaction with DOS. Should the two interact, only carnage can result. To avoid this interaction, you must think like a spy and have the nerves of a race car driver.

TURBO C INTERRUPT FUNCTION MODIFIER

Although not part of the ANSI standard, Turbo C includes a special function type modifier called **interrupt**, which allows a C function to be used as an ISR. (Most major C compiler developers will probably include this type in future releases because it is an important extension.) For example, assume that the function **test( )** is to be used as an interrupt handler. You would declare it as shown here. The parameters, which will contain the values of the respective registers at the time of the interrupt, do not need to be specified if they are not used.

```
void interrupt test(bp, di, si, ds, es, dx, cx, bx,
                    ax, ip, cs, flags)
unsigned bp, di, si, ds, es, dx, cx, bx, ax, ip, cs, flags;
{
    .
    .
    .
}
```

An **interrupt** function automatically saves the contents of all registers and restores them prior to returning. The function also uses the IRET instead of the usual RET instruction to return.

For the examples in this book, the **interrupt** modifier is applied only to those functions that serve as the entry point to the TSR program's interrupt service routines.

If your compiler does not support the **interrupt** modifier, you have to write a short assembly language interface module that saves all the registers, re-enables interrupts, and then calls the proper C function. On exit, it must use an IRET. The means of creating an assembly language function vary with each compiler, so check your user manual.

GENERAL DESIGN OF A TSR PROGRAM

All TSR programs are really two programs in one. The first part of the TSR program is used to initialize the program and then exit via the TSR DOS function call. This part of the program is not executed again unless the TSR program must be reloaded. Part of the initialization always includes putting the address of the TSR program's entry point into the proper location in the vector table.

The second part of the program is the actual pop-up application. Almost without exception, pop-up applications use windows and require window routines. In this way, the screen is not altered when the application exits. Remember, most TSR applications are pop-up utilities, such as notepads and calculators, which should leave the screen in the same condition they found it.

USING THE PRINT SCREEN INTERRUPT

Without a doubt, the easiest interrupt to "steal" is number 5. This interrupt is called when the PT SCR key is pressed. If you are willing to give up the print screen function, you can overlay the address of the print screen routine with the address of your pop-up TSR application. In this way, whenever you press the PT SCR key, your TSR application will be activated.

The example developed here is a pop-up calculator. The same routines used for windows and the calculator in Chapter 2 are applied here with a few simple modifications.

Initialization Portion

The initialization for the pop-up calculator program is quite short and is contained largely in **main( )**, shown here.

```
void interrupt tsr_ap(); /* entry to application */

main()
{
  struct address {
    char far *p;
  } ;
  /* address of the print screen interrupt */
  struct address far *addr = (struct address far *) 20;

  addr->p = (char far *) tsr_ap;
  set_vid_mem();
  tsr(2000);
}
```

The TSR program must first change the address at interrupt 5 to point to the function specified by the TSR program. There are several ways to change an address in the interrupt vector table. One way is to use a DOS call. The trouble with the DOS function is that it requires the address segment to be in the ES register, which is not available for use with **int86( )**. Some compilers, such as Turbo C, include special functions to get or set an address into the interrupt table. However, the method shown here should work with virtually any compiler. The function **tsr—ap( )** is the entry point into the TSR application. It uses a pointer to the location of interrupt 5's vector table location. (Remember, the location of interrupt 5 is at 20 [4 x 5], because all addresses are 4 bytes long.) Some TSR programs have an option that resets the previous interrupt address, but in the programs developed here, you must reboot the system to restore the original interrupts.

In the previous chapters, the video mode was checked dynamically by the routines while they were in use. However, this is no longer possible because it requires a DOS call. Instead, the value of the global pointer **vid—mem** is set by the function **set—vid—mem( )**, shown here.

```
set_vid_mem()
{
  int vmode;

  vmode = video_mode();
  if((vmode!=2) && (vmode!=3) && (vmode!=7)) {
    printf("video must be in 80 column text mode");
    exit(1);
  }
  /* set proper address of video RAM */
  if(vmode==7) vid_mem = (char far *) 0xB0000000;
  else vid_mem = (char far *) 0xB8000000;
}
```

Finally, **main**( ) exits via a call to **tsr**( ), shown here.

```
/* terminate but keep resident */
tsr(size)
unsigned size;
{
  union REGS r;

  r.h.ah = 49;  /* terminate and stay resident */
  r.h.al = 0;   /* return code */
  r.x.dx = size;
  int86(0x21, &r, &r);
}
```

The **size** parameter, specified in DX is used to tell DOS how much memory to allow for the TSR program. It is specified in paragraphs. A paragraph is 16 bytes. It is sometimes difficult to determine the amount of memory required by your program, but generally you will be safe if you divide the size of your program's .EXE file by 16 and then double it. The exact amount of memory is difficult to determine because .EXE files are partially linked when they are loaded into memory and are not necessarily placed in contiguous regions. (If you are planning to market your applications, you certainly want to know exactly how much memory is needed so as not to be wasteful; the easiest way to determine this is to experiment.) The return code specified in AL is returned to the system.

After **main**( ) has executed, the program is still in RAM and cannot be overwritten by any other program. This means that the application portion is ready for execution any time the PT SCR key is pressed.

TSR Application Portion

The first function that needs to be developed, the entry point into the application, must be an **interrupt** function. The one shown here activates the application code by calling **window—main( )**.

```
/* This is the entry point into the TSR application code. */
void interrupt tsr_ap()
{
  if(!busy) {
    busy = !busy;
    window_main();
    busy = !busy;
  }
}
```

The **busy** variable, a global, is initialized to 0. The code to the TSR application is not re-entrant; therefore it must not be activated a second time while it is in use; the **busy** variable prevents this. (Some C compilers may create re-entrant code, but it is safer not to assume this.)

A few changes to the window routines are necessary to allow them to work in a TSR environment. First, it is necessary to statically allocate the memory necessary to store the current contents of the screen by using a global array. You may recall that this memory was allocated dynamically, but this method will not work here because the allocation functions use a DOS call, which is not allowed in a TSR application. For the same reason the **goto—xy( )** function cannot be used to position the cursor. Finally, the standard C functions **sscanf( )** and **sprintf( )** cannot be used (at least in Turbo C) because they appear to make calls to DOS, so **atoi( )** and **itoa( )** are substituted. The entire TSR pop-up calculator program is shown here.

```
/* Terminate and stay resident using the print screen
   interrupt.
*/
#include "dos.h"
#include "stdlib.h"

#define BORDER 1
#define ESC 27
```

```c
#define MAX_FRAME 1
#define REV_VID 0x70
#define NORM_VID 7
#define BKSP 8

void interrupt tsr_ap();
void save_video(), restore_video();
void write_string(), write_char();
void display_header(), draw_border();
void window_gets();
void window_cleol(), window();
void calc();

char far *vid_mem;

struct window_frame {
  int startx, endx, starty, endy;
  int curx, cury; /* current cursor position in window */
  unsigned char *p; /* pointer to buffer */
  char *header; /* header message */
  int border; /* border on/off */
  int active; /* on screen yes/no */
} frame[MAX_FRAME];

char wp[4000]; /* buffer to hold current contents of the screen */

/* busy is set to 1 when the program is active, 0 otherwise */
char busy = 0;

main()
{
  struct address {
    char far *p;
  } ;
  /* address of the print screen interrupt */
  struct address far *addr = (struct address far *) 20;

  addr->p = (char far *) tsr_ap;
  set_vid_mem();
  tsr(2000);
}

set_vid_mem()
{
  int vmode;

  vmode = video_mode();
  if((vmode!=2) && (vmode!=3) && (vmode!=7)) {
    printf("video must be in 80 column text mode");
    exit(1);
  }
  /* set proper address of video RAM */
  if(vmode==7) vid_mem = (char far *) 0xB0000000;
  else vid_mem = (char far *) 0xB8000000;
}

/* this is the entry point into the TSR application code */
void interrupt tsr_ap()
{
```

```
      if(!busy) {
        busy = !busy;
        window_main();
        busy = !busy;
      }
    }

    /* terminate but keep resident */
    tsr(size)
    unsigned size;
    {
      union REGS r;

      r.h.ah = 49;   /* terminate and stay resident */
      r.h.al = 0;    /* return code */
      r.x.dx = size;
      int86(0x21, &r, &r);
    }


    window_main()
    {
      /* first, create the window frames */
      make_window(0, " Calculator ", 8, 20, 12, 60, BORDER);
      /* use window() to activate the specified window */
      calc();
    }


    /**************************************************************/
    /* Window functions                                         */
    /**************************************************************/

    /* Display a pull-down window. */
    void window(num)
    int num; /* window number */
    {

      int   vmode, choice;
      int x, y;

      /* get active window */
      if(!frame[num].active) { /* not currently in use */
        save_video(num);       /* save the current screen */
        frame[num].active = 1; /* set active flag */
      }

      if(frame[num].border) draw_border(num);
      display_header(num); /* display the window */
    }

    /* Construct a pull down window frame
       1 is returned if window frame can be constructed;
       otherwise 0 is returned.
    */
    make_window(num, header, startx, starty, endx, endy, border)
    int num;        /* window number */
    char *header;    /* header text */
```

```
int startx, starty; /* X,Y coordinates of upper left corner */
int endx, endy; /* X,Y coordinates of lower right corner */
int border;      /* no border if 0 */
{
   register int i;
   int choice, vmode;
   unsigned char *p;

   if(num>MAX_FRAME) {
     window_puts(0, "Too many windows\n");
     return 0;
   }

   if((startx>24) || (startx<0) || (starty>70) || (starty<0)) {
     window_puts(0, "range error");
     return 0;
   }

   if((endx>24) || (endy>79)) {
     window_puts(0, "window won't fit");
     return 0;
   }

   /* construct the frame */
   frame[num].startx = startx; frame[num].endx = endx;
   frame[num].starty = starty; frame[num].endy = endy;
   frame[num].p = wp;
   frame[num].header = header;
   frame[num].border = border;
   frame[num].active = 0;
   frame[num].curx = 0; frame[num].cury = 0;
   return 1;
}


/* Deactivate a window and remove it from the screen. */
deactivate(num)
int num;
{
   /* reset the cursor postion to upper left corner */
   frame[num].curx = 0;
   frame[num].cury = 0;
   restore_video(num);
}

/* Display the header message in its proper location. */
void display_header(num)
int num;
{
   register int i, y, len;

   y = frame[num].starty;

   /* Calculate the correct starting position to center
      the header message - if negative, message won't
      fit.
   */
   len = strlen(frame[num].header);
```

```
        len = (frame[num].endy - y - len) / 2;
        if(len<0) return; /* don't display it */
        y = y +len;

        write_string(frame[num].startx, y,
                     frame[num].header, NORM_VID);
}

void draw_border(num)
int num;
{
    register int i;
    char far *v, far *t;

    v = vid_mem;
    t = v;
    for(i=frame[num].startx+1; i<frame[num].endx; i++) {
        v += (i*160) + frame[num].starty*2;
        *v++ = 179;
        *v = NORM_VID;
        v = t;
        v += (i*160) + frame[num].endy*2;
        *v++ = 179;
        *v = NORM_VID;
        v = t;
    }
    for(i=frame[num].starty+1; i<frame[num].endy; i++) {
        v += (frame[num].startx*160) + i*2;
        *v++ = 196;
        *v = NORM_VID;
        v = t;
        v += (frame[num].endx*160) + i*2;
        *v++ = 196;
        *v = NORM_VID;
        v = t;
    }
    write_char(frame[num].startx, frame[num].starty, 218, NORM_VID);
    write_char(frame[num].startx, frame[num].endy, 191, NORM_VID);
    write_char(frame[num].endx, frame[num].starty, 192, NORM_VID);
    write_char(frame[num].endx, frame[num].endy, 217, NORM_VID);
}

/*************************************************************/
/* Window I/O functions                                    */
/*************************************************************/

/* Write a string at the current cursor position
   in the specified window.
   Returns 0 if window not active;
   1 otherwise.
*/
window_puts(num, str)
int num;
char *str;
{
    /* make sure window is active */
    if(!frame[num].active) return 0;
```

```
    for( ; *str; str++)
      window_putchar(num, *str);
    return 1;
}

/* Write a character at the current cursor position
   in the specified window.
   Returns 0 if window not active;
   1 otherwise.
*/
window_putchar(num, ch)
int num;
char ch;
{
  register int x, y;
  char far *v;

  /* make sure window is active */
  if(!frame[num].active) return 0;

  x = frame[num].curx + frame[num].startx + 1;
  y = frame[num].cury + frame[num].starty + 1;

  v = vid_mem;
  v += (x*160) + y*2; /* compute the address */
  if(y>=frame[num].endy) {
    return 1;
  }
  if(x>=frame[num].endx) {
    return 1;
  }

  if(ch=='\n') { /* newline char */
    x++;
    y = frame[num].startx+1;
    v = vid_mem;
    v += (x*160) + y*2; /* compute the address */
    frame[num].curx++;  /* increment X */
    frame[num].cury = 0; /* reset Y */
  }
  else {
    frame[num].cury++;
    *v++ = ch;  /* write the character */
    *v++ = NORM_VID;     /* normal video attribute */
  }
  window_xy(num, frame[num].curx, frame[num].cury);
  return 1;
}

/* Position cursor in a window at specified location.
   Returns 0 if out of range;
   non-zero otherwise.
*/
window_xy(num, x, y)
int num, x, y;
{
```

```
        if(x<0 || x+frame[num].startx>=frame[num].endx-1)
          return 0;
        if(y<0 || y+frame[num].starty>=frame[num].endy-1)
          return 0;
        frame[num].curx = x;
        frame[num].cury = y;
        return 1;
      }

      /* Read a string from a window. */
      void window_gets(num, s)
      int num;
      char *s;
      {
        char ch, *temp;

        temp = s;
        for(;;) {
          ch = window_getche(num);
          switch(ch) {
            case '\r':   /* the ENTER key is pressed */
              *s='\0';
              return;
            case BKSP: /* backspace */
              if(s>temp) {
                s--;
                frame[num].cury--;
                if(frame[num].cury<0) frame[num].cury = 0;
                  window_xy(num, frame[num].curx, frame[num].cury);
                    write_char(frame[num].startx+ frame[num].curx+1,
                      frame[num].starty+frame[num].cury+1, ' ', NORM_VID);
              }
              break;
            default: *s = ch;
              s++;
          }
        }
      }


      /* Input keystrokes inside a window.
         Returns full 16 bit scan code.
      */
      window_getche(num)
      int num;
      {
        union inkey {
          char ch[2];
          int i;
        } c;

        if(!frame[num].active) return 0; /* window not active */

        window_xy(num, frame[num].curx, frame[num].cury);

        c.i = bioskey(0);        /* read the key */
```

```
   if(c.ch[0]) {
     switch(c.ch[0]) {
       case '\r': /* the ENTER key is pressed */
         break;
       case BKSP: /* back space */
         break;
       default:
         if(frame[num].cury+frame[num].starty < frame[num].endy-1) {
         write_char(frame[num].startx+ frame[num].curx+1,
           frame[num].starty+frame[num].cury+1, c.ch[0], NORM_VID);
           frame[num].cury++;
         }
     }
     if(frame[num].curx < 0) frame[num].curx = 0;
     if(frame[num].curx+frame[num].startx > frame[num].endx-2)
       frame[num].curx--;
     window_xy(num, frame[num].curx, frame[num].cury);
   }
   return c.i;
}

/* Clear to end of line. */
void window_cleol(num)
int num;
{
   register int i, x, y;

   x = frame[num].curx;
   y = frame[num].cury;
   window_xy(num, frame[num].curx, frame[num].cury);

   for(i=frame[num].cury; i<frame[num].endy-1; i++)
     window_putchar(num,' ');
   window_xy(num, x, y);
}

/* Move cursor up one line.
   Returns non-zero if successful;
   0 otherwise.
*/
window_upline(num)
int num;
{
   if(frame[num].curx>0) {
     frame[num].curx--;
     window_xy(num, frame[num].curx, frame[num].cury);
     return 1;
   }
   return 0;
}

/* Move cursor down one line.
   Returns non-zero if successful;
   0 otherwise.
*/
window_downline(num)
```

```
      int num;
      {
        if(frame[num].curx<frame[num].endx-frame[num].startx-1) {
          frame[num].curx++;
          window_xy(num, frame[num].curx, frame[num].cury);
          return 1;
        }
        return 1;
      }

      /* back up one character. */
      window_bksp(num)
      int num;
      {
        if(frame[num].cury>0) {
          frame[num].cury--;
          window_xy(num, frame[num].curx, frame[num].cury);
          window_putchar(num, ' ');
          frame[num].cury--;
          window_xy(num, frame[num].curx, frame[num].cury);
        }
      }

      /********************************************************/
      /* Misc. functions                                    */
      /********************************************************/
      /* Display a string with specified attribute. */
      void write_string(x, y, p, attrib)
      int x, y;
      char *p;
      int attrib;
      {
        register int i;
        char far *v;

        v = vid_mem;
        v += (x*160) + y*2; /* compute the address */
        for(i=y; *p; i++) {
          *v++ = *p++;  /* write the character */
          *v++ = attrib;    /* write the attribute */
        }
      }

      /* Write character with specified attribute. */
      void write_char(x, y, ch, attrib)
      int x, y;
      char ch;
      int attrib;
      {
        register int i;
        char far *v;

        v = vid_mem;
        v += (x*160) + y*2;
        *v++ = ch; /* write the character */
        *v = attrib;    /* write the attribute */
      }
```

```c
/* Save a portion of the screen. */
void save_video(num)
int num;
{
  register int i,j;
  char *buf_ptr;
  char far *v, far *t;

  buf_ptr = frame[num].p;
  v = vid_mem;
  for(i=frame[num].starty; i<frame[num].endy+1; i++)
    for(j=frame[num].startx; j<frame[num].endx+1; j++) {
      t = (v + (j*160) + i*2);
      *buf_ptr++ = *t++;
      *buf_ptr++ = *t;
      *(t-1) = ' ';   /* clear the window */
    }
}

/* Restore a portion of the screen. */
void restore_video(num)
int num;
{
  register int i,j;
  char far *v, far *t;
  char *buf_ptr;

  buf_ptr = frame[num].p;
  v = vid_mem;
  t = v;
  for(i=frame[num].starty; i<frame[num].endy+1; i++)
    for(j=frame[num].startx; j<frame[num].endx+1; j++) {
      v = t;
      v += (j*160) + i*2;
      *v++ = *buf_ptr++; /* write the character */
      *v = *buf_ptr++;    /* write the attribute */
    }
  frame[num].active = 0; /* restore_video */
}

/* Returns the current video mode. */
video_mode()
{
  union REGS r;

  r.h.ah = 15;  /* get video mode */
  return int86(0x10, &r, &r) & 255;
}

/*************************************************************
calculator
*************************************************************/

#define MAX 100

int *p;   /* pointer into the stack */
int *tos; /* points to top of stack */
int *bos; /* points to bottom of stack */
```

```
char in[80], out[80];
int stack[MAX];

/* Stack based, postfix notation four-function calculator */
void calc()
{
  int answer;
  int a,b;

  p = stack;
  tos = p;
  bos = p+MAX-1;

  window(0);
  do {
    window_xy(0, 0, 0);
    window_cleol(0);
    window_puts(0, ": "); /* calc prompt */
    window_gets(0, in);
    window_puts(0, "\n ");
    window_cleol(0);
    switch(*in) {
      case '+':
        a = pop();
        b = pop();
        answer = a+b;
        push(a+b);
        break;
      case '-':
        a = pop();
        b = pop();
        answer = b-a;
        push(b-a);
        break;
      case '*':
        a = pop();
        b = pop();
        answer = b*a;
        push(b*a);
        break;
      case '/':
        a = pop();
        b=pop();
        if(a==0) {
            window_puts(0, "divide by 0\n");
            break;
        }
        answer = b/a;
        push(b/a);
        break;
      default:
        push(atoi(in));
        continue;
    }
    itoa(answer, out, 10);
    window_puts(0, out);
  } while(*in);
  deactivate(0);
}
```

```
/* Place a number on the stack.
   Returns 1 if successful;
   0 if stack is full.
*/
push(i)
int i;
{
  if(p>bos) return 0;

  *p=i;
  p++;
  return 1;
}

/* Retrieve top element from the stack.
   Returns 0 on stack underflows.
*/
pop()
{
  p--;
  if(p<tos) {
    p++;
    return 0;
  }
  return *p;
}
```

You should enter this program now. In order to install this TSR application, execute the program. To activate the calculator, press the PT SCR key.

USING THE KEY-PRESS INTERRUPT

The print screen interrupt is easy to use, but it has three major disadvantages. First, it allows only one TSR application to be present in the system. Second, you cannot print screens. Third, it just "feels" wrong, as if the cheap way has been taken. A better way to activate a TSR program is to use interrupt 9, the key-press interrupt. Each time a key is pressed on the keyboard, an interrupt 9 instruction is executed.

Using interrupt 9 to activate a TSR program requires the following basic approach. First, you move the address currently in the vector table associated with interrupt 9 to an interrupt not used by DOS. We will use interrupt 60. Next, put the address of your TSR program's entry point at interrupt 9's location in the vector table. Upon activation, your TSR program first calls, via an interrupt, the keyboard input handler. Then, the character read is checked to see if it is the "hot key" used to activate the TSR application. If it is, the TSR application is executed; otherwise, no action is taken and the TSR program deactivates. Therefore, with each key press the TSR entry function is activated, but the TSR application is executed only if the right key was pressed.

The key-press interrupt has two advantages. First, no functionality is lost. Second, it allows multiple TSR applications to be available simultaneously and selectively activated by different hot keys. The TSR program developed in this chapter uses this approach, and includes both a calculator and a notepad (from Chapter 2), which are activated separately.

Before you can implement this approach, you must know something about the way BIOS inputs keystrokes.

Keystroke Character Buffer

As you know, standard versions of DOS buffer up to 15 characters entered at the keyboard, a process that allows type-ahead. Each time a key is pressed, an interrupt 9 is generated. The keystroke input ISR reads the character from the port and places it in the buffer. When you call a DOS or BIOS keyboard character input function, only the contents of the buffer are examined, not the actual port. It is possible for your routines to directly examine the contents of the keystroke buffer similar to the way the BIOS and DOS routines do, thus allowing your TSR entry function to determine whether a hot key has been pressed or not without actually having to remove the characters from the buffer.

The keystroke input buffer is located at 0000:041E (1054 in decimal). Because all keystrokes generate a 16-bit scan code, it requires 30 bytes for the 15 characters. However, 32 bytes are actually used because the scan code for the RETURN key is automatically appended to the end of the buffer.

The buffer is organized as a circular queue, which is accessed through a head pointer and a tail pointer. The head pointer points to the character last typed. The tail pointer points to the next character to be returned by an input request by DOS or BIOS. The head pointer is stored at location 0000:041A (1050 in decimal) and the tail pointer at 0000:041C (1052 in decimal). The values of the head and tail pointers are actually indexes into the queue, which means that their values are the index of the current position plus 30. (This is due to the way the 8086 processes indirect addressing.) The values of the head and tail pointers are the same when the queue is empty.

Initialization Function

For the TSR application developed in this chapter, little initialization is required; it is contained in the **main( )** function shown here.

```
main()
{
  struct address {
    char far *p;
  } temp;

  /* pointer to interrupt 9's address */
  struct address far *addr = (struct address far *) 36;
  /* pointer to interrupt 60's address */
  struct address far *int9 = (struct address far *) 240;

  /* Move the keyboard interrupt routine's address to int 60.
     If int 60 and int 61 contain the same addresses, then
     the TSR program has not been installed.
  */
  if(int9->p == (int9+1)->p) {
    int9->p = addr->p;
    addr->p = (char far *) tsr_ap;
    printf("tsr installed - F2 for note pad, F3 for calculator");
  } else {
    printf("tsr application already initialized\n");
    exit(1);
  }

  set_vid_mem();
  tsr(2000);
}
```

Notice that this version prevents the TSR program from being installed more than once. This is necessary because a second installation would put a copy of the TSR program's entry point into interrupt 60's vector table location, thus overwriting the keystroke input routine's address. The function works by checking to see if the values in the interrupt vector table for interrupts 60 and 61 are the same. (Interrupt 61 is also unused.) DOS routes all unused interrupts to the same invalid interrupt routine. Therefore, before the TSR program has been installed these addresses will be the same, but after installation they will differ.

TSR Application

This TSR entry function is more complex than the one used in the print screen interrupt method. It must first generate an interrupt 60 so that the key is read by the standard input routine. Most C compilers have a function that generates an interrupt. In Turbo C, this is **geninterrupt( )**, which is called with the number of the interrupt you want to generate. After the interrupt 60 returns, your function must examine the contents of the queue pointed to by the head pointer to see if a hot key was pressed. The hot keys for the program developed here are F2 and F3, with position codes of 60 and 61, respectively. If a hot key is pressed, it must be read so that it is not used by the application. The global variable **busy** is used to prevent both applications from being active at the same time because most C compilers do not generate re-entrant code. If one application is active, the other is denied activation. The **tsr___ap( )** function is shown here.

```
/* This is the entry point into the TSR application code. */
void interrupt tsr_ap()
{
  char far *t = (char far *) 1050; /* address of head pointer */

  geninterrupt(60);

  if(*t != *(t+2)) { /* if not empty */
    t += *t-30+5; /* advance to the character position */
    if(*t == 60 || *t == 61) {
      bioskey(0); /* clear the F2/F3 key */
      if(!busy) {
        busy = !busy;
        window_main(*t);
        busy = !busy;
      }
    }
  }
}
```

Notice that **window__main( )** is called with the position code of the hot key so that it can select the proper application, as shown here.

```
/* create the windows */
window_main(which)
int which;
{
  union inkey {
    char ch[2];
    int i;
  } c;
  int i;
  char ch;

  /* first, create the window frames */
  make_window(0, " Notepad [F1 to exit] ", 5, 20, 17, 60, BORDER);
  make_window(1, " Calculator ", 8, 20, 12, 60, BORDER);

  /* use window() to activate the specified window */
  switch(which) {
    case 60:
      notepad();
      break;
    case 61:
      calc();
      break;
  }
}
```

You should enter the entire program, shown here, at this time. After it is installed, the F2 key selects the notepad and the F3 key activates the calculator.

```
/* Terminate and stay resident using keyboard interrupt 9.
*/
#include "dos.h"
#include "stdlib.h"
#include "ctype.h"

#define BORDER 1
#define ESC 27
#define MAX_FRAME 2
#define REV_VID 0x70
#define NORM_VID 7
#define BKSP 8

void interrupt tsr_ap();
void save_video(), restore_video();
void write_string(), write_char();
void display_header(), draw_border();
void window_gets();
void window_cleol(), window();
void notepad(), calc();
```

```
char far *vid_mem;
char wp[4000]; /* buffer to hold current contents of the screen */

struct window_frame {
  int startx, endx, starty, endy;
  int curx, cury; /* current cursor position in window */
  unsigned char *p; /* pointer to buffer */
  char *header; /* header message */
  int border; /* border on/off */
  int active; /* on screen yes/no */
} frame[MAX_FRAME];
char in[80], out[80];

/* busy is set to 1 when the program is active, 0 otherwise */
char busy = 0;

main()
{
  struct address {
    char far *p;
  } temp;

  /* pointer to interrupt 9's address */
  struct address far *addr = (struct address far *) 36;
  /* pointer to interrupt 60's address */
  struct address far *int9 = (struct address far *) 240;

  /* Move the keyboard interrupt routine's address to int 60.
     If int 60 and int 61 contain the same addresses, then
     the TSR program has not been installed.
  */
  if(int9->p == (int9+1)->p) {
    int9->p = addr->p;
    addr->p = (char far *) tsr_ap;
    printf("tsr installed - F2 for note pad, F3 for calculator");
  } else {
    printf("tsr application already initialized\n");
    exit(1);
  }

  set_vid_mem();
  tsr(800);
}

set_vid_mem()
{
  int vmode;

  vmode = video_mode();
  if((vmode!=2) && (vmode!=3) && (vmode!=7)) {
    printf("video must be in 80 column text mode");
    exit(1);
  }
  /* set proper address of video RAM */
  if(vmode==7) vid_mem = (char far *) 0xB0000000;
  else vid_mem = (char far *) 0xB8000000;
}
```

```
/* This is the entry point into the TSR application code. */
void interrupt tsr_ap()
{
   char far *t = (char far *) 1050; /* address of head pointer */


   geninterrupt(60); /* read the character */

   if(*t != *(t+2)) {/* if not empty */
     t += *t-30+5; /* advance to the character position */
     if(*t == 60 || *t == 61) {
       bioskey(0); /* clear the F2/F3 key */
       if(!busy) {
         busy = !busy;
         window_main(*t);
         busy = !busy;
       }
     }
   }
}


/* terminate but keep resident */
tsr(size)
unsigned size;
{
   union REGS r;

   r.h.ah = 49;  /* terminate and stay resident */
   r.h.al = 0;   /* return code */
   r.x.dx = size; /* size of program/16 */
   int86(0x21, &r, &r);
}


/* create the windows */
window_main(which)
int which;
{
   union inkey {
     char ch[2];
     int i;
   } c;
   int i;
   char ch;

   /* first, create the window frames */
   make_window(0, " Notepad [F1 to exit] ", 5, 20, 17, 60, BORDER);
   make_window(1, " Calculator ", 8, 20, 12, 60, BORDER);

   /* use window() to activate the specified window */
   switch(which) {
     case 60:
       notepad();
       break;
```

```
      case 61:
        calc();
        break;
    }
  }




/**************************************************************/
/* window functions                                         */
/**************************************************************/

/* Display a pull-down window. */
void window(num)
int num; /* window number */
{
  /* get active window */
  if(!frame[num].active) { /* not currently in use */
    save_video(num);        /* save the current screen */
    frame[num].active = 1; /* set active flag */
  }

  if(frame[num].border) draw_border(num);
  display_header(num); /* display the window */
}

/* Construct a pull down window frame
   1 is returned if window frame can be constructed;
   otherwise 0 is returned.
*/
make_window(num, header, startx, starty, endx, endy, border)
int num;         /* window number */
char *header;    /* header text */
int startx, starty; /* X,Y coordinates of upper left corner */
int endx, endy; /* X,Y coordinates of lower right corner */
int border;      /* no border if 0 */
{
  register int i;
  int choice, vmode;
  unsigned char *p;

  if(num>MAX_FRAME) {
    window_puts(0, "Too many windows\n");
    return 0;
  }

  if((startx>24) || (startx<0) || (starty>78) || (starty<0)) {
    window_puts(0, "range error");
    return 0;
  }

  if((endx>24) || (endy>79)) {
    window_puts(0, "window won't fit");
    return 0;
  }
```

```c
    /* allocate enough memory to hold it */
/*  p = (unsigned char *) malloc(2*(endx-startx+1)*(endy-starty+1));
    if(!p) exit(1); /* put your own error handler here */


    /* construct the frame */
    frame[num].startx = startx; frame[num].endx = endx;
    frame[num].starty = starty; frame[num].endy = endy;
    frame[num].p = wp;
    frame[num].header = header;
    frame[num].border = border;
    frame[num].active = 0;
    frame[num].curx = 0; frame[num].cury = 0;
    return 1;
}

/* Deactivate a window and remove it from the screen. */
deactivate(num)
int num;
{
    /* reset the cursor postion to upper left corner */
    frame[num].curx = 0;
    frame[num].cury = 0;
    restore_video(num);
}

/* Display the header message in its proper location. */
void display_header(num)
int num;
{
    register int i, y, len;

    y = frame[num].starty;

    /* Calculate the correct starting position to center
       the header message - if negative, message won't
       fit.
    */
    len = strlen(frame[num].header);
    len = (frame[num].endy - y - len) / 2;
    if(len<0) return; /* don't display it */
    y = y +len;

    write_string(frame[num].startx, y,
                 frame[num].header, NORM_VID);
}

void draw_border(num)
int num;
{
    register int i;
    char far *v, far *t;

    v = vid_mem;
    t = v;
    for(i=frame[num].startx+1; i<frame[num].endx; i++) {
        v += (i*160) + frame[num].starty*2;
        *v++ = 179;
```

```
      *v = NORM_VID;
       v = t;
       v += (i*160) + frame[num].endy*2;
      *v++ = 179;
      *v = NORM_VID;
       v = t;
   }
   for(i=frame[num].starty+1; i<frame[num].endy; i++) {
       v += (frame[num].startx*160) + i*2;
      *v++ = 196;
      *v = NORM_VID;
       v = t;
       v += (frame[num].endx*160) + i*2;
      *v++ = 196;
      *v = NORM_VID;
       v = t;
   }
   write_char(frame[num].startx, frame[num].starty, 218, NORM_VID);
   write_char(frame[num].startx, frame[num].endy, 191, NORM_VID);
   write_char(frame[num].endx, frame[num].starty, 192, NORM_VID);
   write_char(frame[num].endx, frame[num].endy, 217, NORM_VID);
}


/****************************************************************/
/* Window I/O functions                                       */
/****************************************************************/

/* Write a string at the current cursor position
   in the specified window.
   Returns 0 if window not active;
   1 otherwise.
*/
window_puts(num, str)
int num;
char *str;
{
   /* make sure window is active */
   if(!frame[num].active) return 0;

   for( ; *str; str++)
     window_putchar(num, *str);
   return 1;
}

/* Write a character at the current cursor position
   in the specified window.
   Returns 0 if window not active;
   1 otherwise.
*/
window_putchar(num, ch)
int num;
char ch;
{
   register int x, y;
   char far *v;
```

```
        /* make sure window is active */
        if(!frame[num].active) return 0;

        x = frame[num].curx + frame[num].startx + 1;
        y = frame[num].cury + frame[num].starty + 1;

        v = vid_mem;
        v += (x*160) + y*2; /* compute the address */
        if(y>=frame[num].endy) {
          return 1;
        }
        if(x>=frame[num].endx) {
          return 1;
        }

        if(ch=='\n') { /* newline char */
          x++;
          y = frame[num].startx+1;
          v = vid_mem;
          v += (x*160) + y*2; /* compute the address */
          frame[num].curx++;  /* increment X */
          frame[num].cury = 0; /* reset Y */
        }
        else {
          frame[num].cury++;
          *v++ = ch;  /* write the character */
          *v++ = NORM_VID;    /* normal video attribute */
        }
        window_xy(num, frame[num].curx, frame[num].cury);
        return 1;
}

/* Position cursor in a window at specified location.
   Returns 0 if out of range;
   non-zero otherwise.
*/
window_xy(num, x, y)
int num, x, y;
{
  if(x<0 || x+frame[num].startx>=frame[num].endx-1)
    return 0;
  if(y<0 || y+frame[num].starty>=frame[num].endy-1)
    return 0;
  frame[num].curx = x;
  frame[num].cury = y;
  return 1;
}

/* Read a string from a window. */
void window_gets(num, s)
int num;
char *s;
{
  char ch, *temp;
  char out[10];
```

```
            temp = s;
            for(;;) {
              ch = window_getche(num);
              switch(ch) {
                case '\r':  /* the ENTER key is pressed */
                  *s='\0';
                  return;
                case BKSP: /* backspace */
                  if(s>temp) {
                    s--;
                    frame[num].cury--;
                    if(frame[num].cury<0) frame[num].cury = 0;
                      window_xy(num, frame[num].curx, frame[num].cury);
                        write_char(frame[num].startx+ frame[num].curx+1,
                        frame[num].starty+frame[num].cury+1, ' ', NORM_VID);
                  }
                  break;
                default: *s = ch;
                  s++;
              }
            }
          }


/* Input keystrokes inside a window.
   Returns full 16 bit scan code.
*/
window_getche(num)
int num;
{
  union inkey {
    char ch[2];
    int i;
  } c;

  if(!frame[num].active) return 0; /* window not active */

  window_xy(num, frame[num].curx, frame[num].cury);

  c.i = bioskey(0);       /* read the key */

  if(c.ch[0]) {
    switch(c.ch[0]) {
      case '\r': /* the ENTER key is pressed */
        break;
      case BKSP: /* back space */
        break;
      default:
        if(frame[num].cury+frame[num].starty < frame[num].endy-1) {
          write_char(frame[num].startx+ frame[num].curx+1,
            frame[num].starty+frame[num].cury+1, c.ch[0], NORM_VID);
          frame[num].cury++;
        }
    }
    if(frame[num].curx < 0) frame[num].curx = 0;
    if(frame[num].curx+frame[num].startx > frame[num].endx-2)
      frame[num].curx--;
```

```
      window_xy(num, frame[num].curx, frame[num].cury);
   }
   return c.i;
}

/* Clear to end of line. */
void window_cleol(num)
int num;
{
   register int i, x, y;

   x = frame[num].curx;
   y = frame[num].cury;
   window_xy(num, frame[num].curx, frame[num].cury);

   for(i=frame[num].cury; i<frame[num].endy-1; i++)
      window_putchar(num,' ');
   window_xy(num, x, y);
}

/* Move cursor up one line.
   Returns non-zero if successful;
   0 otherwise.
*/
window_upline(num)
int num;
{
   if(frame[num].curx>0) {
      frame[num].curx--;
      window_xy(num, frame[num].curx, frame[num].cury);
      return 1;
   }
   return 0;
}

/* Move cursor down one line.
   Returns non-zero if successful;
   0 otherwise.
*/
window_downline(num)
int num;
{
   if(frame[num].curx<frame[num].endx-frame[num].startx-1) {
      frame[num].curx++;
      window_xy(num, frame[num].curx, frame[num].cury);
      return 1;
   }
   return 1;
}

/* back up one character. */
window_bksp(num)
int num;
{
   if(frame[num].cury>0) {
      frame[num].cury--;
      window_xy(num, frame[num].curx, frame[num].cury);
      window_putchar(num, ' ');
```

```
      frame[num].cury--;
      window_xy(num, frame[num].curx, frame[num].cury);
    }
}


/**********************************************************/
/* Misc. functions                                       */
/**********************************************************/

/* Display a string with specifed attribute. */
void write_string(x, y, p, attrib)
int x, y;
char *p;
int attrib;
{
  register int i;
  char far *v;

  v = vid_mem;
  v += (x*160) + y*2; /* compute the address */
  for(i=y; *p; i++) {
    *v++ = *p++; /* write the character */
    *v++ = attrib;    /* write the attribute */
  }
}


/* Write character with specified attribute. */
void write_char(x, y, ch, attrib)
int x, y;
char ch;
int attrib;
{
  register int i;
  char far *v;

  v = vid_mem;
  v += (x*160) + y*2;
  *v++ = ch; /* write the character */
  *v = attrib;    /* write the attribute */
}


/* Save a portion of the screen. */
void save_video(num)
int num;
{
  register int i,j;
  char *buf_ptr;
  char far *v, far *t;

  buf_ptr = frame[num].p;
  v = vid_mem;
  for(i=frame[num].starty; i<frame[num].endy+1; i++)
    for(j=frame[num].startx; j<frame[num].endx+1; j++) {
      t = (v + (j*160) + i*2);
      *buf_ptr++ = *t++;
```

```
        *buf_ptr++ = *t;
        *(t-1) = ' ';   /* clear the window */
      }
}

/* Restore a portion of the screen. */
void restore_video(num)
int num;
{
  register int i,j;
  char far *v, far *t;
  char *buf_ptr;

  buf_ptr = frame[num].p;
  v = vid_mem;
  t = v;
  for(i=frame[num].starty; i<frame[num].endy+1; i++)
    for(j=frame[num].startx; j<frame[num].endx+1; j++) {
      v = t;
      v += (j*160) + i*2;
      *v++ = *buf_ptr++;   /* write the character */
      *v = *buf_ptr++;     /* write the attribute */
    }

  frame[num].active = 0; /* restore_video */
}


/* Returns the current video mode. */
video_mode()
{
  union REGS r;

  r.h.ah = 15;   /* get video mode */
  return int86(0x10, &r, &r) & 255;
}


/******************************************************/
/* pop-up window functions                           */
/******************************************************/

#define MAX 100

int *p;   /* pointer into the stack */
int *tos; /* points to top of stack */
int *bos; /* points to bottom of stack */
int stack[MAX];

/* Stack based, postfix notation four-function calculator */
void calc()
{
  int answer;
  int a,b;

  p = stack;
  tos = p;
  bos = p+MAX-1;
```

```
        window(1);
        do {
          window_xy(1, 0, 0);
          window_cleol(1);
          window_puts(1, ": "); /* calc prompt */
          window_gets(1, in);
          window_puts(1, "\n ");
          window_cleol(1);
          switch(*in) {
            case '+':
              a = pop();
              b = pop();
              answer = a+b;
              push(a+b);
              break;
            case '-':
              a = pop();
              b = pop();
              answer = b-a;
              push(b-a);
              break;
            case '*':
              a = pop();
              b = pop();
              answer = b*a;
              push(b*a);
              break;
            case '/':
              a = pop();
              b=pop();
              if(a==0) {
                  window_puts(0, "divide by 0\n");
                  break;
              }
              answer = b/a;
              push(b/a);
              break;
            default:
              push(atoi(in));
              continue;
          }
          itoa(answer, out, 10);
          window_puts(1, out);
        } while(*in);
        deactivate(1);
}

/* Place a number on the stack.
   Returns 1 if successful;
   0 if stack is full.
*/
push(i)
int i;
{
   if(p>bos) return 0;

   *p=i;
   p++;
```

```
   return 1;
}

/* Retrieve top element from the stack.
   Returns 0 on stack underflows.
*/
pop()
{
  p--;
  if(p<tos) {
    p++;
    return 0;
  }
  return *p;
}


/*****************************************************/

/* Pop-up note pad. */
#define MAX_NOTE 10
#define BKSP 8
char notes[MAX_NOTE][80];

void notepad()
{
  static first=1;
  register int i, j;
  union inkey {
    char ch[2];
    int i;
  } c;
  char ch;

  /* initialize notes array if necessary */
  if(first) {
    for(i=0; i<MAX_NOTE; i++)
      *notes[i] = '\0';
    first = !first;
  }

  window(0);
  /* display the existing notes */
  for(i=0; i<MAX_NOTE; i++) {
    if(*notes[i]) window_puts(0, notes[i]);
    window_putchar(0, '\n');
  }

  i=0;
  window_xy(0, 0, 0);

  for(;;) {
    c.i = bioskey(0);    /* read the key */
    if(tolower(c.ch[1])==59) { /* F1 to quit */
      deactivate(0);
      break;
    }
```

```
/* if normal key */
if(isprint(c.ch[0]) || c.ch[0]==BKSP) {
  window_cleol(0);
  notes[i][0] = c.ch[0];
  j = 1;
  window_putchar(0, notes[i][0]);
  do {
    ch = window_getche(0);
    if(ch==BKSP) {
      if(j>0) {
        j--;
        window_bksp(0);
      }
    }
    else {
      notes[i][j] = ch;
      j++;
    }
  } while(notes[i][j-1]!='\r');
  notes[i][j-1] = '\0';
  i++;
  window_putchar(0, '\n');
}
else {   /* is special key */
  switch(c.ch[1]) {
    case 72:   /* up arrow */
      if(i>0) {
        i--;
        window_upline(0);
      }
      break;
    case 80:   /* down arrow */
      if(i<MAX_NOTE-1) {
        i++;
        window_downline(0);
      }
      break;
  }
}
```

INT 28H SECRET

An undocumented DOS feature can make TSR programs more reliable
during the periods when they are using many system resources.
Generally, if the TSR application is only doing console I/O, you are fairly
safe, but troubles can arise when using such entities as disk files or I/O

ports. Although it is not described in the DOS technical reference manuals, DOS calls interrupt 28H when DOS is in a "safe" (or idle) state. As you might know, certain functions performed by an operating system, referred to as *critical sections,* must not be interrupted once they begin. Interrupt 28H is never called by DOS when it is in a critical section. You can use this feature to crash-proof your TSR application. Although no code examples are shown here, a discussion of the general method follows.

The main difference you will notice when you use interrupt 28H is the way your TSR application is activated. When interrupt 28H is involved, the TSR application is no longer activated by the keystroke input handler. Instead, the keystroke input routine simply sets a flag (called **is—hotkey** for the rest of this discussion) if a hot key is pressed. Before your TSR application can be activated you must create a new interrupt 28H handler that checks to see if **is—hotkey** is set. If it is, the TSR routine is activated, resetting **is—hotkey** in the process. It is imperative that you do not simply overlay the original interrupt 28H vector. Instead, save it and call it from your interrupt 28H handler. In this way, you still preserve the original ISR associated with interrupt 28H.

If you are going to market your TSR applications, you should definitely use the interrupt 28H because (though undocumented) it appears to avoid accidentally interrupting DOS while it is in a critical section.

TSR PROBLEMS

TSR programs are by their very nature somewhat trouble-prone. For example, using one TSR application developed by one manufacturer frequently precludes simultaneously using another developed by a different manufacturer, because both programs want to overlay the interrupt 9 vector table address with their own routines. Of course, in the TSR applications you create, you can avoid this sort of problem, but be careful when a third-party TSR program is also in your system.

Another trouble spot is that some application programs also intercept the keyboard input routine by routing the interrupt 9 request to their own input routines. For example, a high-performance word processor may do this to allow virtually unlimited type-ahead. If this is done, your TSR application may have no way to be activated.

Finally, depending on what the computer is doing, the stack space of a TSR program may be very limited. If your application uses large local arrays or is heavily recursive, you may need to establish your own stack space by using assembly language interface modules.

CREATING YOUR OWN APPLICATIONS

The best way to do TSR programming is to proceed deliberately. Get the core of your application running and then move ahead slowly. Then, if the program stops working, you will have a good idea what caused the error. Remember, you can find out only by trial and error which C standard library functions are usable and which crash the computer.

If you are thinking of marketing your TSR program, be sure that it is compatible with the most popular ones currently available. With a little thought, you can design your program in such a way that it automatically works with most other TSR programs.

4: Graphics

This chapter introduces a core set of graphics functions that allow the drawing of points, lines, boxes, and circles using either a CGA or EGA graphics adapter. These routines are then used as a foundation on which several higher-level graphics functions are built. For an in-depth treatment of these core graphics functions, refer to *C: The Complete Reference* by Herb Schildt (Osborne/ McGraw-Hill, 1987).

Aside from briefly presenting the core graphics functions, this chapter develops the following routines:

- Saving a graphics image to a disk file

- Loading a graphics image from a disk file

- Rotating an object in two-dimensional space

- Copying or moving a graphics image to a new location

The chapter concludes with a "paint" program that allows the user to draw on the screen using the cursor keys.

Once you have mastered the use of the graphics functions developed in this chapter, you will be able to create some very impressive programs. For example, using the image save and load functions, you will be able to create graphs or diagrams in advance and simply "pop" them up when needed. With the rotation function you can create "Star Wars" type animated graphics that can be very exciting. Or, you can use the functions as a basis for a CAD/CAM application.

For the routines developed in this chapter to run correctly you need an IBM PC XT, AT, or compatible and either a CGA or an EGA graphics board. However, beyond the writing of a point, the routines in the chapter are hardware-independent, and you should have little trouble making them work on other types of graphics hardware.

We'll begin with a brief discussion of the operation of the graphics adapters and the core graphics functions.

MODES AND PALETTES

Before any graphics functions can be used, the computer must be placed into the proper video mode. For the IBM PC, this means selecting the proper mode and palette.

Several different video modes are available on the IBM PC as Table 4-1 shows. The functions developed in this chapter require screen mode 4, which is 320 x 200 four-color graphics. Although the EGA allows greater resolution in other modes, this mode is used because it works with both the CGA and the EGA. To use a different EGA mode, you only need to change the function that writes a point. (For an excellent book on graphics using the EGA, see *Advanced Graphics in C* by Nelson Johnson [Osborne/McGraw-Hill, 1987].) You should keep in mind that in all modes, the upper-left corner is location 0,0.

BIOS interrupt 16, function 0 sets the video mode and is used by the **mode( )** function shown here.

```
/* set the video mode */
void mode(mode_code)
int mode_code;
```

Table 4-1.

Screen Modes for Various IBM PCs

Mode	Type	Dimensions	Adapters
0	text, b/w	40 × 25	CGA, EGA
1	text, 16 colors	40 × 25	CGA, EGA
2	text, b/w	80 × 25	CGA, EGA
3	text, 16 colors	80 × 25	CGA, EGA
4	graphics, 4 colors	320 × 200	CGA, EGA
5	graphics, 4 grey tones	320 × 200	CGA, EGA
6	graphics, b/w	640 × 200	CGA, EGA
7	text, b/w	80 × 25	monochrome
8	graphics, 16 colors	160 × 200	PCjr
9	graphics, 16 colors	320 × 200	PCjr
10	graphics, 4 colors PCjr, 16 colors EGA	640 × 200	PCjr, EGA
13	graphics, 16 colors	320 × 200	EGA
14	graphics, 16 colors	640 × 200	EGA
15	graphics, 4 colors	640 × 350	EGA

```
{
    union REGS r;

    r.h.al = mode_code;
    r.h.ah = 0;
    int86(0x10, &r, &r);
}
```

Two palettes are available in mode 4 graphics. The *palette* determines which four colors are displayed. On the IBM PC, palette 0 provides the colors red, green, and yellow; palette 1 gives white, magenta, and cyan. For each palette the fourth color is the color of the background, usually black. The BIOS interrupt 16, function 11 sets the palette. The function **palette**( ), shown here, selects the palette specified in its argument.

```
/* set the palette */
void palette(pnum)
int pnum;
{
  union REGS r;

  r.h.bh = 1;    /* code for mode 4 graphics */
  r.h.bl = pnum; /* palette number */
  r.h.ah = 11;   /* set palette function */
  int86(0x10, &r, &r);
}
```

WRITING PIXELS

The most fundamental graphics routine is the one that writes a *pixel,* the smallest addressable point on the video monitor screen. For the purposes of this discussion, however, the term *pixel* will be used to describe the smallest addressable point in a specific graphics mode. Because the function that writes to a pixel is used by other, higher-level routines, its efficiency is very important to the overall speed with which the graphics functions operate. On the IBM PC and compatibles, there are two ways to write information to a pixel. The first method, through the use of a ROM-BIOS interrupt, is the easiest but also the slowest — in fact, too slow for our purposes. The second and faster method is to place information directly into the video display RAM; this method is examined below.

Understanding the CGA/EGA
in Graphics Mode

The CGA video RAM always starts at location B8000000h. The EGA uses the same location for those modes that are compatible with the CGA modes. (For complete information on the video hardware, consult the *IBM Technical Reference* manual.) In mode 4, each byte holds the color information for four pixels with each pixel using two bits. Therefore, 16K is needed for a resolution of 320 × 200. Because two bits can hold only four different values, there can be only four colors in mode 4. The value of each two-bit packet determines the color that is displayed according to this table.

Value	Color in Palette 0	Color in Palette 1
0	background	background
1	yellow	blue
2	red	purple
3	green	white

A strange quirk in the CGA causes the even-numbered pixels to be stored in memory beginning at B8000000h, but the odd-numbered pixels are stored 2000h (8152 in decimal) bytes higher, at B8002000h. Therefore, each row of pixels requires 80 bytes, 40 for the even pixels and 40 for the odd. Within each byte, the pixels are stored left to right as they appear on the screen. This means that pixel number 0 occupies bits 6 and 7, while pixel number 3 uses bits 0 and 1.

The direct video RAM write pixel function should support one very interesting feature of the ROM-BIOS write pixel function: If the ROM-BIOS write pixel interrupt is called with the seventh bit (leftmost) of the color code set to 1, then the color specified is XORed with the existing color at the specified location instead of simply overwriting the previous color. The advantage of this feature is that it guarantees that the pixel will be visible. The value of this feature is explained in more detail later in this chapter.

Because four pixels are encoded into each byte, you must preserve the value of the other three when changing the value of one. The best way to do this is to create a bit mask with all bits set except those in the location of the pixel to be changed. This value is ANDed with the original byte, and then this value is ORed with the new information. However, the situation is slightly different if you want to XOR the new value with the old. In this case you simply OR the original byte with 0 and then XOR that result with the new color.

The address of the proper byte is located by first multiplying the X coordinate by 40 and then adding the value of the Y coordinate divided by 4. To determine whether the pixel is in the even or odd bank of memory, the remainder of the X coordinate divided by 2 is used. If the outcome is 0, the number is even so the first bank is used; otherwise it is odd and the second bank must be used. The proper bits within the byte are computed by performing a modulus division by 4. The remainder will be the number of the two-bit packet that contains the information for the desired pixel. Bit shift operations are used to arrange the color code byte and the bit mask into their proper positions. Although the bit manipulations that take place in the function **mempoint( )** are fairly intimidating, if you study the following code carefully, you should have no trouble understanding its operation.

```
/* Write a point directly to the CGA/EGA. */
void mempoint(x, y, color_code)
int x, y, color_code;
{
  union mask {
    char c[2];
    int i;
  } bit_mask;
  int i, index, bit_position;
  unsigned char t;
  char xor; /* xor color in or overwrite */
  char far *ptr = (char far *) 0xB8000000; /* pointer
                                        to CGA memory */
  bit_mask.i = 0xFF3F;  /* 11111111 00111111 in binary */

  /* check range for mode 4 */
  if(x<0 || x>199 || y<0 || y>319) return;

  xor = color_code & 128; /* see if xor mode is set */
  color_code = color_code & 127; /* mask off high bit */

  /* set bit_mask and color_code bits to the right location */
  bit_position = y%4;    /* compute the proper location
                              within the byte */
  color_code<<=2*(3-bit_position); /* shift the color_code
                                    into position */
  bit_mask.i>>=2*bit_position; /* shift the bit_mask into
                                    position */

  /* find the correct byte in screen memory */
  index = x*40 +(y/4);
  if(x % 2) index += 8152; /* if odd use 2nd bank */

  /* write the color */
  if(!xor) { /* overwrite mode */
    t = *(ptr+index) & bit_mask.c[0];
    *(ptr+index) = t | color_code;
  }
  else { /* xor mode */
    t = *(ptr+index) | (char)0;
    *(ptr+index) = t ^ color_code;
  }
}
```

Notice that the pointer to the video memory is declared as **far**; this is necessary if you are compiling with a small data model. You should also note that the special XOR write mode available in the ROM-BIOS function has been preserved in **mempoint( )**.

DRAWING LINES

The line-drawing function, a fundamental graphics routine, is used to draw a line in the specified color given the beginning and ending coordinates of the line. Although it is quite easy to draw lines that are either vertical or horizontal, it is more difficult to create a function that draws lines along a diagonal. For example, to draw a line from 0,0 to 80,120, what are the points in between?

One approach to creating a line-drawing function uses the ratio between the change in the X and Y dimensions. To see how this works, consider a line from 0,0 to 5,10. The change in X is 5 and the change in Y is 10. The ratio is 1/2, and it is used to determine the rate at which the X and Y coordinates change as the line is drawn. In this case it means that the X coordinate is incremented only half as frequently as the Y coordinate. Novice programmers often choose this method when creating a line-drawing function. Although this method is mathematically sound and easy to understand, in order to work properly in all situations floating point variables and arithmetic must be used to avoid serious round-off errors. This means that the line-drawing function will run quite slowly unless a math coprocessor, such as the 8087, is installed in the system. For this reason, it is seldom used.

By far the most common method used to draw a line employs Bresenham's algorithm. Although based conceptually on the ratios between the X and Y distances, no divisions or floating point calculations are required. Instead, the ratio between the change in the X and Y values is handled implicitly through a series of additions and subtractions. The basic idea behind Bresenham's approach is to record the amount of error between the ideal location of each point and where it is actually displayed. The error between the actual and ideal positions is due to the limitations of the hardware — the fact that no display has infinite resolution and therefore the actual location of each dot on the line is the best approximation. In each iteration through the line-drawing loop, two variables called **xerr** and **yerr** are incremented by the changes in magnitude of the X and Y coordinates, respectively. When an error value reaches a predetermined limit, it is reset and the appropriate coordinate counter is incremented. This process continues until the entire line is drawn. The **line( )** function, shown here, implements this method; you should study it until you understand its operation. Notice that it uses the **mempoint( )** function developed earlier to actually write a dot to the screen.

```
/* Draw a line in specified color
   using Bresenham's integer based algorithm.
*/
void line(startx, starty, endx, endy, color)
int startx, starty, endx, endy, color;
{
  register int t, distance;
  int xerr=0, yerr=0, delta_x, delta_y;
  int incx, incy;

  /* compute the distances in both directions */
  delta_x = endx-startx;
  delta_y = endy-starty;

  /* Compute the direction of the increment,
     an increment of 0 means either a vertical or horizontal
     line.
  */
  if(delta_x>0) incx = 1;
  else if(delta_x==0) incx = 0;
  else incx = -1;

  if(delta_y>0) incy = 1;
  else if(delta_y==0) incy = 0;
  else incy = -1;

  /* determine which distance is greater */
  delta_x = abs(delta_x);
  delta_y = abs(delta_y);
  if(delta_x>delta_y) distance = delta_x;
  else distance = delta_y;

  /* draw the line */
  for(t=0; t<=distance+1; t++) {
    mempoint(startx, starty, color);
    xerr+=delta_x;
    yerr+=delta_y;
```

```
    if(xerr>distance) {
      xerr-=distance;
      startx+=incx;
    }
    if(yerr>distance) {
      yerr-=distance;
      starty+=incy;
    }
  }
}
```

DRAWING AND FILLING BOXES

Once you have a line-drawing function, it is easy to create a box-drawing function. The one shown here draws the outline of a box in the specified color given the coordinates of two opposing corners.

```
/* draw a box */
void box(startx,starty, endx, endy, color_code)
int startx,starty,endx,endy,color_code;
{
  line(startx,starty, endx,starty, color_code);
  line(startx,starty, startx,endy, color_code);
  line(startx,endy, endx,endy, color_code);
  line(endx,starty, endx,endy, color_code);
}
```

To fill a box requires that you write to each pixel in the box. The **fill_box( )** routine shown here fills a box with the specified color given the coordinates of two opposing corners. It uses the **line( )** function to actually color in the box.

```
/* fill box with specified color */
void fill_box(startx, starty, endx, endy, color_code)
int startx, starty, endx, endy, color_code;
{
  register int i,begin, end;

  begin = startx<endx ? startx : endx;
  end = startx>endx ? startx : endx;

  for(i=begin; i<=end;i++)
    line(i,starty,i,endy,color_code);
}
```

DRAWING CIRCLES

The easiest and fastest way to draw a circle is to use Bresenham's circle-drawing algorithm, similar to Bresenham's line-drawing algorithm. No floating point calculations are required, except for the aspect ratio, so it is quite fast. Essentially, the algorithm works by incrementing the X and Y coordinates as needed based on the magnitude of the error between them. This value is held in the variable **delta**. The support function **plot_circle( )** actually plots the points. You could place this code in-line for extra speed, but it does make the **circle( )** function harder to read and understand. The variable **asp_ratio** is global because it is used by both **circle( )** and **plot_circle( )**. Also, you may find it useful to set its value outside of the **circle( )** function for some applications. By varying the **asp_ratio** you can draw ellipses. The **circle( )** function is called with the coordinates of the center of the circle, the radius (in pixels) of the circle, and its color. The **circle( )** and **plot_circle( )** functions are shown here.

```
double asp_ratio;

/* Draw a circle using Bresenham's integer based Algorithm. */
void circle(x_center, y_center, radius,  color_code)
int x_center, y_center, radius, color_code;
{
  register int x, y, delta;

  asp_ratio = 1.0;   /* for different aspect ratios, alter
                        this number */

  y = radius;
  delta = 3 - 2 * radius;

  for(x=0; x<y; ) {
    plot_circle(x, y, x_center, y_center, color_code);

    if (delta < 0)
      delta += 4*x+6;
    else {
      delta += 4*(x-y)+10;
      y--;
    }
    x++;
  }
  x=y;
  if(y) plot_circle(x, y, x_center, y_center, color_code);
}
```

```
/* plot_circle actually prints the points that
   define the circle */
void plot_circle(x, y, x_center, y_center, color_code)
int x, y, x_center, y_center, color_code;
{
  int startx, endx, x1, starty, endy, y1;

  starty = y*asp_ratio;
  endy = (y+1)*asp_ratio;
  startx = x*asp_ratio;
  endx = (x+1)*asp_ratio;

  for (x1=startx; x1<endx; ++x1)  {
    mempoint(x1+x_center, y+y_center, color_code);
    mempoint(x1+x_center, y_center-y, color_code);
    mempoint(x_center-x1, y_center-y, color_code);
    mempoint(x_center-x1, y+y_center, color_code);
  }

  for (y1=starty; y1<endy; ++y1) {
    mempoint(y1+x_center, x+y_center, color_code);
    mempoint(y1+x_center, y_center-x, color_code);
    mempoint(x_center-y1, y_center-x, color_code);
    mempoint(x_center-y1, x+y_center, color_code);
  }
}
```

It is possible to fill a circle by repeatedly calling **circle( )** with increasingly smaller radiuses. This is the method used by **fill_circle( )** shown here.

```
/* fill a circle by repeatedly calling circle()
   with smaller radiuses
*/
void fill_circle(x, y, r, c)
int x, y, r, c;
{
  while(r) {
    circle(x, y, r, c);
    r--;
  }
}
```

A SIMPLE TEST PROGRAM

The following program illustrates the previously described graphics functions. Its output is shown in Figure 4-1.

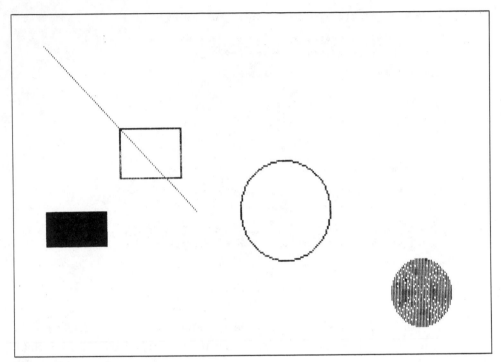

Figure 4-1.

Sample output from the simple
graphics test program

```
/* A simple program to illustrate the core graphics
   functions.
 */
#include "dos.h"
#include "stdio.h"

void mode(), line(), box(),fill_box();
void mempoint(), palette(), xhairs();
void circle(), plot_circle(), fill_circle();

double asp_ratio; /* holds aspect ratio for circles */

main()
{
  mode(4);
  palette(0);
```

```
    line(0, 0, 100, 100, 1);
    box(50, 50, 80, 90, 2);
    fill_box(100, 0, 120, 40, 3);
    circle(100, 160, 30, 2);
    fill_circle(150, 250, 20, 1);

    getchar();
    mode(2);
}

/* Set the palette. */
void palette(pnum)
int pnum;
{
    union REGS r;

    r.h.bh = 1;    /* code for mode 4 graphics */
    r.h.bl = pnum;
    r.h.ah = 11;   /* set palette function */
    int86(0x10, &r, &r);
}

/* Set the video mode. */
void mode(mode_code)
int mode_code;
{
    union REGS r;

    r.h.al = mode_code;
    r.h.ah = 0;
    int86(0x10, &r, &r);
}


/* Draw a box. */
void box(startx, starty, endx, endy, color_code)
int startx, starty, endx, endy, color_code;
{
    line(startx, starty, endx, starty, color_code);
    line(startx, starty, startx, endy, color_code);
    line(startx, endy, endx, endy, color_code);
    line(endx, starty, endx, endy, color_code);
}


/* Draw a line in specified color
   using Bresenham's integer based algorithm.
*/
void line(startx, starty, endx, endy, color)
int startx, starty, endx, endy, color;
{
    register int t, distance;
    int x=0, y=0, delta_x, delta_y;
    int incx, incy;

    /* compute the distances in both directions */
    delta_x = endx-startx;
    delta_y = endy-starty;
```

```
/* Compute the direction of the increment,
   an increment of 0 means either a vertical or horizontal
   line.
*/
if(delta_x>0) incx = 1;
else if(delta_x==0) incx = 0;
else incx=-1;

if(delta_y>0) incy = 1;
else if(delta_y==0) incy = 0;
else incy = -1;

/* determine which distance is greater */
delta_x = abs(delta_x);
delta_y = abs(delta_y);
if(delta_x>delta_y) distance = delta_x;
else distance = delta_y;

/* draw the line */
for(t=0; t<=distance+1; t++) {
  mempoint(startx, starty, color);
  x+=delta_x;
  y+=delta_y;
  if(x>distance) {
    x-=distance;
    startx+=incx;
  }
  if(y>distance) {
    y-=distance;
    starty+=incy;
  }
}
}

/* Fill box with specified color. */
void fill_box(startx, starty, endx, endy, color_code)
int startx, starty, endx, endy, color_code;
{
  register int i, begin, end;

  begin = startx<endx ? startx : endx;
  end = startx>endx ? startx : endx;

  for(i=begin; i<=end;i++)
    line(i, starty, i, endy, color_code);
}

/* Draw a circle using Bresenham's integer based Algorithm. */
void circle(x_center, y_center, radius,  color_code)
int x_center, y_center, radius, color_code;
{
  register int x, y, delta;

  asp_ratio = 1.0;  /* for different aspect ratios, alter
                       this number */

  y = radius;
  delta = 3 - 2 * radius;

  for(x=0; x<y; ) {
    plot_circle(x, y, x_center, y_center, color_code);
```

```
      if (delta < 0)
        delta += 4*x+6;
      else {
        delta += 4*(x-y)+10;
        y--;
      }
      x++;
    }
    x = y;
    if(y) plot_circle(x, y, x_center, y_center, color_code);
}

/* Plot_circle actually prints the points that
    define the circle. */
void plot_circle(x, y, x_center, y_center, color_code)
int x, y, x_center, y_center, color_code;
{
    int startx, endx, x1, starty, endy, y1;

    starty = y*asp_ratio;
    endy = (y+1)*asp_ratio;
    startx = x*asp_ratio;
    endx = (x+1)*asp_ratio;

    for (x1=startx; x1<endx; ++x1)  {
      mempoint(x1+x_center, y+y_center, color_code);
      mempoint(x1+x_center, y_center-y, color_code);
      mempoint(x_center-x1, y_center-y, color_code);
      mempoint(x_center-x1, y+y_center, color_code);
    }

    for (y1=starty; y1<endy; ++y1) {
      mempoint(y1+x_center, x+y_center, color_code);
      mempoint(y1+x_center, y_center-x, color_code);
      mempoint(x_center-y1, y_center-x, color_code);
      mempoint(x_center-y1, x+y_center, color_code);
    }
}

/* Fill a circle by repeatedly calling circle()
    with smaller radius.
*/
void fill_circle(x, y, r, c)
int x, y, r, c;
{
    while(r) {
      circle(x, y, r, c);
      r--;
    }
}

/* Write a point directly to the CGA/EGA */
void mempoint(x, y, color_code)
int x, y, color_code;
{
    union mask {
      char c[2];
      int i;
    } bit_mask;
    int i, index, bit_position;
    unsigned char t;
```

```
char xor; /* xor color in or overwrite */
char far *ptr = (char far *) 0xB8000000; /* pointer
                                       to CGA memory */

bit_mask.i=0xFF3F;     /* 11111111 00111111 in binary */

/* check range for mode 4 */
if(x<0 || x>199 || y<0 || y>319) return;

xor=color_code & 128; /* see if xor mode is set */
color_code = color_code & 127; /* mask off high bit */

/* set bit_mask and color_code bits to the right location */
bit_position = y%4;
color_code<<=2*(3-bit_position);
bit_mask.i>>=2*bit_position;


/* find the correct byte in screen memory */
index = x*40 +(y >> 2);
if(x % 2) index += 8152; /* if odd use 2nd bank */

/* write the color */
if(!xor) { /* overwrite mode */
  t = *(ptr+index) & bit_mask.c[0];
  *(ptr+index) = t | color_code;
}
else { /* xor mode */
  t = *(ptr+index) | (char)0;
  *(ptr+index) = t ^ color_code;
}
}
```

SAVING AND LOADING A GRAPHICS IMAGE

It is a simple matter to save or load a graphics image. Since what is displayed on the screen is held in the video RAM, the contents of that RAM are easily copied to a disk file, or vice versa. The biggest problem is to let the user enter a file name because both the prompting message and the file name entered by the user cause part of the image to be overwritten. To avoid this, the functions save_pic( ) and load_pic( ), shown here, first save the top 14 rows of the image, clear that area, prompt for the file name, and then restore the image after the file name has been entered.

```
/* save part of the video graphics display */
void save_pic()
{
  char fname[80];
  FILE *fp;
  register int i, j;
  char far *ptr = (char far *) 0xB8000000; /* pointer
                                         to CGA memory */
  char far *temp;
  unsigned char buf[14][80]; /* hold the contents of screen */

  temp = ptr;
  /* save the top of the current screen */
  for(i=0; i<14; i++)
    for(j=0; j<80; j+=2) {
      buf[i][j] = *temp; /* even byte */
      buf[i][j+1] = *(temp+8152); /* odd byte */
      *temp = 0; *(temp+8152) = 0;  /* clear top of screen */
      temp++;
    }

  goto_xy(0, 0);
  printf("Filename: ");
  gets(fname);
  if(!(fp=fopen(fname, "wb"))) {
    printf("cannot open file\n");
    return;
  }

  temp = ptr;
  /* restore the top of the current screen */
  for(i=0; i<14; i++)
    for(j=0; j<80; j+=2) {
      *temp = buf[i][j];
      *(temp+8152) = buf[i][j+1];
      temp++;
    }

  /* save image to file */
  for(i=0; i<8152; i++) {
    putc(*ptr, fp); /* even byte */
    putc(*(ptr+8152), fp); /* odd byte */
    ptr++;
  }

  fclose(fp);
}

/* load the video graphics display */
void load_pic()
{
  char fname[80];
  FILE *fp;
  register int i, j;
  char far *ptr = (char far *) 0xB8000000; /* pointer
                                         to CGA memory */
  char far *temp;
  unsigned char buf[14][80]; /* hold the contents of screen */
```

```
  temp = ptr;
  /* save the top of the current screen */
  for(i=0; i<14; i++)
    for(j=0; j<80; j+=2) {
      buf[i][j] = *temp;
      buf[i][j+1] = *(temp+8152);
      *temp = 0; *(temp+8152) = 0; /* clear the top of the screen */
      temp++;
    }

  goto_xy(0, 0);
  printf("Filename: ");
  gets(fname);
  if(!(fp=fopen(fname, "rb"))) {
    goto_xy(0, 0);
    printf("cannot open file\n");
    temp = ptr;
    /* restore the top of the current screen */
    for(i=0; i<14; i++)
      for(j=0; j<80; j+=2) {
        *temp = buf[i][j];
        *(temp+8152) = buf[i][j+1];
        temp++;
      }
    return;
  }

  /* load image from file */
  for(i=0; i<8152; i++) {
    *ptr = getc(fp); /* even byte */
    *(ptr+8152) = getc(fp); /* odd byte */
    ptr++;
  }

  fclose(fp);
}
```

The routines operate by assigning a pointer to the starting address of the video RAM and then by writing or reading each even and odd byte in ascending order. This allows the image to be loaded into RAM in a natural, visually pleasing way. If the video memory was accessed in a strictly ascending fashion, the even pixels would be displayed first, followed by the odd ones. Although an interesting effect, it would be a bit unsettling for general use.

DUPLICATING PART OF THE SCREEN

It is sometimes useful to be able to copy a graphics image in one part of the screen to another location. This is easily accomplished using the **copy( )** function shown here.

```
/* Copy one region to another location. */
void copy(startx, starty, endx, endy, x, y)
int startx, starty; /* upper left coordinate */
int endx, endy;  /* lower right coordinate of region to copy */
int x, y; /* upper left coordinate of region to copy to */
{
  int i, j;
  unsigned char c;

  for(; startx<=endx; startx++, x++)
    for(i=starty, j=y; i<=endy; i++, j++) {
      c = read_point(startx, i); /* read point */
      mempoint(x, j, c); /* write it to new location */
    }
}
```

As you can see, it is called with the upper-left and lower-right corner coordinates of the region to be copied and the upper-left coordinates of the location to which it is being copied.

As you might surmise, with only a slight change it is possible to transform **copy( )** into **move( )**. The **move( )** function moves a region to another place and erases the original as it does so. The **move( )** function is shown here.

```
/* Move one region to another location. */
void move(startx, starty, endx, endy, x, y)
int startx, starty; /* upper left coordinate */
int endx, endy; /* lower right coordinate of region to move */
int x, y; /* upper left of region receiving the image */
{
  int i, j;
  unsigned char c;

  for(; startx<=endx; startx++, x++)
    for(i=starty, j=y; i<=endy; i++, j++) {
      c = read_point(startx, i); /* read point */
      mempoint(startx, i, 0); /* erase old image */
      mempoint(x, j, c); /* write it to new location */
    }
}
```

TWO-DIMENSIONAL ROTATION

The rotation of an object in two-dimensional space is actually quite easy in the Cartesian coordinate system. You might recall from your high school analytic geometry class that the rotation of a point through an angle *theta* around the origin is described by these equations:

new__x = old__x * cos(theta) − old__y * sin(theta)
new__y = old__x * sin(theta) + old__y * cos(theta)

The only problem when you apply these formulas to the graphics display is that the screen is not technically a Cartesian space. A Cartesian axis defines four quadrants, as shown in Figure 4-2. However, the graphics screen only defines one quadrant — and in this quadrant the X and Y axes are reversed. To solve this problem it is necessary to establish a new origin and to normalize the screen X, Y coordinates to it. Any point on the screen can be used as an origin, but generally you want to define an origin that is near (or at) the center of the object that you wish to rotate. The function **rotate__point( )**, shown here, computes the proper new X,Y value for a specified angle of rotation.

```
/* Rotate a point around the origin, specified by
   x_org and y_org, by angle theta. */
void rotate_point(theta, x, y, x_org, y_org)
double theta, *x, *y;
int x_org, y_org;
{
  double tx, ty;

  /* normalize x and y to origin */
  tx = *x - x_org;
  ty = *y - y_org;

  /* rotate */
  *x = tx * cos(theta) - ty * sin(theta);
  *y = tx * sin(theta) + ty * cos(theta);

  /* return to PC coordinate values */
  *x += x_org;
  *y += y_org;

}
```

Notice that **rotate__point( )** modifies the **x** and **y** parameters by setting them to their proper value for the given angle of rotation specified by **theta**. The angle of rotation is specified in radians.

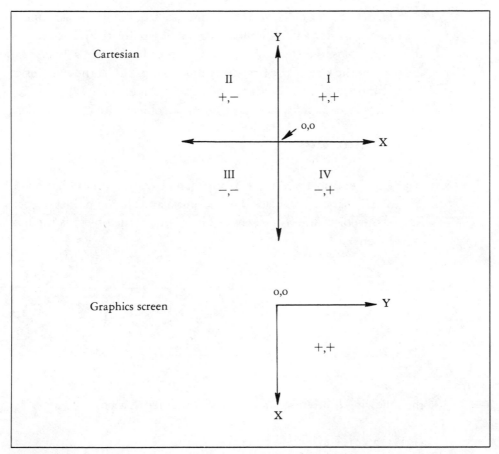

Figure 4-2.

Cartesian axis versus the graphics
screen

Rotating an Object

Although the function **rotate_point**( ) will compute the proper X,Y
coordinates that a rotated point will occupy, another function is needed if
entire objects are to be rotated. For the purposes of this discussion, an

object is defined as a collection of one or more straight lines. Each line in the object is held in a two-dimensional floating point array. Each row in the array holds the starting and ending coordinates for a line. This means that the size of the first array dimension will be the number of lines comprising the object and the second dimension will be 4. For example, the array shown here can define an object with up to 10 sides.

```
double object[10][4];
```

By convention, the array will be organized as shown in Figure 4-3.

To define an object, place the beginning and ending points of each line of the object into the array. For example, if the object is the box shown here

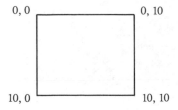

the following code creates an array that defines that box:

```
object[0][0] = 0;  object[0][1] = 0;
object[0][0] = 0;  object[0][3] = 10;

object[1][0] = 0;  object[1][1] = 10;
object[1][0] = 10; object[1][3] = 10;

object[2][0] = 10; object[2][1] = 10;
object[2][0] = 10; object[2][3] = 0;

object[3][0] = 10; object[3][1] = 0;
object[3][0] = 0;  object[3][3] = 0;
```

Once you have defined an object, the function **rotate_object( )**, shown here, can be used to rotate it in either a clockwise or counter-clockwise direction by pressing either the R or L key, respectively.

First index	Second index			
	0	1	2	3
0	start__X1	start__Y1	end__X1	end__Y1
1	start__X2	start__Y2	end__X2	end__Y2
2	start__X3	start__Y3	end__X3	end__Y3
3	start__X4	start__Y4	end__X4	end__Y4
.	.	.		
.	.	.		
.	.	.		
n	start__Xn	start__Yn	end__Xn	end__Yn

Figure 4-3.

Conventional organization of an array

```
/* Rotate the specified object. */
void rotate object(ob, theta, x, y, sides)
double ob[][4]; /* object definition */
double theta; /* angle of rotation in radians */
int x, y; /* location of origin */
int sides;
{
  register int i, j;
  double tempx, tempy;  /* these help with the type conversions */
  char ch;

  for(;;) {
    ch = getch(); /* see which direction to rotate */
    switch(tolower(ch)) {
      case 'l': /* rotate counterclockwise */
        theta = theta < 0 ? -theta : theta;
        break;
      case 'r': /* rotate clockwise */
        theta = theta > 0 ? -theta : theta;
        break;
      default: return;
    }

    for(j=0; j<sides; j++) {
      /* erase old line */
      line((int) ob[j][0], (int) ob[j][1],
        (int) ob[j][2], (int) ob[j][3], 0);
```

```
      rotate_point(theta, &ob[j][0],
        &ob[j][1], x, y);

      rotate_point(theta, &ob[j][2],
        &ob[j][3], x, y);

      line((int)ob[j][0], (int) ob[j][1],
        (int) ob[j][2], (int) ob[j][3], 2);
    }
  }
}
```

As indicated by the function parameter declarations, **rotate__ object( )** will rotate the object about the origin specified in X and Y by the angle **theta**. Remember, **theta** must be specified in radians. The smallest practical value of **theta** is 0.01. Notice that the object is erased from its previous position and then moved to its new position. If this were not done, the screen would quickly become a blur of color. You must be sure to specify the number of sides an object has in the parameter **sides**.

Although not technically part of the rotation functions, **display__ object( )**, shown here, is useful when working with objects. It displays the object defined in **ob**.

```
/* Display an object. */
void display_object(ob, sides)
double ob[][4];
int sides;
{
  register int i;

  for(i=0; i<sides; i++)
    line((int) ob[i][0], (int) ob[i][1],
      (int) ob[i][2], (int) ob[i][3], 2);
}
```

To illustrate the usefulness of the rotation functions, the following program uses them to rotate a house about its center. A series of screen images at different points in the rotation is shown in Figure 4-4. The box around the house helps define the perspective.

```
/* An example of object rotation using the
   CGA/EGA in graphics mode 4 */

#include "dos.h"
#include "stdio.h"
#include "math.h"
```

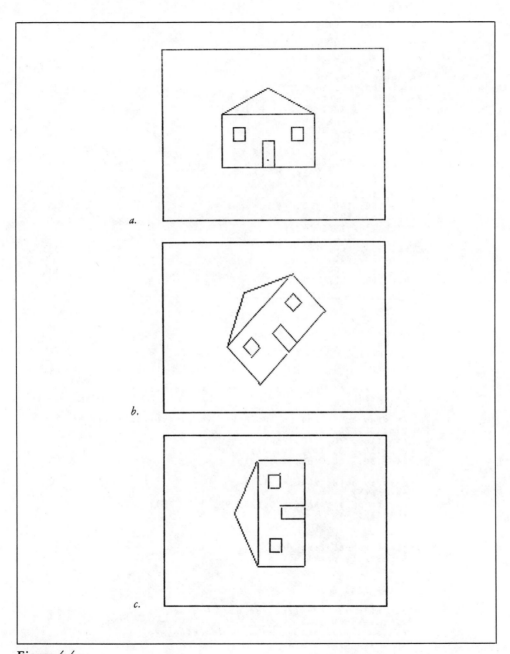

a.

b.

c.

Figure 4-4.

Rotating an object

```
void mode(), line();
void mempoint(), palette();
void rotate_point(), rotate_object();
void display_object();

/* house array */
double house[][4] ={
/* startx, starty, endx, endy */
  120, 120, 120, 200, /* house */
  120, 200, 80, 200,
  80, 120, 80, 200,
  80, 120, 120, 120,
  60, 160, 80, 120, /* roof */
  60, 160, 80, 200,
  120, 155, 100, 155, /* door */
  100, 155, 100, 165,
  100, 165, 120, 165,
  90, 130, 100, 130, /* windows */
  90, 130, 90, 140,
  100, 130, 100, 140,
  90, 140, 100, 140,
  90, 180, 100, 180,
  90, 180, 90, 190,
  100, 180, 100, 190,
  90, 190, 100, 190
};

main()
{
  union k{
    char c[2];
    int i;
  } key;

  mode(4);  /* mode 4 graphics, palette 0 */
  palette(0);

  /* draw a box around the house to give perspective */
  line(30, 70, 30, 260, 2);
  line(160, 70, 160, 260, 2);
  line(30, 70, 160, 70, 2);
  line(30, 260, 160, 260, 2);

  display_object(house, 17);
  getche();
  rotate_object(house, 0.025, 90, 160, 17);
  mode(3);
}

/* Set the palette. */
void palette(pnum)
int pnum;
{
  union REGS r;

  r.h.bh = 1;   /* code for mode 4 graphics */
  r.h.bl = pnum;
  r.h.ah = 11;  /* set palette function */
  int86(0x10, &r, &r);
}
```

```
/* Set the video mode. */
void mode(mode_code)
int mode_code;
{
  union REGS r;

  r.h.al = mode_code;
  r.h.ah = 0;
  int86(0x10, &r, &r);
}



/* Draw a line in specified color
   using Bresenham's integer based algorithm.
*/
void line(startx, starty, endx, endy, color)
int startx, starty, endx, endy, color;
{
  register int t, distance;
  int x=0, y=0, delta_x, delta_y;
  int incx, incy;

  /* compute the distances in both directions */
  delta_x=endx-startx;
  delta_y=endy-starty;

  /* Compute the direction of the increment,
     an increment of 0 means either a vertical or horizontal
     line.
  */
  if(delta_x>0) incx=1;
  else if(delta_x==0) incx=0;
  else incx=-1;

  if(delta_y>0) incy=1;
  else if(delta_y==0) incy=0;
  else incy=-1;

  /* determine which distance is greater */
  delta_x=abs(delta_x);
  delta_y=abs(delta_y);
  if(delta_x>delta_y) distance=delta_x;
  else distance=delta_y;

  /* draw the line */
  for(t=0; t<=distance+1; t++) {
    mempoint(startx, starty, color);
    x+=delta_x;
    y+=delta_y;
    if(x>distance) {
      x-=distance;
      startx+=incx;
    }
    if(y>distance) {
      y-=distance;
      starty+=incy;
    }
  }
}
```

```
/* Write a point directly to the CGA/EGA. */
void mempoint(x,y,color_code)
int x,y,color_code;
{
  union mask {
    char c[2];
    int i;
  } bit_mask;
  int i, index, bit_position;
  unsigned char t;
  char xor; /* xor color in or overwrite */
  char far *ptr = (char far *) 0xB8000000; /* pointer
                                              to CGA memory */

  bit_mask.i=0xFF3F;    /* 11111111 00111111 in binary */

  /* check range for mode 4 */
  if(x<0 || x>199 || y<0 || y>319) return;

  xor=color_code & 128; /* see if xor mode is set */
  color_code=color_code & 127; /* mask off high bit */

  /* set bit_mask and color_code bits to the right location */
  bit_position=y%4;
  color_code<<=2*(3-bit_position);
  bit_mask.i>>=2*bit_position;


 /* find the correct byte in screen memory */
  index=x*40 +(y >> 2);
  if(x % 2) index += 8152; /* if odd use 2nd bank */

  /* write the color */
  if(!xor) { /* overwrite mode */
    t=*(ptr+index) & bit_mask.c[0];
    *(ptr+index)=t | color_code;
  }
  else { /* xor mode */
    t=*(ptr+index) | (char)0;
    *(ptr+index)=t ^ color_code;
  }
}

/* Rotate a point around the origin, specified by
   x_org and y_org, by angle theta. */
void rotate_point(theta, x, y, x_org, y_org)
double theta, *x, *y;
int x_org, y_org;
{
  double tx, ty;

  /* normalize x and y */
  tx = *x - x_org;
  ty = *y - y_org;

  /* rotate */
  *x = tx * cos(theta) - ty * sin(theta);
  *y = tx * sin(theta) + ty * cos(theta);
```

```
      /* return to PC coordinate values */
      *x += x_org;
      *y += y_org;

}


/* Rotate the specified object. */
void rotate_object(ob, theta, x, y, sides)
double ob[][4]; /* object definition */
double theta; /* angle of rotation in radians */
int x, y; /* location of origin */
int sides;
{
   register int i, j;
   double tempx, tempy;  /* these help with the type conversions */
   char ch;

   for(;;) {
     ch = getch(); /* see which direction to rotate */
     switch(tolower(ch)) {
       case 'l':  /* counterclockwise */
         theta = theta < 0 ? -theta : theta;
         break;
       case 'r': /* clockwise */
         theta = theta > 0 ? -theta : theta;
         break;
       default: return;
     }

     for(j=0; j<sides; j++) {
       /* erase old line */
       line((int) ob[j][0], (int) ob[j][1],
         (int) ob[j][2], (int) ob[j][3], 0);

       rotate_point(theta, &ob[j][0],
         &ob[j][1], x, y);

       rotate_point(theta, &ob[j][2],
         &ob[j][3], x, y);

       line((int)ob[j][0], (int) ob[j][1],
         (int) ob[j][2], (int) ob[j][3], 2);
     }
   }
}


/* Display an object. */
void display_object(ob, sides)
double ob[][4];
int sides;
{
   register int i;

   for(i=0; i<sides; i++)
     line((int) ob[i][0], (int) ob[i][1],
       (int) ob[i][2], (int) ob[i][3], 2);
}
```

COMBINING THE ROUTINES

This final section presents a simple "paint" program that uses the graphics routines developed in this chapter. You are probably familiar with some of the popular paint-type programs that are available. A paint program generally uses a mouse to allow the user to "brush" lines onto the screen. However, since not everyone has a mouse, the paint program developed here relies on the cursor keys for its operation.

In a paint program, you must be able to see where the current X,Y position is. (In graphics mode, there is no cursor.) To do this requires the use of a locator which resembles the crosshairs of a rifle scope. The function **xhairs( )**, shown here, places a small crosshairs on the screen at the current X,Y position. Notice that the color code is ORed with 128, causing bit 7 to be set to 1. This tells the **mempoint( )** function to XOR the color onto the screen instead of overwriting the current color. This arrangement achieves two very important objectives. First, the locator is always visible because it always has a color different than the surrounding color. Second, it makes it easy to return the pixels occupied by the locator to their former color by simply writing them a second time. (Recall that a sequence of two XOR operations always produce the original value.)

```
/* display crosshair locator */
void xhairs(x,y)
int x,y;
{
   line(x-4, y, x+3, y, 1 | 128);
   line(x, y+4, x, y-3, 1 | 128);
}
```

The paint program shown here lets you

- Draw lines

- Draw boxes

- Fill boxes

- Draw circles

- Fill circles

- Select color

- Select palette

- Turn the brush on and off

- Set a speed of motion parameter

- Save a graphics image

- Load a graphics image

- Rotate an object around any point of origin

- Copy and move graphics images

The main loop of the program is shown here.

```
main()
{
  union k{
    char c[2];
    int i;
  } key;

  int x=10, y=10; /* current screen position */
  int cc=2; /* current color */
  int on_flag=1; /* pen on or off */
  int pal_num=1; /* palette number */
  /* the end points of a defined line, circle, or box */
  int startx=0, starty=0, endx=0, endy=0, first_point=1;
  int inc=1; /* movement increment */
  int sides=0; /* number of sides of a defined object */
  int i;

  mode(4);  /* switch to mode 4 CGA/EGA graphics */
  palette(0); /* palette 0 */

  xhairs(x, y); /* show the crosshairs */
  do {
    key.i = bioskey(0);
    xhairs(x, y);    /* plot the crosshairs */
    if(!key.c[0]) switch(key.c[1]) {
      case 75: /* left */
        if(on_flag) line(x, y, x, y-inc, cc);
        y -= inc;
        break;
      case 77: /* right */
        if(on_flag) line(x, y, x, y+inc, cc);
        y += inc;
        break;
      case 72: /* up */
        if(on_flag) line(x, y, x-inc, y, cc);
        x -= inc;
        break;
```

```
        case 80: /* down */
          if(on_flag) line(x, y, x+inc, y, cc);
          x += inc;
          break;
        case 71: /* up left */
          if(on_flag) line(x, y, x-inc, y-inc, cc);
          x -= inc; y -= inc;
          break;
        case 73: /* up right */
          if(on_flag) line(x, y, x-inc, y+inc, cc);
          x -= inc; y += inc;
          break;
        case 79: /* down left*/
          if(on_flag) line(x, y, x+inc, y-inc, cc);
          x += inc; y -= inc;
          break;
        case 81: /* down right */
          if(on_flag) line(x, y, x+inc, y+inc, cc);
          x += inc; y += inc;
          break;
        case 59: inc = 1;  /* F1 - slow speed */
          break;
        case 60: inc = 5;  /* F2 - fast speed */
          break;
      }
      else switch(tolower(key.c[0])) {
        case 'o': on_flag = !on_flag; /* toggle brush */
          break;
        case '1': cc = 1; /* color 1 */
          break;
        case '2': cc = 2; /* color 2 */
          break;
        case '3': cc = 3; /* color 3 */
          break;
        case '0': cc = 0; /* color 0 */
          break;
        case 'b': box(startx, starty, endx, endy, cc);
          break;
        case 'f': fill_box(startx, starty, endx, endy, cc);
          break;
        case 'l': line(startx, starty, endx, endy, cc);
          break;
        case 'c': circle(startx, starty, endy-starty, cc);
          break;
        case 'h': fill_circle(startx, starty, endy-starty, cc);
          break;
        case 's': save_pic();
          break;
        case 'r': load_pic();
          break;
        case 'm': /* move a region */
          move(startx, starty, endx, endy, x, y);
          break;
        case 'x': /* copy a region */
          copy(startx, starty, endx, endy, x, y);
          break;
        case 'd':  /* define an object to rotate */
          sides = define_object(object, x, y);
          break;
        case 'a': /* rotate the object */
          rotate_object(object, 0.05, x, y, sides);
          break;
```

```
    case '\r': /* set endpoints for line, circle, or box */
      if(first_point) {
        startx = x, starty = y;
      }
      else {
        endx = x; endy = y;
      }
      first_point = !first_point;
      break;
    case 'p': pal_num = pal_num==1 ? 2:1;
      palette(pal_num);
  }
  xhairs(x, y);
} while (key.c[0]!='q');
getchar();
mode(2);
}
```

The paint program works like this. The screen is first set to graphics mode 4. Palette 0 is selected and the locator is displayed in the upper-left corner. The brush is on with a default color of 2 (red in palette 0). Therefore, moving the cursor leaves a trail of pixels. This is the way color is "brushed" onto the screen. Each time a cursor key is struck, the locator moves one pixel in the indicated direction. This can be rather slow at times, so the program allows you to move five pixels at a time by striking the F2 function key. To return to single pixel moves, strike the F1 function key. Different colors may be selected by typing the numbers 0 through 3 on the keyboard. In palette 0, 0 is blank, 1 is green, 2 is red, and 3 is yellow. The brush may be turned off and on by typing the O key. The HOME, PGUP, PGDN, and END keys move the locator at 45-degree angles in the expected direction.

The program uses the **bioskey( )** function to read scan codes. If your compiler does not include this function, refer to Chapter 1 for a version that you can use.

The program supports several special commands that draw boxes, fill boxes, draw lines, draw circles, fill circles, copy or move images, save or load the contents of the screen, and define and rotate an object. Let's see how these commands operate.

To draw lines, boxes, and circles automatically, you must first define two coordinates. For boxes and filled boxes, you must specify the location of two opposing corners. For lines, you select the beginning and ending points. For circles and filled circles you specify the center and a point on the circle directly left or right of the center. The selection process is performed by hitting the RETURN key when the locator is over the desired spot. For example, to define the end points of a line, you move the locator to the point where the line will begin and press the RETURN key. Next, you position the locator at the point where the line will end and press the RETURN key again. Pressing the RETURN key loads the variables **startx**, **starty**, **endx**, and **endy**, which are then used as parameters to the appropriate function. Once the locations have been recorded, typing a B draws a box, an F draws a filled box, an L draws a line, C draws a circle, and H fills a circle.

To move or copy a region of the screen, you must define the upper-left and lower-right corner of the region by pressing the RETURN key at the appropriate locations. Next, move the locator to the upper-left corner of the region where you want to move or copy the image. To move the image, press M; to copy the image press X. Remember, what was previously in the destination region will be overwritten.

To rotate an object, you must first define the object by pressing the D key. Next, using the RETURN key, define each line segment in the object. That is, trace the object, pressing the ENTER key at the beginning and ending point of each line in the object. When you have defined the object, press the F1 key to stop the definition process. The definition process is performed by the **define_object( )** function, which is found in the complete program shown here. Once the object is defined, it can be rotated by pressing the A key and using the L or R key to rotate the object about an origin defined by the current position of the locator. To stop the rotate procedure, press any key other than L or A.

The program is terminated by typing a Q.

The entire paint program is shown here. You might find it enjoyable to add other high-level commands or to interface it to a mouse. Sample output is shown in Figure 4-5.

```
/* A paint program for the CGA/EGA that allows
   lines, boxes, and circles to be drawn.  You may
   define an object and rotate it in either a clockwise
   or counterclockwise direction.  Also, the
   graphics image may be saved to disk and loaded
   at a later date.
*/
```

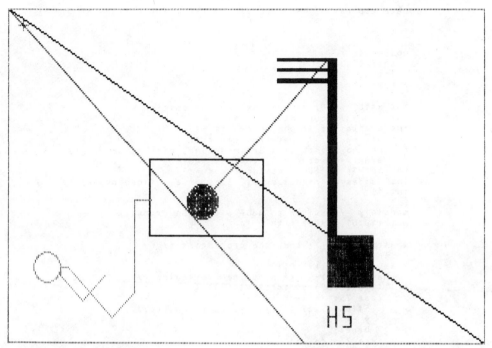

Figure 4-5.

Sample output from the paint
program

```
#define NUM_SIDES 20 /* Number of sides an object may
                         have.  Enlarge as needed */

#include "dos.h"
#include "stdio.h"
#include "math.h"

void mode(), line(), box(),fill_box();
void mempoint(), palette(), xhairs();
void circle(), plot_circle(), fill_circle();
void rotate_point(), rotate_object(), goto_xy();
void display_object(), copy(), move();
void save_pic(), load_pic();
unsigned char read_point();

/* This array will hold the coordinates of an object
   defined dynamcially.
*/
double object[NUM_SIDES][4];
```

```
double asp_ratio; /* holds aspect ratio for circles */

main()
{
  union k{
    char c[2];
    int i;
  } key;

  int x=10, y=10; /* current screen position */
  int cc=2; /* current color */
  int on_flag=1; /* pen on or off */
  int pal_num=1; /* palette number */
  /* the end points of a defined line, circle, or box */
  int startx=0, starty=0, endx=0, endy=0, first_point=1;
  int inc=1; /* movement increment */
  int  sides=0; /* number of sides of a defined object */
  int i;

  mode(4);   /* switch to mode 4 CGA/EGA graphics */
  palette(0); /* palette 0 */

  xhairs(x, y); /* show the crosshairs */
  do {
    key.i = bioskey(0);
    xhairs(x, y);    /* plot the crosshairs */
    if(!key.c[0]) switch(key.c[1]) {
      case 75: /* left */
        if(on_flag) line(x, y, x, y-inc, cc);
        y -= inc;
        break;
      case 77: /* right */
        if(on_flag) line(x, y, x, y+inc, cc);
        y += inc;
        break;
      case 72: /* up */
        if(on_flag) line(x, y, x-inc, y, cc);
        x -= inc;
        break;
      case 80: /* down */
        if(on_flag) line(x, y, x+inc, y, cc);
        x += inc;
        break;
      case 71: /* up left */
        if(on_flag) line(x, y, x-inc, y-inc, cc);
        x -= inc; y -= inc;
        break;
      case 73: /* up right */
        if(on_flag) line(x, y, x-inc, y+inc, cc);
        x -= inc; y += inc;
        break;
      case 79: /* down left*/
        if(on_flag) line(x, y, x+inc, y-inc, cc);
        x += inc; y -= inc;
        break;
      case 81: /* down right */
        if(on_flag) line(x, y, x+inc, y+inc, cc);
        x += inc; y += inc;
        break;
      case 59: inc = 1;  /* F1 - slow speed */
        break;
      case 60: inc = 5;  /* F2 - fast speed */
        break;
```

```
      }
    else switch(tolower(key.c[0])) {
      case 'o': on_flag = !on_flag; /* toggle brush */
        break;
      case '1': cc = 1; /* color 1 */
        break;
      case '2': cc = 2; /* color 2 */
        break;
      case '3': cc = 3; /* color 3 */
        break;
      case '0': cc = 0; /* color 0 */
        break;
      case 'b': box(startx, starty, endx, endy, cc);
        break;
      case 'f': fill_box(startx, starty, endx, endy, cc);
        break;
      case 'l': line(startx, starty, endx, endy, cc);
        break;
      case 'c': circle(startx, starty, endy-starty, cc);
        break;
      case 'h': fill_circle(startx, starty, endy-starty, cc);
        break;
      case 's': save_pic();
        break;
      case 'r': load_pic();
        break;
      case 'm': /* move a region */
        move(startx, starty, endx, endy, x, y);
        break;
      case 'x': /* copy a region */
        copy(startx, starty, endx, endy, x, y);
        break;
      case 'd':  /* define an object to rotate */
        sides = define_object(object, x, y);
        break;
      case 'a': /* rotate the object */
        rotate_object(object, 0.05, x, y, sides);
        break;
      case '\r': /* set endpoints for line, circle, or box */
        if(first_point) {
          startx = x, starty = y;
        }
        else {
          endx = x; endy = y;
        }
        first_point = !first_point;
        break;
      case 'p': pal_num = pal_num==1 ? 2:1;
        palette(pal_num);
    }
    xhairs(x, y);
  } while (key.c[0]!='q');
  getchar();
  mode(2);
}


/* Set the palette. */
void palette(pnum)
int pnum;
{
  union REGS r;
```

```
   r.h.bh = 1;    /* code for mode 4 graphics */
   r.h.bl = pnum;
   r.h.ah = 11;   /* set palette function */
   int86(0x10, &r, &r);
}

/* Set the video mode. */
void mode(mode_code)
int mode_code;
{
  union REGS r;

  r.h.al = mode_code;
  r.h.ah = 0;
  int86(0x10, &r, &r);
}


/* Draw a box. */
void box(startx, starty, endx, endy, color_code)
int startx, starty, endx, endy, color_code;
{
  line(startx, starty, endx, starty, color_code);
  line(startx, starty, startx, endy, color_code);
  line(startx, endy, endx, endy, color_code);
  line(endx, starty, endx, endy, color_code);
}


/* Draw a line in specified color
   using Bresenham's integer based algorithm.
*/
void line(startx, starty, endx, endy, color)
int startx, starty, endx, endy, color;
{
  register int t, distance;
  int x=0, y=0, delta_x, delta_y;
  int incx, incy;

  /* compute the distances in both directions */
  delta_x = endx-startx;
  delta_y = endy-starty;

  /* Compute the direction of the increment,
     an increment of 0 means either a vertical or horizontal
     line.
  */
  if(delta_x>0) incx = 1;
  else if(delta_x==0) incx = 0;
  else incx=-1;

  if(delta_y>0) incy = 1;
  else if(delta_y==0) incy = 0;
  else incy = -1;

  /* determine which distance is greater */
  delta_x = abs(delta_x);
  delta_y = abs(delta_y);
  if(delta_x>delta_y) distance = delta_x;
  else distance = delta_y;
```

```
     /* draw the line */
     for(t=0; t<=distance+1; t++) {
       mempoint(startx, starty, color);
       x+=delta_x;
       y+=delta_y;
       if(x>distance) {
         x-=distance;
         startx+=incx;
       }
       if(y>distance) {
         y-=distance;
         starty+=incy;
       }
     }
}


/* Fill box with specified color. */
void fill_box(startx, starty, endx, endy, color_code)
int startx, starty, endx, endy, color_code;
{
  register int i, begin, end;

  begin = startx<endx ? startx : endx;
  end = startx>endx ? startx : endx;

  for(i=begin; i<=end;i++)
    line(i, starty, i, endy, color_code);
}


/* Draw a circle using Bresenham's integer based Algorithm. */
void circle(x_center, y_center, radius, color_code)
int x_center, y_center, radius, color_code;
{
  register int x, y, delta;

  asp_ratio = 1.0;   /* for different aspect ratios, alter
                        this number */

  y = radius;
  delta = 3 - 2 * radius;

  for(x=0; x<y; ) {
    plot_circle(x, y, x_center, y_center, color_code);

    if (delta < 0)
      delta += 4*x+6;
    else {
      delta += 4*(x-y)+10;
      y--;
    }
    x++;
  }
  x = y;
  if(y) plot_circle(x, y, x_center, y_center, color_code);
}


/* Plot_circle actually prints the points that
   define the circle. */
void plot_circle(x, y, x_center, y_center, color_code)
int x, y, x_center, y_center, color_code;
```

```
{
  int startx, endx, x1, starty, endy, y1;

  starty = y*asp_ratio;
  endy = (y+1)*asp_ratio;
  startx = x*asp_ratio;
  endx = (x+1)*asp_ratio;

  for (x1=startx; x1<endx; ++x1)  {
    mempoint(x1+x_center, y+y_center, color_code);
    mempoint(x1+x_center, y_center-y, color_code);
    mempoint(x_center-x1, y_center-y, color_code);
    mempoint(x_center-x1, y+y_center, color_code);
  }

  for (y1=starty; y1<endy; ++y1) {
    mempoint(y1+x_center, x+y_center, color_code);
    mempoint(y1+x_center, y_center-x, color_code);
    mempoint(x_center-y1, y_center-x, color_code);
    mempoint(x_center-y1, x+y_center, color_code);
  }
}

/* Fill a circle by repeatedly calling circle()
   with smaller radius.
*/
void fill_circle(x, y, r, c)
int x, y, r, c;
{
  while(r) {
    circle(x, y, r, c);
    r--;
  }
}

/* Display crosshair locator. */
void xhairs(x,y)
int x, y;
{
  line(x-4, y, x+3, y, 1 | 128);
  line(x, y+4, x, y-3, 1 | 128);
}

/* Write a point directly to the CGA/EGA */
void mempoint(x, y, color_code)
int x, y, color_code;
{
  union mask {
    char c[2];
    int i;
  } bit_mask;
  int i, index, bit_position;
  unsigned char t;
  char xor; /* xor color in or overwrite */
  char far *ptr = (char far *) 0xB8000000; /* pointer
                                       to CGA memory */

  bit_mask.i=0xFF3F;      /* 11111111 00111111 in binary */

  /* check range for mode 4 */
  if(x<0 || x>199 || y<0 || y>319) return;

  xor=color_code & 128; /* see if xor mode is set */
  color_code = color_code & 127; /* mask off high bit */
```

```c
   /* set bit_mask and color_code bits to the right location */
   bit_position = y%4;
   color_code<<=2*(3-bit_position);
   bit_mask.i>>=2*bit_position;


   /* find the correct byte in screen memory */
   index = x*40 +(y >> 2);
   if(x % 2) index += 8152; /* if odd use 2nd bank */

   /* write the color */
   if(!xor) { /* overwrite mode */
     t = *(ptr+index) & bit_mask.c[0];
     *(ptr+index) = t | color_code;
   }
   else { /* xor mode */
     t = *(ptr+index) | (char)0;
     *(ptr+index) = t ^ color_code;
   }
}

/* Read byte directly from the CGA/EGA in mode 4. */
unsigned char read_point(x, y)
int x, y;
{
   union mask {
     char c[2];
     int i;
   } bit_mask;
   int i, index, bit_position;
   unsigned char t;
   char xor; /* xor color in or overwrite */
   char far *ptr = (char far *) 0xB8000000; /* pointer
                                               to CGA memory */

   bit_mask.i=3; /* 11111111 00111111 in binary */

   /* check range for mode 4 */
   if(x<0 || x>199 || y<0 || y>319) return 0;

   /* set bit_mask and color_code bits to the right location */
   bit_position = y%4;
   bit_mask.i<<=2*(3-bit_position);
   /* find the correct byte in screen memory */
   index = x*40 +(y >> 2);
   if(x % 2) index += 8152; /* if odd use 2nd bank */

   /* read the color */
   t = *(ptr+index) & bit_mask.c[0];
   t >>=2*(3-bit_position);
   return t;
}


/* save the video graphics display */
void save_pic()
{
   char fname[80];
   FILE *fp;
   register int i, j;
   char far *ptr = (char far *) 0xB8000000; /* pointer
                                               to CGA memory */
   char far *temp;
```

```
      unsigned char buf[14][80]; /* hold the contents of screen */

      temp = ptr;
      /* save the top of the current screen */
      for(i=0; i<14; i++)
        for(j=0; j<80; j+=2) {
          buf[i][j] = *temp; /* even byte */
          buf[i][j+1] = *(temp+8152); /* odd byte */
          *temp = 0; *(temp+8152) = 0;  /* clear top of screen */
          temp++;
        }

      goto_xy(0, 0);
      printf("Filename: ");
      gets(fname);
      if(!(fp=fopen(fname, "wb"))) {
        printf("cannot open file\n");
        return;
      }

      temp = ptr;
      /* restore the top of the current screen */
      for(i=0; i<14; i++)
        for(j=0; j<80; j+=2) {
          *temp = buf[i][j];
          *(temp+8152) = buf[i][j+1];
          temp++;
        }

    /* save image to file */
    for(i=0; i<8152; i++) {
      putc(*ptr, fp); /* even byte */
      putc(*(ptr+8152), fp); /* odd byte */
      ptr++;
    }

      fclose(fp);
    }


    /* load the video graphics display */
    void load_pic()
    {
      char fname[80];
      FILE *fp;
      register int i, j;
      char far *ptr = (char far *) 0xB8000000; /* pointer
                                          to CGA memory */
      char far *temp;
      unsigned char buf[14][80]; /* hold the contents of screen */

      temp = ptr;
      /* save the top of the current screen */
      for(i=0; i<14; i++)
        for(j=0; j<80; j+=2) {
          buf[i][j] = *temp;
          buf[i][j+1] = *(temp+8152);
          *temp = 0; *(temp+8152) = 0; /* clear the top of the screen */
          temp++;
        }

      goto_xy(0, 0);
      printf("Filename: ");
```

```
   gets(fname);
   if(!(fp=fopen(fname, "rb"))) {
     goto_xy(0, 0);
     printf("cannot open file\n");
     temp = ptr;
     /* restore the top of the current screen */
     for(i=0; i<14; i++)
       for(j=0; j<80; j+=2) {
         *temp = buf[i][j];
         *(temp+8152) = buf[i][j+1];
         temp++;
       }
     return;
   }

   /* load image from file */
   for(i=0; i<8152; i++) {
     *ptr = getc(fp); /* even byte */
     *(ptr+8152) = getc(fp); /* odd byte */
     ptr++;
   }

   fclose(fp);
}

/* Send the cursor to the specified X,Y position. */
void goto_xy(x, y)
int x, y;
{
   union REGS r;

   r.h.ah=2; /* cursor addressing function */
   r.h.dl = y; /* column coordinate */
   r.h.dh = x; /* row coordinate */
   r.h.bh = 0; /* video page */
   int86(0x10, &r, &r);
}

/* Move one region to another location. */
void move(startx, starty, endx, endy, x, y)
int startx, starty; /* upper left coordinate */
int endx, endy; /* lower right coordinate of region to move */
int x, y; /* upper left of region receiving the image */
{
   int i, j;
   unsigned char c;

   for(; startx<=endx; startx++, x++)
     for(i=starty, j=y; i<=endy; i++, j++) {
       c = read_point(startx, i); /* read point */
       mempoint(startx, i, 0); /* erase old image */
       mempoint(x, j, c); /* write it to new location */
     }
}

/* Copy one region to another location. */
void copy(startx, starty, endx, endy, x, y)
int startx, starty; /* upper left coordinate */
int endx, endy; /* lower right coordinate of region to copy */
int x, y; /* upper left of region receiving the image */
{
   int i, j;
   unsigned char c;
```

```
      for(; startx<=endx; startx++, x++)
        for(i=starty, j=y; i<=endy; i++, j++) {
          c = read_point(startx, i); /* read point */
          mempoint(x, j, c); /* write it to new location */
        }
    }


/* Rotate a point around the origin, specified by
   x_org and y_org,  by angle theta. */
void rotate_point(theta, x, y, x_org, y_org)
double theta, *x, *y;
int x_org, y_org;
{
  double tx, ty;

  /* normalize x and y to origin */
  tx = *x - x_org;
  ty = *y - y_org;

  /* rotate */
  *x = tx * cos(theta) - ty * sin(theta);
  *y = tx * sin(theta) + ty * cos(theta);

  /* return to PC coordinate values */
  *x += x_org;
  *y += y_org;

}

/* Rotate the specified object. */
void rotate_object(ob, theta, x, y, sides)
double ob[][4]; /* object definition */
double theta; /* angle of rotation in radians */
int x, y; /* location of origin */
int sides;
{
  register int i, j;
  double tempx, tempy;  /* these help with the type conversions */
  char ch;

  for(;;) {
    ch = getch(); /* see which direction to rotate */
    switch(tolower(ch)) {
      case 'l': /* rotate counterclockwise */
        theta = theta < 0 ? -theta : theta;
        break;
      case 'r': /* rotate clockwise */
        theta = theta > 0 ? -theta : theta;
        break;
      default: return;
    }

    for(j=0; j<sides; j++) {
      /* erase old line */
      line((int) ob[j][0], (int) ob[j][1],
        (int) ob[j][2], (int) ob[j][3], 0);

      rotate_point(theta, &ob[j][0],
        &ob[j][1], x, y);

      rotate_point(theta, &ob[j][2],
        &ob[j][3], x, y);
```

```
      line((int)ob[j][0], (int) ob[j][1],
        (int) ob[j][2], (int) ob[j][3], 2);
    }
  }
}

/* Display an object. */
void display_object(ob, sides)
double ob[][4];
int sides;
{
  register int i;

  for(i=0; i<sides; i++)
    line((int) ob[i][0], (int) ob[i][1],
      (int) ob[i][2], (int) ob[i][3], 2);
}

/* Define an object by specifying its endpoints */
define_object(ob, x, y)
double ob[][4];
int x, y;
{

  union k{
    char c[2];
    int i;
  } key;
  register int i, j;
  char far *ptr = (char far *) 0xB8000000; /* pointer
                                             to CGA memory */
  char far *temp;
  unsigned char buf[14][80]; /* hold the contents of screen */
  int sides=0;

  temp = ptr;
  /* save the top of the current screen */
  for(i=0; i<14; i++)
    for(j=0; j<80; j+=2) {
      buf[i][j] = *temp;
      buf[i][j+1] = *(temp+8152);
      *temp = 0; *(temp+8152) = 0; /* clear the top of the screen */
      temp++;
    }

  i = 0;
  xhairs(x, y);
  do {
    goto_xy(0, 0);
    printf("Define side %d,", sides+1);
    if(i==0) printf(" enter first endpoint");
    else printf(" enter second endpoint");

    key.i = bioskey(0);
    xhairs(x, y);    /* plot the crosshairs */
    if(key.c[0]==13) {
      ob[sides][i++] = (double) x;
      ob[sides][i++] = (double) y;
      if(i==4) {
        i = 0;
        sides++;
      }
    }
```

```
        /* if arrow key, move the crosshairs */
        if(!key.c[0]) switch(key.c[1]) {
          case 75: /* left */
            y-=1;
            break;
          case 77: /* right */
            y+=1;
            break;
          case 72: /* up */
            x-=1;
            break;
          case 80: /* down */
            x+=1;
            break;
          case 71: /* up left */
            x-=1; y-=1;
            break;
          case 73: /* up right */
            x-=1; y+=1;
            break;
          case 79: /* down left*/
            x+=1;y-=1;
            break;
          case 81: /* down right */
            x+=1;y+=1;
            break;
        }
    if(key.c[1]!=59) xhairs(x, y);
  } while(key.c[1]!=59); /* F1 to stop */

  temp = ptr;
  /* restore the top of the current screen */
  for(i=0; i<14; i++)
    for(j=0; j<80; j+=2) {
      *temp = buf[i][j];
      *(temp+8152) = buf[i][j+1];
      temp++;
    }
  return sides;
}
```

Even though the paint program requires a lot of code, you should enter it into your computer because it is really a fun program to use. (It can be quite addictive.) Also, it gives you a powerful graphics toolbox that you can draw upon at any time.

5: Video Games

Video games are either a blessing or a curse, depending on your point of view! However, the art of video game programming is an exciting and rewarding pursuit. (In fact, one good way to get rich quick is to write the next hit video game!) A good video game combines animated graphics with some logic that can be very complex to produce an enjoyable challenge to the player. Some of the best games even apply artificial intelligence techniques to allow the computer's strategy to respond to user input.

In this chapter you will learn some basic programming techniques that you can use to develop your own video games. In the process, you will learn how to animate objects on the screen. Also, a complete video game is developed for you to use as a starting point. Many of the principles used to create video games can be applied to your application programs to add excitement or interest.

The code examples developed in this chapter require an IBM PC or compatible with either a CGA, EGA, or VGA color graphics adapter. Many of the graphics functions used in this chapter are developed in Chapter 4. So, if you haven't read Chapter 4, you might want to do so at this time.

SPRITES

Many arcade-style video games consist of two main components: the environment (hereafter referred to as the "game board") and *sprites*. A sprite is a small, animated object that moves about the game board according to some rules and for some purpose. For example, when a rocket ship fires a photon torpedo, the image of the fast-moving "torpedo" is accomplished by animating a sprite across the screen.

For the purposes of this chapter, a sprite is assumed to consist solely of straight-line segments. However, it is possible to create sprites based on circular patterns. A sprite's definition will be held in a two-dimensional integer array. For example, the one shown here can hold a sprite consisting of four lines.

int sprite[4][4];

The first dimension specifies a particular line, and the second dimension specifies the beginning and ending coordinates of that line. (This is similar to an object's definition as described in Chapter 4.) In other words, each second dimension will be, by convention, organized like this:

start__x, start__y, end__x, end__y

Therefore, if the first line segment of a sprite went from location 0,0 to 0,10, you would define it as shown here in the **sprite** array.

```
sprite[0][0] = 0;   /* start_x */
sprite[0][1] = 0;   /* start_y */
sprite[0][2] = 0;   /* end_x */
sprite[0][3] = 10;  /* end_y */
```

THE GAME BOARD

In most video games, the game board consists of an unchanging (or slowly changing) graphics image inside of which the action of the game takes place. The actual layout of the game board can be created by another program and simply loaded by the video game at start-up. In this way, the video game need not actually contain all the overhead necessary to dynamically create the game board. This is the approach taken in this chapter. The paint program developed in Chapter 4 is used to create a graphics image, which is then saved to disk. The video game then loads this image and begins play.

SCREEN-LEVEL ANIMATION

The key (and excitement) to video games is their animation. Indeed, the animated graphics images set a video game apart from a non-computerized board game. The general method of animation is quite easy: Erase the part of the screen that currently displays the object and redisplay the object in its new position, which must be very close to its old position. The catch is that the process must be accomplished very fast. For this reason, it is again necessary to bypass the ROM-BIOS video service interrupts in favor of the direct video RAM accessing routines shown in Chapter 4.

By far the best approach to displaying, erasing, and redisplaying an object is to XOR each point in the object onto the screen. In this way, the first time an object is written to the screen it is displayed, and the second time it is written to the same location the previous contents of the screen are restored. In this way, it is possible to create sprites that move across the entire game board, no matter what color is currently in a specific location, without destroying what is already there.

The routine that actually displays a sprite is a slightly modified version of **display_object( )**, developed in Chapter 4. The modified version is shown here.

```
/* Display an object using XOR write mode. */
void display_object(ob, sides, cc)
int ob[][4]; /* object */
int sides; /* number of sides */
int cc; /* color of object */
{
  register int i;

  for(i=0; i<sides; i++)
    line((int) ob[i][0], (int) ob[i][1],
      (int) ob[i][2], (int) ob[i][3], cc | 128);
}
```

As you can see, this function draws all the lines in the object using the **line( )** function (also from Chapter 4). Notice, however, that the color parameter **cc** is ORed with 128 in order to set the high-order bit. This causes the **mempoint( )** function (used by **line( )** to actually write each pixel) to XOR the color with what is already there and allows the sprite to be visible no matter what the background color.

To see how the animation process works, enter the following program into your computer at this time. (If your compiler does not include the **bioskey( )** function, refer to Chapter 1 for a version you can use.) The program allows you to move a sprite about the screen using the cursor keys. The sprite is a small 6 pixel by 6 pixel plus sign.

```c
/* Animated sprite example. */

#include "dos.h"
#include "stdio.h"

void mode(), line();
void mempoint(), palette();
void display_object(), update_object();
unsigned char read_point();


int sprite[2][4] = {
  3, 0, 3, 5,
  0, 3, 5, 3
};

main()
{
  union k{
    char c[2];
    int i;
  } key;

  int deltax=0, deltay=0; /* direction of movement */

  mode(4);  /* switch to mode 4 CGA/EGA graphics */
  palette(0); /* palette 0 */

  display_object(sprite, 2, 1);
  do {
    deltay=deltax=0;
    key.i = bioskey(0);
    if(!key.c[0]) switch(key.c[1]) {
      case 75: /* left */
        deltay = -1;
        break;
      case 77: /* right */
        deltay = 1;
        break;
```

```c
      case 72: /* up */
        deltax = -1;
        break;
      case 80: /* down */
        deltax = 1;
        break;
      case 71: /* up left */
        deltax = -1; deltay = -1;
        break;
      case 73: /* up right */
        deltax = -1; deltay = 1;
        break;
      case 79: /* down left*/
        deltax = 1; deltay = -1;
        break;
      case 81: /* down right */
        deltax = 1; deltay = 1;
        break;
    }
    /* erase sprite's current position */
    display_object(sprite, 2, 1);
    /* if move is legal, update object definition */
    if(is_legal(sprite, deltax, deltay, 2))
      update_object(sprite, deltax, deltay, 2);
    /* redisplay sprite in new position */
    display_object(sprite, 2, 1);
  } while (key.c[0]!='q');
  getchar();
  mode(2);
}

/* Set the palette. */
void palette(pnum)
int pnum;
{
  union REGS r;

  r.h.bh = 1;    /* code for mode 4 graphics */
  r.h.bl = pnum;
  r.h.ah = 11;   /* set palette function */
  int86(0x10, &r, &r);
}

/* Set the video mode. */
void mode(mode_code)
int mode_code;
{
  union REGS r;

  r.h.al = mode_code;
  r.h.ah = 0;
  int86(0x10, &r, &r);
}

/* Draw a line in specified color
   using Bresenham's integer based algorithm.
*/
void line(startx, starty, endx, endy, color)
int startx, starty, endx, endy, color;
{
  register int t, distance;
  int x=0, y=0, delta_x, delta_y;
  int incx, incy;
```

```
      /* compute the distances in both directions */
      delta_x = endx-startx;
      delta_y = endy-starty;

      /* Compute the direction of the increment,
         an increment of 0 means either a vertical or horizontal
         line.
      */
      if(delta_x>0) incx = 1;
      else if(delta_x==0) incx = 0;
      else incx=-1;

      if(delta_y>0) incy = 1;
      else if(delta_y==0) incy = 0;
      else incy = -1;

      /* determine which distance is greater */
      delta_x = abs(delta_x);
      delta_y = abs(delta_y);
      if(delta_x>delta_y) distance = delta_x;
      else distance = delta_y;

      /* draw the line */
      for(t=0; t<=distance+1; t++) {
        mempoint(startx, starty, color);
        x+=delta_x;
        y+=delta_y;
        if(x>distance) {
          x-=distance;
          startx+=incx;
        }
        if(y>distance) {
          y-=distance;
          starty+=incy;
        }
      }
    }


    /* Write a point directly to the CGA/EGA */
    void mempoint(x, y, color_code)
    int x, y, color_code;
    {
      union mask {
        char c[2];
        int i;
      } bit_mask;
      int i, index, bit_position;
      unsigned char t;
      char xor; /* xor color in or overwrite */
      char far *ptr = (char far *) 0xB8000000; /* pointer
                                             to CGA memory */

      bit_mask.i=0xFF3F;    /* 11111111 00111111 in binary */

      /* check range for mode 4 */
      if(x<0 || x>199 || y<0 || y>319) return;

      xor=color_code & 128; /* see if xor mode is set */
      color_code = color_code & 127; /* mask off high bit */
```

```
    /* set bit_mask and color_code bits to the right location */
    bit_position = y%4;
    color_code<<=2*(3-bit_position);
    bit_mask.i>>=2*bit_position;


    /* find the correct byte in screen memory */
    index = x*40 +(y >> 2);
    if(x % 2) index += 8152; /* if odd use 2nd bank */

    /* write the color */
    if(!xor) { /* overwrite mode */
      t = *(ptr+index) & bit_mask.c[0];
      *(ptr+index) = t | color_code;
    }
    else { /* xor mode */
      t = *(ptr+index) | (char)0;
      *(ptr+index) = t ^ color_code;
    }
}

/* Read byte directly from the CGA/EGA in mode 4. */
unsigned char read_point(x, y)
int x, y;
{
  union mask {
    char c[2];
    int i;
  } bit_mask;
  int i, index, bit_position;
  unsigned char t;
  char xor; /* xor color in or overwrite */
  char far *ptr = (char far *) 0xB8000000; /* pointer
                                              to CGA memory */

  bit_mask.i=3; /* 11111111 00111111 in binary */

  /* check range for mode 4 */
  if(x<0 || x>199 || y<0 || y>319) return 0;

  /* set bit_mask and color_code bits to the right location */
  bit_position = y%4;
  bit_mask.i<<=2*(3-bit_position);
  /* find the correct byte in screen memory */
  index = x*40 +(y >> 2);
  if(x % 2) index += 8152; /* if odd use 2nd bank */

  /* read the color */
  t = *(ptr+index) & bit_mask.c[0];
  t >>=2*(3-bit_position);
  return t;
}

/* Display an object using XOR write mode. */
void display_object(ob, sides, cc)
int ob[][4]; /* object */
int sides; /* number of sides */
int cc; /* color of object */
{
  register int i;
```

```
      for(i=0; i<sides; i++)
        line((int) ob[i][0], (int) ob[i][1],
           (int) ob[i][2], (int) ob[i][3], cc | 128);
}

/* Update an object by specified x, y */
void update_object(ob, x, y, sides)
int ob[][4]; /* object */
int x, y; /* increment */
register int sides; /* number of sides */
{
  sides--;
  for( ; sides>=0; sides--) {
    ob[sides][0] += x;
    ob[sides][1] += y;
    ob[sides][2] += x;
    ob[sides][3] += y;
  }
}

/* Return 1 if prospective move is legal; 0 otherwise */
is_legal(ob, x, y, sides)
int ob[][4]; /* object */
int x, y; /* increment to move */
int sides; /* number of sides the object has */
{
  if(x==0 && y==0) return 1;
  sides--;
  for( ; sides>=0; sides--) {
    if(ob[sides][0]+x>199 || ob[sides][1]+y >319) return 0;
    if(ob[sides][2]+x<0 || ob[sides][3]+y<0) return 0;
  }
  return 1;
}
```

The program works like this: The arrow keys plus the HOME, PGUP, END, and PGDN keys control the position of the sprite. Each time a key is pressed, the sprite moves one pixel in the desired direction. The arrow keys control horizontal and vertical movement while the others control diagonal motion. The **is—legal**( ) function determines whether a prospective move is legal. If the move would take the sprite off the screen, the move is not allowed. All the other functions in the program work as described in Chapter 4.

It is usually necessary to keep the size of the object that you animate fairly small so that it can be redrawn quickly enough to appear to move smoothly. If the object is too big, it will seem to move in a jerky fashion. Keep in mind that the faster the computer or the graphics adapter, the larger the animated object can be.

SPRITE-LEVEL ANIMATION

The ability to move the sprite about the screen only takes you halfway to professional-quality animation. Generally, the sprite should appear to be doing something that helps create the illusion of motion. For example, a sprite that looks like a person may move its legs so as to appear to be walking. This type of animation is best (and most easily) accomplished by creating object definitions for two (or more) variations of the same sprite. The only differences between the variations are in the part of the sprite that will move. The program will then switch between the variations, in sequence, as the sprite is moved across the screen.

For example, add the second sprite and substitute this **main( )** in the previously shown program. The second sprite displays a "+" rotated by 45 degrees. If you run this program, the "+" seems to turn around as it moves across the screen. The **swap** variable is used to select which sprite is used.

```
int sprite2[2][4] = {
  0, 0, 5, 5,
  0, 5, 5, 0
};

main()
{
  union k{ /* holds both scan and key codes */
    char c[2];
    int i;
  } key;

  int deltax=0, deltay=0; /* direction of movement */
  int swap=0; /* controls which sprite is used. */

  mode(4);  /* switch to mode 4 CGA/EGA graphics */
  palette(0); /* palette 0 */

  display_object(sprite, 2, 1);
  do {
    deltay = deltax = 0;
    key.i = bioskey(0);
    if(!key.c[0]) switch(key.c[1]) {
      case 75: /* left */
        deltay = -1;
        break;
```

```
      case 77: /* right */
        deltay = 1;
        break;
      case 72: /* up */
        deltax = -1;
        break;
      case 80: /* down */
        deltax = 1;
        break;
      case 71: /* up left */
        deltax = -1; deltay = -1;
        break;
      case 73: /* up right */
        deltax = -1; deltay = 1;
        break;
      case 79: /* down left*/
        deltax = 1; deltay = -1;
        break;
      case 81: /* down right */
        deltax = 1; deltay = 1;
        break;
    }
    /* erase sprite's current position */
    if(!swap) display_object(sprite, 2, 1);
    else display_object(sprite2, 2, 1);
    /* change the object database if move is legal */
    if(is_legal(sprite, deltax, deltay, 2)) {
      update_object(sprite, deltax, deltay, 2);
      update_object(sprite2, deltax, deltay, 2);
    }
    swap = !swap; /* switch between sprites */
    /* redisplay sprite in new location */
    if(!swap) display_object(sprite, 2, 1);
    else display_object(sprite2, 2, 1);
  } while (key.c[0]!='q');
  getchar();
  mode(2);
}
```

ORGANIZING THE VIDEO GAME DATA

Like most programs, video games involve both code and data. Aside
from the current score and the status of various consumable game
resources (such as how many photon torpedos remain, for example),
most of the data related to a video game consists of the screen positions
of the various objects. Generally, the screen position of an object that
moves must be stored explicitly in a set of variables. However, most
often the information about fixed objects on the game board is implicitly
stored in the video RAM. Therefore, if your game needs information
about the game board (as most do) you can access the video RAM as a
large array to see what is there.

Recognizing Boundaries

Most video games have a sprite that is under the player's control. Generally, however, you are not allowed to move the sprite through certain environmental objects on the game board or through another sprite. There are two ways to restrict the destination of the sprite. The first is to keep a set of variables that hold the end points to various boundaries and check those coordinates against the location into which the sprite will move in order to determine if a boundary will be violated. Frankly, this method is fairly tedious, and in games with a large number of objects it can be very slow. The better solution is to simply see if an intended screen location already contains something by checking its corresponding location in the video RAM. Since all the information about the game board is already in the video RAM, it seems senseless to duplicate the information elsewhere.

A second advantage to using the screen image in the video RAM as the only (or at least main) source of information about the game, is that it allows new game boards to be loaded dynamically during play without having to reset — or worse, compute — new settings for several variables.

Color Counts

Often, you will want different colors to have different meanings. For example, you might use red to indicate noncrossable boundaries, green for your sprite, and yellow for the opponent's sprite. Though it is possible to use a set of variables to specify which objects are what, it is often possible (and much easier) to let objects be defined by their color. Not only does this make the game code easier, it also makes it faster. For example, if purple indicates the color of a mine, to determine if your sprite has hit a mine, check if the color of one of the pixels next to it is purple.

The use of color-coding for different objects has a long history in video games. For example, the first "ping-pong" video game used the most simple approach conceivable: black and white. In the old "ping-pong" game, white repelled white, but white could move through black. Therefore, the white ball could move through the black playing space unless it was struck by the white paddle, or if it hit the white wall behind the paddle. The same basic principles are expanded when other colors are used. By color-coding the objects in the game, the routines that must determine what is happening in the game become much easier to write and run faster.

SCOREKEEPER VERSUS ACTIVE PARTICIPANT

The computer's role in a video game depends to a great extent on whether the game is a two-player game or a single-player game. If two players are involved, the computer's role is largely that of scorekeeper and referee. However, in a single-player game the computer also becomes an active participant. From a programming point of view, the computer-as-participant is of the most interest.

DEVELOPING A VIDEO GAME

In this section we develop a complete video game that illustrates many of the principles discussed in this chapter.

Defining the Game

The first step in creating a video game is deciding the nature of the game and how it will be played. The game developed here is a computerized version of the traditional childhood game of tag. The player and the computer each control one "person." Whoever is "it" chases the other until contact is made, in which case the other person becomes "it." The winner of the game is the person who is not "it" for the longest period of time.

The score is kept by monitoring the system time: For each second that passes, one is added to the score of the person who is not "it." The score is displayed continuously at the bottom of the screen. The game ends when one player reaches 999 seconds. For convenience, the game can also be terminated by pressing Q.

The player controls the sprite with the arrow keys.

The game board is not created by the game itself. Rather, it is created with the paint program developed in Chapter 4; the board is loaded by the game. In this way, you can create several different playing environments.

Color-Coding the Game

Tag lends itself to a color-coded approach for identifying objects. For example, we can make the player's sprite green, the computer's sprite yellow, and boundaries and objects red. With this approach, it is not necessary to keep a separate database on the location of obstacles — the routines simply check to see what is in the video RAM. It then becomes a simple matter to restrict a sprite from moving into a red region by making a small addition to the is__legal( ) function developed earlier, as shown here.

```
/* See if a prospective move is legal.
   Returns 1 if legal; 0 otherwise.
*/
is_legal(ob, x, y, sides)
int ob[][4]; /* object */
int x, y; /* increment to move */
int sides; /* number of sides the object has */
{
  if(x==0 && y==0) return 1;
  sides--;
  for( ; sides>=0; sides--) {
    /* check for out of range */
    if(ob[sides][0]+x>199 || ob[sides][1]+y >319) return 0;
    if(ob[sides][2]+x<0 || ob[sides][3]+y<0) return 0;
    /* check for obstacle */
    if(read_point(ob[sides][0]+x, ob[sides][1] + y)==2) return 0;
    if(read_point(ob[sides][2]+x, ob[sides][3] + y)==2) return 0;
  }
  return 1;
}
```

Remember, the color code for yellow is 1, red is 2, green is 3, and black (background) is 0.

Defining the Sprites

The sprites used in the game should be designed to resemble people running. A sprite used by the program is shown here.

The program creates two versions of the sprite. In the second version, the legs are slightly closer together. Quickly alternating between the two makes the "person" seem to run.

The player's sprite begins near the upper-left corner, and the computer's sprite starts near the lower-left corner. Their object definitions are shown here.

```
int human[4][4] = { /* your sprites */
   1, 6, 6, 6,
   4, 2, 3, 9,
   9, 1, 6, 6,
   9, 11, 6, 6
};

int human2[4][4] = {
   1, 6, 6, 6,
   4, 2, 3, 9,
   9, 3, 6, 6,
   9, 9, 6, 6
};

int computer[4][4] = { /* computer's sprites */
   180, 6, 185, 6,
   183, 2, 182, 9,
   188, 1, 185, 6,
   188, 11, 185, 6
};
```

```
int computer2[4][4] = {
  180, 6, 185, 6,
  183, 2, 182, 9,
  188, 3, 185, 6,
  188, 9, 185, 6
};
```

The Main Loop

As you create your own video games, you quickly discover that they all have one thing in common — a fairly complex main loop that drives the game. The reason for this is that the program must continuously update the display, watch for keyboard input, check for illegal moves, display the score, and generate its own moves. The Tag game's main loop, inside the **main( )** function, is shown here.

```
int directx, directy; /* direction of human */

main()
{
  union k{ /* holds both scan and key codes */
    char c[2];
    int i;
  } key;

  int deltax=0, deltay=0; /* direction of movement */
  int swaph=0, swapc=0;
  int it=COMPUTER;
  long htime, ctime, starttime, curtime; /* score timers */
  int count; /* used to let the players separate slightly
                after a tag */

  mode(4);  /* switch to mode 4 CGA/EGA graphics */
  palette(0); /* palette 0 */

  load_pic(); /* get the game board */

  time(&starttime); /* setup the clocks */
  htime = ctime = 0;

  display_object(human, 4, 1);
  display_object(computer, 4, 3);
  count = 0;

  /* main loop of the game */
  do {
    /* update the score counters */
    time(&curtime);
    if(it==COMPUTER) htime += curtime-starttime;
    else ctime += curtime-starttime;
    time(&starttime);
    show_score(it, htime, ctime);
```

```
if(bioskey(1)) { /* if keypressed */
  directx = directy = IDLE; /* reset direction for each move */
  key.i = bioskey(0); /* read the key */
  deltax = 0; deltay = 0;
  if(!key.c[0]) switch(key.c[1]) {
    case 75: /* left */
      deltay = -1;
      directy = LEFT;
      break;
    case 77: /* right */
      deltay = 1;
      directy = RIGHT;
      break;
    case 72: /* up */
      deltax = -1;
      directx = UP;
      break;
    case 80: /* down */
      deltax = 1;
      directx = DOWN;
      break;
    case 71: /* up left */
      deltax = -1; deltay = -1;
      directx = UP; directy = LEFT;
      break;
    case 73: /* up right */
      deltax = -1; deltay = 1;
      directx = UP; directy = RIGHT;
      break;
    case 79: /* down left*/
      deltax = 1; deltay = -1;
      directx = DOWN; directy = LEFT;
      break;
    case 81: /* down right */
      deltax = 1; deltay = 1;
      directx = DOWN; directy = RIGHT;
      break;
  }
}
/* turn off player's person */
if(!swaph) display_object(human, 4, 1);
else display_object(human2, 4, 1);
if(is_legal(human, deltax, deltay, 4)) {
  update_object(human, deltax, deltay, 4);
  update_object(human2, deltax, deltay, 4);
}
/* see if a tag has occurred */
if(!count && tag(human, computer)) {
  it = !it; /* switch who is "it" */
  count = 6; /* don't allow an instant re-tag */
}
swaph = !swaph; /* swap figures to simulate running */
/* redisplay person in new position */
if(!swaph) display_object(human, 4, 1);
else display_object(human2, 4, 1);

/* turn off computer's person */
if(!swapc) display_object(computer, 4, 3);
else display_object(computer2, 4, 3);
```

```
/* generate the computer's move */
if(it==COMPUTER) it_comp_move(computer, computer2, human, 4);
else not_it_comp_move(computer, computer2, directx, directy, 4);
if(!count && tag(human, computer)) {
  it = !it; /* switch who is "it" */
  count = 6; /* don't allow an instant re-tag */
  /* if computer tags person, shift computer's  X
     position by 2 so that it is not trivial to re-tag.
  */
  if(is_legal(computer, 2, 0, 4)) {
    update_object(computer, 2, 0, 4);
    update_object(computer2, 2, 0, 4);
  }
  else {
    update_object(computer, -2, 0, 4);
    update_object(computer2, -2, 0, 4);
  }

}
swapc = !swapc; /* swap figures to simulate running */
/* display computer's person */
if(!swapc) display_object(computer, 4, 3);
else display_object(computer2, 4, 3);
if(count) count--;
} while (key.c[0]!='q' && htime<999 && ctime<999);
mode(2);
if(ctime>htime) printf("Computer wins!");
else printf("You win!");
}
```

Before filling in all the functions, let's examine the main loop to see how the game operates. In the **main( )** function, prior to the main loop, the screen is switched to mode 4 graphics, palette 0, and the score timer variables are initialized. Also, the two sprites are displayed in their starting positions.

The variable **htime** holds the score of the human player and **ctime** holds the computer's score. The variables **swapc** and **swaph** are used to switch between the two versions of the sprites. The variables **deltax** and **deltay** hold the direction of the player's last key press. The global variables **directx** and **directy** hold the direction that the player's sprite travels. This information is used by the computer to generate its own defensive moves. The **it** variable contains the current "it" of the game. It will have either the value COMPUTER or HUMAN, which are macros defined elsewhere, near the start of the program. The **count** variable is used to provide a short delay between tags so that the sprites have time to separate slightly. This delay prevents instant retags from occurring.

When the loop begins, it displays the current scores. Next, it checks to see if there has been a key press. If so, it reads the key and sets the appropriate variables accordingly. Keep in mind that the loop does not pause, waiting for a key press, but rather continues to run. Next, the player's sprite is moved in the direction indicated by the last key press, if possible, and a check for tag is made. It is important to understand that the player's sprite continues to move in the direction indicated by the last key press even if no key is held down. For example, if the RIGHT ARROW key is pressed and released, the sprite will move from its current position to the far right side of the screen if no other directional key is pressed. Thus, the sprite is always moving — making for a very fast and exciting game.

After the player's move has been processed, the computer's move is generated and its sprite is moved, if possible. Notice that different functions are called when the computer is "it" and when it isn't because different strategies are used. Also, a check for a tag must be made.

Now let's look at some of the support routines.

Generating the Computer's Move

If the computer is "it," its next move is generated by the function **it__comp__move( )**. The computer's general, if somewhat simplistic, strategy is to move its sprite in the direction of the player's sprite. It will try to go around objects that separate it from the player's sprite. However, as the function stands, the computer's sprite cannot go around all types of objects, an intentional feature that helps balance the skill level of the game. In designing video games, it is sometimes hard to "hold the computer back." The human player should have a reasonable chance of winning the game without the game being boring.

The function **it__comp__move( )** is shown here.

```
/* Generate the computer's move when it is "it". */
void it_comp_move(ob1, ob2, human, sides)
int ob1[][4], ob2[][4], human[][4], sides;
{
  register int  x, y, direction;
  static skip = 0;
```

```
skip++;
if(skip==3) {
  skip = 0;
  return; /* skip every third time to slow computer */
}
x = 0; y = 0;

/* move toward the human */
if(human[0][0]<ob1[0][0]) x = -1;
else if(human[0][0]>ob1[0][0]) x = 1;

if(human[0][1]<ob1[0][1]) y = -1;
else if(human[0][1]>ob1[0][1]) y = 1;

if(is_legal(ob1, x, y, sides)) {
  update_object(ob1, x, y, sides);
  update_object(ob2, x, y, sides);
}
else { /* if not legal, try to go around */
  if(x && is_legal(ob1, x, 0, sides)) {
    update_object(ob1, x, 0, sides);
    update_object(ob2, x, 0, sides);
  }
  else if(is_legal(ob1, 0, y, sides)) {
    update_object(ob1, 0, y, sides);
    update_object(ob2, 0, y, sides);
  }
}
}
```

Notice that the function only changes the position of the computer's sprite one-third of the time. This is necessary to slow the computer to a level a human player can deal with.

The function that generates the computer's moves when it is not "it" works by always moving the computer's sprite in the opposite direction of the player's sprite. Although this is not the most sophisticated approach, it actually presents a fairly challenging game that requires good timing on the player's part to "tag" the computer's sprite. The function is shown here.

```
/* Generate the computer's move when it is not "it". */
void not_it_comp_move(ob1, ob2, directx, directy, sides)
int ob1[][4], ob2[][4];
int directx, directy; /* direction of human's last move */
int sides;
{
  register int  x, y, direction;
  static skip = 1;

  skip++;
  if(skip==3) {
    skip = 0;
```

```
      return; /* skip every third time to slow computer */
   }
   x = 0; y = 0;

   /* move in opposite direction as human */
   x = -directx;
   y = -directy;

   if(is_legal(ob1, x, y, sides)) {
     update_object(ob1, x, y, sides);
     update_object(ob2, x, y, sides);
   }
   else { /* if not legal, try to go around */
     if(x && is_legal(ob1, x, 0, sides)) {
       update_object(ob1, x, 0, sides);
       update_object(ob2, x, 0, sides);
     }
     else if(is_legal(ob1, 0, y, sides)) {
       update_object(ob1, 0, y, sides);
       update_object(ob2, 0, y, sides);
     }
   }
}
```

Again, notice that the function is delayed slightly and only executes once
out of every three calls.

Check for Tag

In this game, a tag occurs when one sprite is within one pixel in any
direction of being directly on top of the other sprite. (A tag can be
defined as one sprite being exactly on top of the other, but for most
players this constraint proves too difficult to be enjoyable.) The function
tag, shown here, returns 1 if a tag has occurred and 0 otherwise.

```
/* See if a tag has taken place. */
tag(ob1, ob2)
int ob1[][4], ob2[][4];
{
  register int i;

  /* To tag, one figure must be within one pixel
     of being directly on top of the other.
  */
  for(i=-1; i<2; i++) {
    if(ob1[0][0]==ob2[0][0]+i && ob1[0][1]==ob2[0][1]+i) {
      return 1;
    }
  }
  return 0;
}
```

You may wish to modify this function's operation to suit your personal taste.

The Entire Tag Program

The entire Tag game is shown here. You should enter it into your computer at this time. Remember that it does require a graphics adapter for operation.

```
/* A simple animated video game of TAG.

   The object of the game is for your "person" to
   tag the other "person" by running into it.

   Your person is green, the computer's is yellow. No
   red boundary may be crossed.

   For the tag to count, the two "people" must be within
   one pixel of being directly on top of one another.
*/

#define COMPUTER 0
#define HUMAN 1

#define IDLE 0
#define DOWN 1
#define UP -1
#define LEFT -1
#define RIGHT 1

#include "dos.h"
#include "stdio.h"
#include "math.h"
#include "time.h"

void mode(), line();
void mempoint(), palette(), xhairs();
void goto_xy(), show_score();
void display_object(), update_object();
void save_pic(), load_pic();
void it_comp_move(), not_it_comp_move();
unsigned char read_point();

int human[4][4] = { /* your sprites */
  1, 6, 6, 6,
  4, 2, 3, 9,
  9, 1, 6, 6,
  9, 11, 6, 6
};

int human2[4][4] = {
  1, 6, 6, 6,
  4, 2, 3, 9,
```

```
     9, 3, 6, 6,
     9, 9, 6, 6
};

int computer[4][4] = { /* computer's sprites */
   180, 6, 185, 6,
   183, 2, 182, 9,
   188, 1, 185, 6,
   188, 11, 185, 6
};

int computer2[4][4] = {
   180, 6, 185, 6,
   183, 2, 182, 9,
   188, 3, 185, 6,
   188, 9, 185, 6
};

int directx, directy; /* direction of human */

main()
{
  union k{ /* holds both scan and key codes */
    char c[2];
    int i;
  } key;

  int deltax=0, deltay=0; /* direction of movement */
  int swaph=0, swapc=0;
  int it=COMPUTER;
  long htime, ctime, starttime, curtime;
  int count; /* used to let the players separate slightly
                after a tag */

  mode(4);  /* switch to mode 4 CGA/EGA graphics */
  palette(0); /* palette 0 */

  load_pic(); /* get the game board */

  time(&starttime); /* setup the clocks */
  htime = ctime = 0;

  display_object(human, 4, 1);
  display_object(computer, 4, 3);
  count = 0;

  /* main game loop */
  do {
    /* update the score counters */
    time(&curtime);
    if(it==COMPUTER) htime += curtime-starttime;
    else ctime += curtime-starttime;
    time(&starttime);
    show_score(it, htime, ctime);

    if(bioskey(1)) { /* if keypressed */
      directx = directy = IDLE; /* reset direction for each move */
      key.i = bioskey(0); /* read the key */
      deltax = 0; deltay = 0;
      if(!key.c[0]) switch(key.c[1]) {
```

```
    case 75: /* left */
      deltay = -1;
      directy = LEFT;
      break;
    case 77: /* right */
      deltay = 1;
      directy = RIGHT;
      break;
    case 72: /* up */
      deltax = -1;
      directx = UP;
      break;
    case 80: /* down */
      deltax = 1;
      directx = DOWN;
      break;
    case 71: /* up left */
      deltax = -1; deltay = -1;
      directx = UP; directy = LEFT;
      break;
    case 73: /* up right */
      deltax = -1; deltay = 1;
      directx = UP; directy = RIGHT;
      break;
    case 79: /* down left*/
      deltax = 1; deltay = -1;
      directx = DOWN; directy = LEFT;
      break;
    case 81: /* down right */
      deltax = 1; deltay = 1;
      directx = DOWN; directy = RIGHT;
      break;
  }
}
/* turn off player's person */
if(!swaph) display_object(human, 4, 1);
else display_object(human2, 4, 1);
if(is_legal(human, deltax, deltay, 4)) {
  update_object(human, deltax, deltay, 4);
  update_object(human2, deltax, deltay, 4);
}
/* see if a tag has occurred */
if(!count && tag(human, computer)) {
  it = !it;  /* switch who is "it" */
  count = 6; /* don't allow an instant re-tag */
}
swaph = !swaph; /* swap figures to simulate running */
/* redisplay person in new position */
if(!swaph) display_object(human, 4, 1);
else display_object(human2, 4, 1);

/* turn off computer's person */
if(!swapc) display_object(computer, 4, 3);
else display_object(computer2, 4, 3);
/* generate the computer's move */
if(it==COMPUTER) it_comp_move(computer, computer2, human, 4);
else not_it_comp_move(computer, computer2, directx, directy, 4);
if(!count && tag(human, computer)) {
  it = !it; /* switch who is "it" */
  count = 6; /* don't allow an instant re-tag */
```

```
        /* if computer tags person, shift computer's  X
           position by 2 so that it is not trivial to re-tag.
        */
        if(is_legal(computer, 2, 0, 4)) {
          update_object(computer, 2, 0, 4);
          update_object(computer2, 2, 0, 4);
        }
        else {
          update_object(computer, -2, 0, 4);
          update_object(computer2, -2, 0, 4);
        }

      }
      swapc = !swapc; /* swap figures to simulate running */
      /* display computer's person */
      if(!swapc) display_object(computer, 4, 3);
      else display_object(computer2, 4, 3);
      if(count) count--;
    } while (key.c[0]!='q' && htime<999 && ctime<999);
    getchar();
    mode(2);
    if(ctime>htime) printf("Computer wins!");
    else printf("You win!");
}

/* Display the score.
   When the YOU or ME is in caps, points
   are scored.
*/
void show_score(it, htime, ctime)
int it;
long htime, ctime;
{
    goto_xy(24,6);
    if(it==COMPUTER) printf("YOU:%ld", htime);
    else printf("you:%ld", htime);
    goto_xy(24,26);
    if(it==HUMAN) printf("ME:%ld", ctime);
    else printf("me:%ld", ctime);
}

/* Set the palette. */
void palette(pnum)
int pnum;
{
    union REGS r;

    r.h.bh = 1;    /* code for mode 4 graphics */
    r.h.bl = pnum;
    r.h.ah = 11;   /* set palette function */
    int86(0x10, &r, &r);
}

/* Set the video mode. */
void mode(mode_code)
int mode_code;
{
    union REGS r;
```

```
   r.h.al = mode_code;
   r.h.ah = 0;
   int86(0x10, &r, &r);
}


/* Draw a line in specified color
   using Bresenham's integer based algorithm.
*/
void line(startx, starty, endx, endy, color)
int startx, starty, endx, endy, color;
{
   register int t, distance;
   int x=0, y=0, delta_x, delta_y;
   int incx, incy;

   /* compute the distances in both directions */
   delta_x = endx-startx;
   delta_y = endy-starty;

   /* Compute the direction of the increment,
      an increment of 0 means either a vertical or horizontal
      line.
   */
   if(delta_x>0) incx = 1;
   else if(delta_x==0) incx = 0;
   else incx=-1;

   if(delta_y>0) incy = 1;
   else if(delta_y==0) incy = 0;
   else incy = -1;

   /* determine which distance is greater */
   delta_x = abs(delta_x);
   delta_y = abs(delta_y);
   if(delta_x>delta_y) distance = delta_x;
   else distance = delta_y;

   /* draw the line */
   for(t=0; t<=distance+1; t++) {
     mempoint(startx, starty, color);
     x+=delta_x;
     y+=delta_y;
     if(x>distance) {
       x-=distance;
       startx+=incx;
     }
     if(y>distance) {
       y-=distance;
       starty+=incy;
     }
   }
}


/* Write a point directly to the CGA/EGA */
void mempoint(x, y, color_code)
int x, y, color_code;
{
   union mask {
```

```
      char c[2];
      int i;
} bit_mask;
int i, index, bit_position;
unsigned char t;
char xor; /* xor color in or overwrite */
char far *ptr = (char far *) 0xB8000000; /* pointer
                                              to CGA memory */

bit_mask.i=0xFF3F;      /* 11111111 00111111 in binary */

/* check range for mode 4 */
if(x<0 || x>199 || y<0 || y>319) return;

xor=color_code & 128; /* see if xor mode is set */
color_code = color_code & 127; /* mask off high bit */

/* set bit_mask and color_code bits to the right location */
bit_position = y%4;
color_code<<=2*(3-bit_position);
bit_mask.i>>=2*bit_position;

/* find the correct byte in screen memory */
index = x*40 +(y >> 2);
if(x % 2) index += 8152; /* if odd use 2nd bank */

/* write the color */
if(!xor) { /* overwrite mode */
  t = *(ptr+index) & bit_mask.c[0];
  *(ptr+index) = t | color_code;
}
else { /* xor mode */
  t = *(ptr+index) | (char)0;
  *(ptr+index) = t ^ color_code;
}
}

/* Read byte directly from the CGA/EGA in mode 4. */
unsigned char read_point(x, y)
int x, y;
{
  union mask {
    char c[2];
    int i;
  } bit_mask;
  int i, index, bit_position;
  unsigned char t;
  char xor; /* xor color in or overwrite */
  char far *ptr = (char far *) 0xB8000000; /* pointer
                                               to CGA memory */

  bit_mask.i=3; /* 11111111 00111111 in binary */

  /* check range for mode 4 */
  if(x<0 || x>199 || y<0 || y>319) return 0;

  /* set bit_mask and color_code bits to the right location */
  bit_position = y%4;
  bit_mask.i<<=2*(3-bit_position);
  /* find the correct byte in screen memory */
  index = x*40 +(y >> 2);
  if(x % 2) index += 8152; /* if odd use 2nd bank */
```

```
    /* read the color */
    t = *(ptr+index) & bit_mask.c[0];
    t >>=2*(3-bit_position);
    return t;
}

/* load the video graphics display */
void load_pic()
{
  char fname[80];
  FILE *fp;
  register int i, j;
  char far *ptr = (char far *) 0xB8000000; /* pointer
                                            to CGA memory */
  char far *temp;
  unsigned char buf[14][80]; /* hold the contents of screen */

  temp = ptr;
  /* save the top of the current screen */
  for(i=0; i<14; i++)
    for(j=0; j<80; j+=2) {
      buf[i][j] = *temp;
      buf[i][j+1] = *(temp+8152);
      *temp = 0; *(temp+8152) = 0; /* clear the top of the screen */
      temp++;
    }

  goto_xy(0, 0);
  printf("Game board?: ");
  gets(fname);
  if(!(fp=fopen(fname, "rb"))) {
    goto_xy(0, 0);
    printf("cannot open file\n");
    temp = ptr;
    /* restore the top of the current screen */
    for(i=0; i<14; i++)
      for(j=0; j<80; j+=2) {
        *temp = buf[i][j];
        *(temp+8152) = buf[i][j+1];
        temp++;
      }
    return;
  }

  /* load image from file */
  for(i=0; i<8152; i++) {
    *ptr = getc(fp); /* even byte */
    *(ptr+8152) = getc(fp); /* odd byte */
    ptr++;
  }

  fclose(fp);
}

/* Send the cursor to the specified X,Y position. */
void goto_xy(x, y)
int x, y;
{
  union REGS r;

  r.h.ah=2; /* cursor addressing function */
  r.h.dl = y; /* column coordinate */
```

```
      r.h.dh = x; /* row coordinate */
      r.h.bh = 0; /* video page */
      int86(0x10, &r, &r);
   }


   /* Display an object. */
   void display_object(ob, sides, cc)
   int ob[][4]; /* object */
   int sides; /* number of sides */
   int cc; /* color of object */
   {
      register int i;

      for(i=0; i<sides; i++)
        line((int) ob[i][0], (int) ob[i][1],
          (int) ob[i][2], (int) ob[i][3], cc | 128);
   }


   /* Update an object's position as specified in x, y. */
   void update_object(ob, x, y, sides)
   int ob[][4]; /* object */
   int x, y; /* amount to update */
   register int sides; /* number of sides */
   {
      sides--;
      for( ; sides>=0; sides--) {
        ob[sides][0] += x;
        ob[sides][1] += y;
        ob[sides][2] += x;
        ob[sides][3] += y;
      }
   }


   /* See if a prospective move is legal.
      Returns 1 if legal; 0 otherwise.
   */
   is_legal(ob, x, y, sides)
   int ob[][4]; /* object */
   int x, y; /* increment to move */
   int sides; /* number of sides the object has */
   {
      if(x==0 && y==0) return 1;
      sides--;
      for( ; sides>=0; sides--) {
        /* check for out of range */
        if(ob[sides][0]+x>199 || ob[sides][1]+y >319) return 0;
        if(ob[sides][2]+x<0 || ob[sides][3]+y<0) return 0;
        /* check for obstacle */
        if(read_point(ob[sides][0]+x, ob[sides][1] + y)==2) return 0;
        if(read_point(ob[sides][2]+x, ob[sides][3] + y)==2) return 0;
      }
      return 1;
   }


   /* Generate the computer's move when it is "it". */
   void it_comp_move(ob1, ob2,  human, sides)
   int ob1[][4], ob2[][4], human[][4], sides;
   {
      register int  x, y, direction;
      static skip = 0;
```

```
  skip++;
  if(skip==3) {
    skip = 0;
    return; /* skip every other time to slow computer */
  }
  x = 0; y = 0;

  /* move toward the human */
  if(human[0][0]<ob1[0][0]) x = -1;
  else if(human[0][0]>ob1[0][0]) x = 1;

  if(human[0][1]<ob1[0][1]) y = -1;
  else if(human[0][1]>ob1[0][1]) y = 1;

  if(is_legal(ob1, x, y, sides)) {
    update_object(ob1, x, y, sides);
    update_object(ob2, x, y, sides);
  }
  else { /* if not legal, try to go around */
    if(x && is_legal(ob1, x, 0, sides)) {
      update_object(ob1, x, 0, sides);
      update_object(ob2, x, 0, sides);
    }
    else if(is_legal(ob1, 0, y, sides)) {
      update_object(ob1, 0, y, sides);
      update_object(ob2, 0, y, sides);
    }
  }
}

/* Generate the computer's move when it is not "it". */
void not_it_comp_move(ob1, ob2, directx, directy, sides)
int ob1[][4], ob2[][4];
int directx, directy; /* direction of human's last move */
int sides;
{
  register int  x, y, direction;
  static skip = 1;

  skip++;
  if(skip==3) {
    skip = 0;
    return; /* skip every other time to slow computer */
  }
  x = 0; y = 0;

  /* move in opposite direction as human */
  x = -directx;
  y = -directy;

  if(is_legal(ob1, x, y, sides)) {
    update_object(ob1, x, y, sides);
    update_object(ob2, x, y, sides);
  }
    else { /* if not legal, try to go around */
      if(x && is_legal(ob1, x, 0, sides)) {
        update_object(ob1, x, 0, sides);
        update_object(ob2, x, 0, sides);
      }
      else if(is_legal(ob1, 0, y, sides)) {
```

```
      update_object(ob1, 0, y, sides);
      update_object(ob2, 0, y, sides);
    }
  }
}

/* See if a tag has taken place. */
tag(ob1, ob2)
int ob1[][4], ob2[][4];
{
  register int i;

  /* To tag, one figure must be within one pixel
     of being directly on top of the other.
  */
  for(i=-1; i<2; i++) {
    if(ob1[0][0]==ob2[0][0]+i && ob1[0][1]==ob2[0][1]+i) {
      return 1;
    }
  }
  return 0;
}
```

To use the program, you must first create one or more game boards using the paint program from Chapter 4. (You can use a blank screen, but that is much less fun!) Use red for obstacles that cannot be penetrated by the sprites. You may use yellow and green for decoration, but they will have no effect on the game. Figures 5-1 and 5-2 show two game boards, so that you can see how the game looks on the screen.

On a fast computer, such as an AT or PS/2 model 50, 60, or 80, the game is quite snappy. It will be a bit slow on a standard PC, however, and you will probably want to try to speed it up a bit.

FOR FURTHER EXPLORATION

You will probably want to create your own video games, but you might want to try improving the Tag game first. For example, the computer's ability to go around objects or follow a maze can be improved. The basic approach is to create a function that follows the side of an object. Although this task is not especially difficult, it does require a fair amount of code because a database of points visited must be maintained to prevent the computer from following the same object endlessly.

A second improvement would be to give the computer the ability to predict the player's moves so that it has a better chance of tagging.

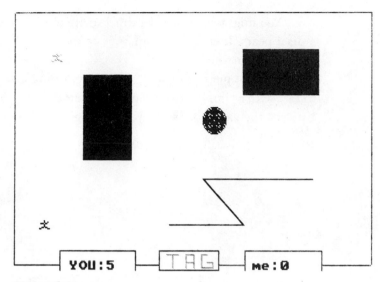

Figure 5-1.

The Tag game with the first
game board

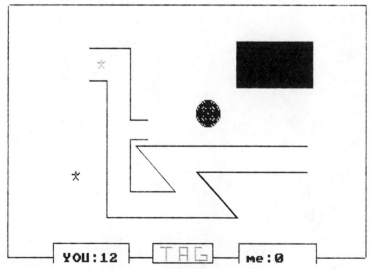

Figure 5-2.

The Tag game with the second
game board

You might want to add a third sprite that appears briefly and then disappears. If either the computer or the player tag this sprite, bonus points are earned.

One last piece of advice: When developing video games it is best to start with a simple, well-designed, skeleton of the game. Once you have played the game for awhile you can begin adding enhancements.

6: Using the Serial Port: File Transfers and a Poor Man's LAN

Perhaps no other standard feature causes as much grief for the programmer as the asynchronous serial port. Unlike the much simpler parallel port, a serial port can experience several types of transmission errors. To complicate matters, the "handshaking" capabilities of the serial port, which help provide reliable communication, are often bypassed by the wiring in the cable that connects the serial port to the external device. Even with these problems, the serial port is widely used because it is the least expensive way to link two devices that are separated by more than a couple of feet.

The goal of this chapter is to explain the basics of the serial port's operation, including initialization, transmission, and reception of data, and to discuss some common errors that can occur. Once the operation of the serial port is covered, two separate applications that use the port are developed. The first is a file transfer program that you can use to transfer any type of file (including binary files) between two computers. The file transfer program is especially useful to those readers that have several different types of computers. The second is the creation of a "poor man's" local area network (LAN), which includes a file server and two new commands that allow remote computers to load files from, or save them to, the server.

The examples in this chapter once again assume an IBM PC, XT, AT, or PS/2 environment running DOS. However, you should be able to generalize to other systems including OS/2.

ASYNCHRONOUS SERIAL TRANSMISSION OF DATA

Before learning about the asynchronous serial port itself, you need to understand asynchronous communications. (Hereafter, the asynchronous serial port will simply be called the "serial port.") Data is transmitted through a serial port one bit at a time. This differs from the transmission of data through a parallel port, which sends one byte at a time. The transmission is called *asynchronous* because the length of time between the transmission of a byte of data (one bit at a time) does not matter. However, both the timing and sequence of the transmission of the bits that compose the byte and some other information is critical.

Each byte of data transmitted by the serial port uses this sequence of signals:

1. One start bit

2. Eight data bits (seven in some situations)

3. Optional parity bit

4. One or two stop bits

Between the transmission of each byte, any amount of time may pass.

The idle state of the transmission line is high. A bit set to zero drives the line low; a bit set to one leaves the line high. The start bit signals the start of the transmission of a new byte by driving the line low for one cycle. The data bits are then transmitted, followed by an optional parity bit. Finally, one or two stop bits are sent, which also drive the line low. The stop bits determine the shortest time between bytes. Usually, it does not matter a great deal whether you use one or two stop bits, as long as both the transmitting port and the receiving port use the same number.

The parity bit, if supplied, is used to check for errors in transmission. Parity can be either even or odd. If even parity is selected, the parity bit is set in such a way that the transmitted byte plus the parity bit will be an even number. If odd parity is used, the byte plus the parity bit will be an odd number.

The rate at which bits are transmitted is measured in *baud* (bits per second). The slowest baud rate in general use is 300, which is used mostly with older, slower modems. (Most modems today use either 1200 or 2400 baud.) The IBM PC family of computers is capable of bauds up to 9600. Other types of computers may have speeds up to 38,400 baud!

RS-232 STANDARD

Although it is not critical to understand the RS-232 asynchronous serial communications standard in any great detail for the purposes of this chapter, it is important to understand it well enough to see how and why so many problems occur when serial ports are used.

The configuration of most serial ports is based, often loosely, upon the RS-232 standard using a 25-pin connector on each end. (The IBM AT uses a 9-pin connector.) However, a great many serial ports do not support all the signals specified by the RS-232 standard. Some signals are not supported because they don't apply to the intended usage; others are not supported because the manufacturer sometimes elects not to provide full RS-232 support, offering instead a minimal subset. The most common RS-232 signals are

Signal	Abbreviation	Pin on Connector
Request to send	RTS	4
Clear to send	CTS	5
Data set ready	DSR	6
Data terminal ready	DTR	20
Transmit data	TxD	2
Receive data	RxD	3
Ground	GRD	7

There are so many signals because the serial port was initially designed as a device to support a modem. Therefore, when it is used with other devices, several of these signals are not applicable. These signals are generally used to establish a hardware protocol between the modem and the computer so that the computer (1) does not send information to it before it is ready to transmit it or (2) does not read data from the modem before it is ready.

A *framing error* is caused if the internal clocks that control the two ports are very different from each other. As you can guess, the serial port, upon seeing the start bit, samples the input register once every cycle to read the next bit. The length of that cycle is determined by the baud rate. However, the time each bit is actually in the register is determined by the clock that controls the system. If the receiving computer's clock rate is not close enough to the transmitter's clock, a bit gets overwritten, resulting in a framing error.

Hardware Handshaking

The proper way to transmit data over a serial port is to monitor the status of the clear-to-send signal of the receiving port. You must not send data until the clear-to-send signal indicates that it is safe to do so. Therefore, when hardware handshaking is used, the transmit routine, in pseudo-C code, looks like this:

```
do {
   while(not CTS) wait;
   send(byte);
} while(bytes to send);
```

If you have a properly wired cable and the hardware on both ends supports the RS-232 standard, you should definitely use hardware handshaking. However, in a less-than-perfect world it is not always possible to do so.

COMMUNICATIONS PROBLEMS

To allow modem communications, several signals are used to determine when data is ready or when the next byte can be sent. However, when communication is occurring between computers, it is possible (though not necessarily advisable) to use only the GRD, TxD, and RxD signals. The reasoning behind this is that running three wires is much less expensive than running five or six. If two computers of the same type are communicating with each other, when one is ready to send data, the other will, in theory, be ready to receive it. However, by bypassing the protocol signals built into the RS-232 standard, you open a Pandora's box of trouble. The worst of these is the *overrun* error.

Overrunning the Receive Register

When only three wires are used to connect two serial ports together, it is necessary to "trick" the transmitting port into believing that the receiving port is always ready for data. This is usually accomplished by hooking together pins 6, 8, and 20 of the 25-pin connector. Unfortunately, this procedure makes a data overrun error very likely. Assume that computer A is faster than computer B. If no hardware handshaking is being used, computer A can conceivably send a second byte to computer B before computer B has read the information from the input register of its serial port. This is called an *overrun error*. This type of error can occur even when computer B is faster than A if computer B's software is too slow.

This problem occurs because pins 6, 8, and 20 have been tied together, and the transmitting port thinks the receiving port is always ready for data. Shortly, you will be shown a way around this difficulty.

ACCESSING THE PC SERIAL PORTS THROUGH BIOS

The serial ports on a PC or compatible can be accessed through DOS, through the ROM-BIOS, or by bypassing DOS and BIOS and directly controlling the hardware. Accessing serial ports through DOS is not generally a good idea because DOS provides no feedback on the status of the port; it provides only blind reads or writes to the port. As such, the DOS interrupts will not be used. Although previous chapters have opted for direct hardware control of system resources, this method is not necessary for serial ports because high performance can be achieved through the ROM-BIOS interrupts.

Four ROM-BIOS services support access to the serial ports. These services are reached through interrupt 14H. Let's look at each now.

Port Initialization

Before using the serial port, you will probably want to initialize it to a setting different from the default setting. (The default setting of the first serial port is generally 1200 baud, even parity, seven data bits, and one stop bit.) Interrupt 14H, service 0 is used to initialize a serial port. As with other BIOS interrupts, the AH register is used to hold the service number. The AL register holds the initialization parameters that are encoded into one byte as shown here.

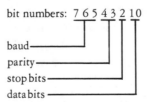

The baud is encoded as shown in Table 6-1. The parity bits are encoded as shown in Table 6-2.

Table 6-1.

The Encoding of the Baud in Bits 7, 6,
and 5 of the Serial Port Initialization
Byte

Baud	Bit Pattern
9600	1 1 1
4800	1 1 0
2400	1 0 1
1200	1 0 0
600	0 1 1
300	0 1 0
150	0 0 1
110	0 0 0

The number of stop bits is determined by bit 2 of the serial port initialization byte. If bit 2 is 1, two stop bits are used; otherwise, one stop bit is used. Finally, the number of data bits is set by the code in bits 1 and 0 of the initialization byte. Of the four possible bit patterns, only two are valid. If bits 1 and 0 contain the pattern "1 0," seven data bits are used. If they contain the pattern "1 1," eight data bits are used.

Table 6-2.

The Encoding of the Parity in Bits 4
and 3 of the Serial Port Initialization
Byte

Parity	Bit Pattern
no parity	0 0 or 1 0
odd	0 1
even	1 1

For example, if you want to set the port to 9600 baud, even parity, one stop bit, and eight data bits, you would use the bit pattern shown here. In decimal form, this value is 251.

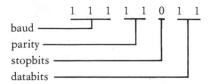

Up to seven serial ports are available on a standard PC (more on newer types of machines). You specify which serial port you want to use in the DX register. The first serial port is 0, the second is 1, and so on. The function shown here, called **init—port( )**, is used to initialize the value of any serial port in the system.

```
/* Initialize the port.
*/
void port_init(port, code)
int port;
unsigned char code;
{
  union REGS r;

  r.x.dx = port; /* serial port */
  r.h.ah = 0;  /* initialize port function */
  r.h.al = code; /* initialization code - see text for details */
  int86(0x14, &r, &r);
}
```

This function relies upon the **int86( )** function, which is found in many compilers including Turbo C and MicroSoft C, though the function may be called something else if you are using a different compiler. You might also be provided with a specific function that initializes the serial port. (For example, the **bioscom( )** function in Turbo C allows port initialization.)

Transmitting Bytes

BIOS interrupt 14H, service 1 transmits one byte through the serial port specified in DX. The byte you wish to send must be in AL. The status of the transmission is returned in the AH register. The function **sport( )**, shown here, transmits one byte through the specified serial port.

```
/* Send a character out the serial port */
void sport(port, c)
int port; /* i/o port */
char c; /* character to send */
{
  union REGS r;

  r.x.dx = port; /* serial port */
  r.h.al = c; /* char to send */
  r.h.ah = 1;   /* send character function */
  int86(0x14, &r, &r);
  if(r.h.ah & 128) { /* check bit 7 */
    printf("send error detected in serial port");
    exit(1);
  }
}
```

If bit 7 of AH is set upon return from the interrupt, a transmission error has occurred. To determine the cause of the error, you must read the status of the port; the method for doing this is discussed shortly. Athough **sport( )** simply exits upon an error, you could write an error handler routine that would attempt to recover from certain types of errors.

Checking a Port's Status

BIOS interrupt 14H, service 3 is used to check a port's status. The port to be checked is specified in the DX register. Upon return from the interrupt, AH and AL will hold the port's status encoded as shown in Table 6-3.

Table 6-3.

The Status Bytes of a Serial Port

Line Status (AH)	
Meaning when set	**Bit**
Data ready	0
Overrun error	1
Parity error	2
Framing error	3
Break-detect error	4
Transfer holding register empty	5
Transfer shift register empty	6
Time-out error	7

Modem Status (AL)	
Meaning when set	**Bit**
Change in clear-to-send	0
Change in data-set-ready	1
Trailing-edge ring detector	2
Change in line signal	3
Clear-to-send	4
Data-set-ready	5
Ring indicator	6
Line signal detected	7

As you can see, most of the status conditions apply to modems and are less important when you are using the serial port to communicate with other devices. However, there is one status condition that is very important: "data ready." By checking this condition, you can determine when a byte of data has been received by a port and is ready for reading. The function **rport( )**, used to read data from a port, illustrates the use of the data ready status condition, as you'll see in the next section.

Receiving a Byte

BIOS interrupt 14H, service 2 is used to read a byte from a serial port. Again, the serial port to use is specified in the DX register. Upon return from the interrupt, the character read is in AL. As with transmitting a character, upon return, bit 7 of AH is used to indicate success or failure.

The function **rport( )**, shown here, reads a byte from the specified port.

```
/* Read a character from a port */
rport(port)
int port; /* i/o port */
{
  union REGS r;

  /* wait for a character */
  while(!(check_stat(PORT)&256))
    if(kbhit()) { /* abort on keypress */
      getch();
      exit(1);
    }

  r.x.dx = port; /* serial port */
  r.h.ah = 2;  /* read character function */
  int86(0x14, &r, &r);
  if(r.h.ah & 128)
    printf("read error detected in serial port");
  return r.h.al;
}
```

The read port interrupt waits until a byte has been received by the serial port before it returns. However, certain types of errors, such as an unplugged cable, can cause the computer to lock up. To avoid this problem, **rport( )** reads the status of the specified port, checking the data ready bit. At the same time, the function **kbhit( )** checks to see if a keypress has occurred. If a key has been hit, the function exits. (In some cases, you may want it to call a custom error-handling function.) This gives you a way to abort if no data is received. As soon as data is received, interrupt 14H, service 2 is called and the byte is read. Once again, bit 7 of AH is checked to see if the operation was a success. Finally, the byte is returned by the function.

TRANSFERRING FILES BETWEEN COMPUTERS

Today, many offices and individuals own more than one microcomputer, and these computers are frequently different brands or models with incompatible disk formats. For example, the 3 1/2-inch diskettes of the PS/2 systems are incompatible with the 5 1/5-inch diskettes of the older PC, XT, and AT line of IBM computers. When multiple computers are used, it is very helpful to have the computers communicate with each other via the serial ports in order to share information and/or programs. For various reasons, the creation of programs that allow the transfer of files through the serial port is problematic.

Although faster and more efficient file transfer programs exist, the one developed in this chapter has several significant advantages: It works for all types of files, with all types of computers — even those with different speeds — and *requires no hardware handshaking.* This last feature is important because it allows the use of three wire cables. In addition, the program will work even when hardware handshaking is completely disabled and unavailable.

Although you should take advantage of hardware handshaking whenever possible, because it lets you achieve the highest level of performance with the greatest reliability, it is not used here because often the proper signals are either unavailable or have been defeated. This situation is slowly changing but it is still quite common.

The file transfer routines developed here operate by performing *software handshaking* and work in virtually any environment. Sometimes it is better to sacrifice some performance to gain reliability.

Software Handshaking

When hardware handshaking is either unavailable or disabled, the only way to be sure that an overrun error will not occur during transmission is to implement handshaking in software. Software handshaking works like this: The transmitting computer sends the first byte and waits for the receiving computer to return an acknowledgment byte. Once the acknowledgment is received, the sender transmits the next byte and then waits again for acknowledgment. This process continues until the file has been transferred. In pseudo-C code, the sending and receiving routines look like this:

```
send( )
{
    while (there are bytes to send) {
        send(a byte);
        wait( );
    }
}
receive( )
{
    do {
        receive__byte( );
        send(acknowledgment):
    } while(there are still bytes to read);
}
```

In this way, the transmitter never overruns the receiver, no matter how much the two computers differ in speed of operation.

The only drawback to this type of handshaking is that it effectively halves the transmission rate because two bytes must be transmitted for each byte of information transferred.

Seven Versus Eight Data Bits

If you only want to transfer text files, you need to use only seven data bits because no letter or punctuation mark requires the eighth bit. By sending only seven bits, you slightly increase the speed at which a file is sent, but a problem arises when you want to send a nontext file, such as a program file.

All program files and some data files contain information that uses all eight bits of the byte. To transmit these files you must send the full eight bits. For this reason, the file transfer program will transmit all eight bits. However, there is one slight problem when sending binary files: the EOF mark cannot be used to signal the end of the file. To solve this problem, a count of the number of bytes to be transferred must be sent to the receiver prior to sending the file.

Sending a File

The first routine needed is a function that transmits a file through the serial port. In general, it must open the file to be transmitted, count the file, transmit the count, and finally send the file. The function **send — file( )**, shown here, accomplishes these tasks.

```c
/* Send the specified file. */
void send_file(fname)
char *fname;
{
  FILE *fp;
  char ch;
  union {
    char c[2];
    unsigned int count;
  } cnt;

  if(!(fp=fopen(fname,"rp"))) {
    printf("cannot open input file\n");
    exit(1);
  }

  send_file_name(fname); /* send the name of the file */

  wait(PORT);  /* wait for receiver to acknowledge */

  /* found out the size of the file */
  cnt.count = filesize(fp);
  /* send size */
  sport(PORT, cnt.c[0]);
  wait(PORT);
  sport(PORT, cnt.c[1]);

  do {
    ch = getc(fp);
    if(ferror(fp)) {
      printf("error reading input file");
      break;
    }

    /* wait until receiver is ready */
    if(!feof(fp)) {
      wait(PORT);
      sport(PORT, ch);
    }
  } while(!feof(fp));
```

```
    wait(PORT);/* read the last period from port */
    fclose(fp);
}
```

The function **send—file—name( )**, shown here, establishes connection with the receiver and transmits the file name.

```
/* send the file name */
void send_file_name(f)
char *f;
{
  printf("Transmitter waiting...\n");
  do {
    sport(PORT, '?');
  } while(!kbhit() && !(check_stat(PORT)&256));
  if(kbhit()) {
    getch();
    exit(1);
  }
  wait(PORT);  /* wait for receiver to acknowledge */
  printf("sending %s\n\n",f);

  /* actually send the name */
  while(*f) {
    sport(PORT, *f++);
    wait(PORT); /* wait for receiver to acknowledge */
  }
  sport(PORT,'\0'); /* null terminator */
}
```

The **send—file—name( )** function has two purposes. First, it establishes communication with the receiver by sending question marks until the receiver responds with a period. (The period is the acknowledgment symbol in the transfer program, but you can use any value you like.) Once communication has been established, the file name is transmitted. Note that this function can be aborted by striking any key.

The function **check—stat( )** used by **send—file—name( )** returns the status of the specified port. The code for **check—stat( )** will be shown in the complete listing.

The function **wait( )**, shown here, waits for an acknowledgment from the receiver, thus implementing the software handshaking.

```
/* Wait for a response. */
void wait(port)
int port;
{
```

```
if(rport(port)!='.') {
  printf("communication error\n");
  exit(1);
}
}
```

Although this function exists on error, you could substitute your own error handler, if your application requires it.

The **filesize( )** function returns the size of the file in bytes. It is possible that your compiler will supply a file length function, so feel free to substitute it. The **union** variable **cnt** is needed because the size of the file is a two-byte quantity, but you may only send one byte at a time through the serial port.

Receiving a File

Receiving a file is just the opposite of sending one. First, the receiving function waits until it receives a question mark. It replies with a period (the acknowledgment symbol). Then the file name is read, followed by the number of bytes in the file. Finally, the file is read. Keep in mind that after each byte is received, an acknowledgment is sent. This creates the software handshaking. The **rec__file( )** function is shown here.

```
/* Receive a file. */
void rec_file()
{
  FILE *fp;
  char ch;
  char fname[14];
  union {
    char c[2];
    unsigned int count;
  } cnt;
  get_file_name(fname); /* get the file name */

  printf("receiving file %s\n",fname);
  remove(fname);
  if(!(fp=fopen(fname, "wb"))) {
    printf("cannot open output file\n");
    exit(1);
  }

  /* get file length */
  sport(PORT, '.'); /* acknowledge */
  cnt.c[0] = rport(PORT);
  sport(PORT, '.'); /* acknowledge */
  cnt.c[1] = rport(PORT);
  sport(PORT, '.'); /* acknowledge */
```

```
   for(; cnt.count; cnt.count--) {
     ch = rport(PORT);
     putc(ch, fp);
     if(ferror(fp)) {
       printf("error writing file");
       exit(1);
     }
     sport(PORT, '.'); /* acknowledge */
   }
   fclose(fp);
}
```

The function **get — file — name( )** is shown here.

```
/* Receive the file name */
void get_file_name(f)
char *f;
{
  printf("receiver waiting...\n");
  while(rport(PORT)!='?') ;
  sport(PORT, '.'); /* acknowledge */
  while((*f=rport(PORT))) {
    if(*f!='?') {
      f++;
      sport(PORT, '.'); /* acknowledge */
    }
  }
}
```

The Transfer Program

The entire file transfer program, including all necessary support functions, is shown here. As it stands, port 0 — the first serial port — is used; however, you can change the definition of **PORT** near the top of the program if you wish to use a different port.

```
/* File transfer program using software handshaking.

   Port initialized to
     9600 baud,
     no parity,
     eight data bits,
     two stop bits.

 */

#define PORT 0

#include "dos.h"
#include "stdio.h"
```

```c
unsigned int filesize();
void sport(), send_file(), rec_file(), send_file_name();
void get_file_name(), port_init(), wait();

main(argc,argv)
int argc;
char *argv[];
{
  if(argc<2) {
    printf("Usage: trans s filename OR trans r\n");
    exit(1);
  }

  printf("File transfer program in operation.  To abort,\n");
  printf("press any key.\n\n");

  port_init(PORT, 231); /* initalize the serial port */

  if(tolower(*argv[1]) == 's') send_file(argv[2]);
  else rec_file();
}

/* Send the specified file. */
void send_file(fname)
char *fname;
{
  FILE *fp;
  char ch;
  union {
    char c[2];
    unsigned int count;
  } cnt;

  if(!(fp=fopen(fname,"rb"))) {
    printf("cannot open input file\n");
    exit(1);
  }

  send_file_name(fname); /* send the name of the file */

  wait(PORT);  /* wait for receiver to acknowledge */

  /* found out the size of the file */
  cnt.count = filesize(fp);
  /* send size */
  sport(PORT, cnt.c[0]);
  wait(PORT);
  sport(PORT, cnt.c[1]);

  do {
    ch = getc(fp);
    if(ferror(fp)) {
      printf("error reading input file");
      break;
    }

    /* wait until receiver is ready */
    if(!feof(fp)) {
      wait(PORT);
      sport(PORT, ch);
    }
  } while(!feof(fp));
  wait(PORT);/* read the last period from port */
```

```
    fclose(fp);
}

/* Receive a file. */
void rec_file()
{
  FILE *fp;
  char ch;
  char fname[14];
  union {
    char c[2];
    unsigned int count;
  } cnt;

  get_file_name(fname); /* get the file name */

  printf("receiving file %s\n",fname);
  remove(fname);
  if(!(fp=fopen(fname, "wb"))) {
    printf("cannot open output file\n");
    exit(1);
  }

  /* get file length */
  sport(PORT, '.'); /* acknowledge */
  cnt.c[0] = rport(PORT);
  sport(PORT, '.'); /* acknowledge */
  cnt.c[1] = rport(PORT);
  sport(PORT, '.'); /* acknowledge */

  for(; cnt.count; cnt.count--) {
    ch = rport(PORT);
    putc(ch, fp);
    if(ferror(fp)) {
      printf("error writing file");
      exit(1);
    }
    sport(PORT, '.'); /* acknowledge */
  }
  fclose(fp);
}

/* Return the length, in bytes, of a file */
unsigned int filesize(fp)
FILE *fp;
{
  unsigned long int i;

  i = 0;
  do {
    getc(fp);
    i++;
  } while(!feof(fp));
  rewind(fp);
  return i-1; /* don't count EOF char */
}

/* Send the file name */
void send_file_name(f)
char *f;
{
  printf("Transmitter waiting...\n");
  do {
```

```c
      sport(PORT, '?');
  } while(!kbhit() && !(check_stat(PORT)&256));
  if(kbhit()) {
    getch();
    exit(1);
  }
  wait(PORT);  /* wait for receiver to acknowledge */
  printf("sending %s\n\n",f);

  /* actually send the name */
  while(*f) {
    sport(PORT, *f++);
    wait(PORT); /* wait for receiver to acknowledge */
  }
  sport(PORT, '\0'); /* null terminator */
}

/* Receive the file name */
void get_file_name(f)
char *f;
{
  printf("receiver waiting...\n");
  while(rport(PORT)!='?') ;
  sport(PORT, '.'); /* acknowledge */
  while((*f=rport(PORT))) {
    if(*f!='?') {
      f++;
      sport(PORT, '.'); /* acknowledge */
    }
  }
}

/* Wait for a response. */
void wait(port)
int port;
{
  if(rport(port)!='.') {
    printf("communication error\n");
    exit(1);
  }
}

/* Send a character out the serial port */
void sport(port, c)
int port; /* i/o port */
char c; /* character to send */
{
  union REGS r;

  r.x.dx = port; /* serial port */
  r.h.al = c; /* char to send */
  r.h.ah = 1;  /* send character function */
  int86(0x14, &r, &r);
  if(r.h.ah & 128) {
    printf("send error detected in serial port");
    exit(1);
  }
}

/* Read a character from a port */
rport(port)
```

```
int port; /* i/o port */
{
  union REGS r;

  /* wait for a character */
  while(!(check_stat(PORT)&256))
    if(kbhit()) { /* abort on keypress */
      getch();
      exit(1);
    }

  r.x.dx = port; /* serial port */
  r.h.ah = 2;  /* read character function */
  int86(0x14, &r, &r);
  if(r.h.ah & 128)
    printf("read error detected in serial port");
  return r.h.al;
}

/* Check the status of the serial port. */
check_stat(port)
int port; /* i/o port */
{
  union REGS r;

  r.x.dx = port; /* serial port */
  r.h.ah = 3;  /* read status */
  int86(0x14, &r, &r);
  return r.x.ax;
}

/* Initialize the port.
*/
void port_init(port, code)
int port;
unsigned char code;
{
  union REGS r;

  r.x.dx = port; /* serial port */
  r.h.ah = 0;  /* initialize port function */
  r.h.al = code; /* initialization code - see text for details */
  int86(0x14, &r, &r);
}
```

Using the Transfer Program

The transfer program operates with command line parameters.
Assume that the transfer program is called TRANS. To send a file, use
this general form:

TRANS S <*filename*>

where <*filename*> is the name of the file you wish to transfer.

To receive a file, use this command line:

TRANS R

When receiving a file, the file name need not be specified, because it is sent by the sending computer.

ENHANCEMENTS

The transfer program presented above is fully functional and quite reliable. However, in highly critical situations that have no margin for error, you might want to add a few enhancements.

One way to insure that the file has been correctly received is to echo each byte received back to the transmitter as acknowledgment instead of using the period. The transmitting routine has to be modified to check this byte against the one just transmitted. If a discrepancy is found, an error should be reported.

You might also want to add automatic retry on errors. Automatic retry greatly complicates both the sending and receiving functions but may be worth the effort when one or both of the systems is operating unattended.

Finally, you might want to print the specific nature of any error that occurs. This could be valuable when trying to diagnose problems.

A POOR MAN'S LAN

Local area networks have become increasingly popular in situations where multiple computers are in use. These networks allow the sharing of both data files and programs among several computers. There are two basic approaches to a LAN. One method interconnects all computers in the network and allows any computer to access any other computer. This is sometimes called a *ring network*. Although this type of network has several advantages, its three main disadvantages are often cited as the reason it is seldom used. First, security in a ring network is difficult (though not impossible) to achieve. Second, the management of data and programs becomes very complex because no central location for the files is defined. Third, each computer in the network must spend some of its computing resources transferring other users' files, which degrades performance. The second, and more common, method of creating LANs is called the *star network*. This method uses a central computer solely for storing files and serving them to the other computers in the network. The central computer is often called the *file server*. The computers that access the file server are called *nodes, terminals,* or *workstations*.

The two approaches to LANs are illustrated in Figure 6-1. Here, we will examine the star network — the simple, reliable, file-server based LAN.

Actually, the title to this section is somewhat of an overstatement. In a true LAN, the file server is "transparent," that is, to a great extent each workstation appears to have direct access to the files on the file server. In the programs developed in this section, the user at a workstation must explicitly request a file. However, this approach has the advantage of being easy to develop and does not require any special hardware. You could also use it as a starting point for a full-featured LAN.

The File Server

At the center of a star network is the file server, which sequentially checks the status of each port in the system. A workstation makes a file request by placing either an "r" or an "s" in its port. An "s" is a request for the file server to send a file; an "r" is a request for the file server to

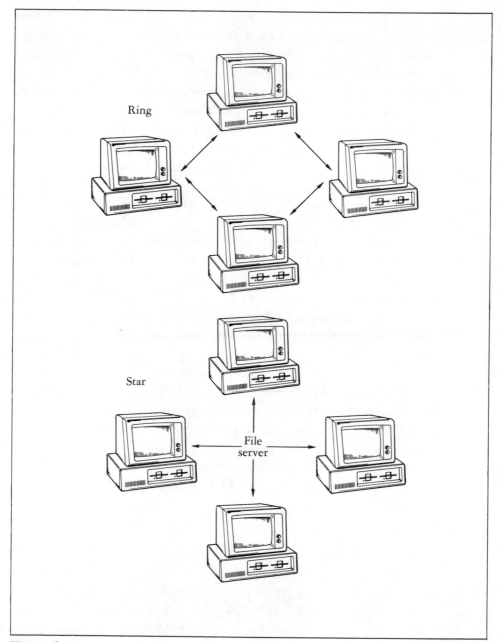

Figure 6-1.

The star and ring networks

receive a file (and store it). When a request is made, the file server fulfills the request and then returns to checking the status of the ports, waiting for the next request. The actual transmission or reception of a file is virtually the same as used in the file transfer program developed in the first part of this chapter.

The main loop of the file server is shown here. The code inserted as a comment shows how additional ports are added to the loop.

```
main()
{

  printf("File server in operation.\n");
  printf("To abort, press any key.\n\n");

  port_init(PORT); /* initalize the serial port */

  do {
    /* wait until a request is received */
    if(check_stat(PORT)&256) {
      switch(rport(PORT)) {
        case 's': send_file(PORT);
          break;
        case 'r': rec_file(PORT);
          break;
      }
    }


/**********************************
Add additional workstations by checking more ports
as shown here.
    if(check_stat(PORT1)&256) {
      switch(rport(PORT1)) {
        case 's': send_file(PORT1);
          break;
        case 'r': rec_file(PORT1);
          break;
      }
    }
   .
   .
   .

    if(check_stat(PORTn)&256) {
      switch(rport(PORTn)) {
        case 's': send_file(PORTn);
          break;
        case 'r': rec_file(PORTn);
          break;
      }
    }
**********************************/
  } while(!kbhit());
}
```

As shown, the file server works with only one workstation, but as the comments indicate you can add as many as necessary. Notice that the file server program runs continuously until a key is pressed. This means that it is always ready to act upon a file request.

As you can see, the functions **send—file**( ) and **rec—file**( ) now accept the port with which they will communicate as an argument. This is necessary because the file server must be able to service several different ports. They must also send acknowledgment to the workstation that the request has been received. The reworked **send—file**( ) and **rec—file**( ) functions are shown here.

```
/* Send the specified file through specified port. */
void send_file(port)
int port;
{
  FILE *fp;
  char ch, fname[14];
  union {
    char c[2];
    unsigned int count;
  } cnt;

  sport(port, '.'); /* acknowledge */

  get_file_name(fname, PORT);
  if(!(fp=fopen(fname,"rb"))) {
    printf("cannot open input file\n");
    exit(1);
  }

  if(rport(port)!='.') {
    printf("remote file failure\n");
    exit(1);
  }

  printf("sending file %s\n", fname);
  /* found out the size of the file */
  cnt.count = filesize(fp);
  /* send size */
  sport(port, cnt.c[0]);
  wait(port);

  sport(port, cnt.c[1]);
  do {
    ch = getc(fp);
    if(ferror(fp)) {
      printf("error reading input file");
      break;
    }
```

```
      /* wait until receiver is ready */
      if(!feof(fp)) {
        wait(port);
        sport(port, ch);
      }
    } while(!feof(fp));
    wait(port);/* read the last period from port */
    fclose(fp);
}

/* Receive a file through the specified port. */
void rec_file(port)
int port;
{
  FILE *fp;
  char ch;
  char fname[14];
  union {
    char c[2];
    unsigned int count;
  } cnt;

  sport(port, '.'); /* acknowledge */

  get_file_name(fname, PORT);

  printf("receiving file %s\n",fname);
  remove(fname);
  if(!(fp=fopen(fname, "wb"))) {
    printf("cannot open output file\n");
    exit(1);
  }

  /* get file length */
  sport(port, '.');
  cnt.c[0] = rport(port);
  sport(port, '.');
  cnt.c[1] = rport(port);
  sport(port, '.');

  for(; cnt.count; cnt.count--) {
    ch = rport(port);
    putc(ch, fp);
    if(ferror(fp)) {
      printf("error writing file");
      exit(1);
    }
    sport(port, '.');
  }
  fclose(fp);
}
```

The entire file server program, for use with port 0, is shown here. If you have more than one workstation, be sure to add the appropriate extra code.

```
/* Poor man's LAN file server.  Port settings:

    9600 baud,
    no parity,
    eight data bits,
    two stop bits.
*/

#define PORT 0

#include "dos.h"
#include "stdio.h"

unsigned int filesize();
void sport(), send_file(), rec_file(), send_file_name();
void get_file_name(), port_init(), wait();

main()
{

  printf("File server in operation.\n");
  printf("To abort, press any key.\n\n");

  port_init(PORT); /* initalize the serial port */

  do {
    /* wait until a request is received */
    if(check_stat(PORT)&256) {
      switch(rport(PORT)) {
        case 's': send_file(PORT);
          break;
        case 'r': rec_file(PORT);
          break;
      }
    }
/***********************************
Add additional workstations by checking more ports
as shown here.
    if(check_stat(PORT1)&256) {
      switch(rport(PORT1)) {
        case 's': send_file(PORT1);
          break;
        case 'r': rec_file(PORT1);
          break;
      }
    }
  .
  .
  .
    if(check_stat(PORTn)&256) {
      switch(rport(PORTn)) {
        case 's': send_file(PORTn);
          break;
        case 'r': rec_file(PORTn);
          break;
      }
    }

*******************************/
  } while(!kbhit());
}
```

```
/* Send the specified file through specified port. */
void send_file(port)
int port;
{
  FILE *fp;
  char ch, fname[14];
  union {
    char c[2];
    unsigned int count;
  } cnt;

  sport(port, '.'); /* acknowledge */

  get_file_name(fname, PORT);
  if(!(fp=fopen(fname,"rb"))) {
    printf("cannot open input file\n");
    exit(1);
  }

  if(rport(port)!='.') {
    printf("remote file failure\n");
    exit(1);
  }

  printf("sending file %s\n", fname);
  /* found out the size of the file */
  cnt.count = filesize(fp);
  /* send size */
  sport(port, cnt.c[0]);
  wait(port);

  sport(port, cnt.c[1]);
  do {
    ch = getc(fp);
    if(ferror(fp)) {
      printf("error reading input file");
      break;
    }

    /* wait until receiver is ready */
    if(!feof(fp)) {
      wait(port);
      sport(port, ch);
    }
  } while(!feof(fp));
  wait(port);/* read the last period from port */
  fclose(fp);
}


/* Receive a file through the specified port. */
void rec_file(port)
int port;
{
  FILE *fp;
  char ch;
  char fname[14];
  union {
    char c[2];
    unsigned int count;
  } cnt;
```

```
    sport(port, '.'); /* acknowledge */

    get_file_name(fname, PORT);

    printf("receiving file %s\n",fname);
    remove(fname);
    if(!(fp=fopen(fname, "wb"))) {
      printf("cannot open output file\n");
      exit(1);
    }

    /* get file length */
    sport(port, '.');
    cnt.c[0] = rport(port);
    sport(port, '.');
    cnt.c[1] = rport(port);
    sport(port, '.');

    for(; cnt.count; cnt.count--) {
      ch = rport(port);
      putc(ch, fp);
      if(ferror(fp)) {
        printf("error writing file");
        exit(1);
      }
      sport(port, '.');
    }
    fclose(fp);
}

/* Return the length, in bytes, of a file */
unsigned int filesize(fp)
FILE *fp;
{
  unsigned long int i;

  i = 0;
  do {
    getc(fp);
    i++;
  } while(!feof(fp));
  rewind(fp);
  return i-1; /* don't count the EOF char */
}

/* Send the file name */
void send_file_name(f, port)
char *f;
int port;
{
  do {
    sport(port, '?');
  } while(!kbhit() && !(check_stat(port)&256));
  if(kbhit()) {
    getch();
    exit(1);
  }
  wait(port);

  while(*f) {
    sport(port, *f++);
```

```
      wait(port);
  }
  sport(port, 0);
}

/* Receive the file name */
void get_file_name(f, port)
char *f;
int port;
{

  while(rport(port)!='?') printf(".");
  sport(port, '.');
  while((*f=rport(port))) {
    if(*f!='?') {
      f++;
      sport(port, '.');
    }
  }
  sport(port, '.');
}

/* Wait for a response. */
void wait(port)
int port;
{
  if(rport(port)!='.') {
    printf("communication error\n");
    exit(1);
  }
}

/* Send a character out the serial port */
void sport(port, c)
int port; /* i/o port */
char c; /* character to send */
{
  union REGS r;

  r.x.dx = port; /* serial port */
  r.h.al = c; /* byte to send */
  r.h.ah = 1;  /* send character function */
  int86(0x14, &r, &r);
  if(r.h.ah & 128) {
    printf("send error detected in serial port %d", r.h.ah);
    exit(1);
  }
}

/* Read a character from a port */
rport(port)
int port; /* i/o port */
{
  union REGS r;

  /* wait for a character */
  while(!(check_stat(port)&256))
    if(kbhit()) {
      getch();
      exit(1);
    }
```

```
    r.x.dx = port; /* serial port */
    r.h.ah = 2;  /* read character function */
    int86(0x14, &r, &r);
    if(r.h.ah & 128)
      printf("read error detected in serial port");
    return r.h.al;
}

/* Check the status of the serial port. */
check_stat(port)
int port; /* i/o port */
{
  union REGS r;

  r.x.dx = port; /* serial port */
  r.h.ah = 3;  /* read status */
  int86(0x14, &r, &r);
  return r.x.ax;
}

/* Initialize port to 9600 baud, two stop-bits,

   no parity, 8 data bits.
*/
void port_init(port)
int port;
{
  union REGS r;

  r.x.dx = port; /* serial port */
  r.h.ah = 0;  /* initialize port function */
  r.h.al = 231; /* initialization code - see text for details */
  int86(0x14, &r, &r);
}
```

Loading Files

In order for a workstation to request and download a file from the file server, a special program is required. This program is called GET and is run by the workstation to request a file. It can be thought of as an extension to the DOS command set. The general form for using GET is

GET <*filename*>

where <*filename*> is the file to be downloaded.

There are two differences in the operation of the GET functions and those used in the file server. First, the **rec_file( )** function sends the name of the file to the server. Second, the ports are hardcoded into the routines, not passed as in the file server.

The entire code to the GET program is shown here.

```c
/* Load a file from the file server.
*/

#define PORT 0

#include "dos.h"
#include "stdio.h"

void sport(), rec_file(), send_file_name();
void get_file_name(), port_init(), wait();

main(argc,argv)
int argc;
char *argv[];
{
  if(argc!=2) {
    printf("Usage: get <filename>");
    exit(1);
  }

port_init(PORT); /* initialize the serial port */

  rec_file(argv[1]);
}


/* Receive a file. */
void rec_file(fname)
char *fname;
{
  FILE *fp;
  char ch;
  union {
    char c[2];
    unsigned int count;
  } cnt;

  printf("loading file %s\n",fname);
  remove(fname);
  if(!(fp=fopen(fname, "wb"))) {
    printf("cannot open output file\n");
    exit(1);
  }

  sport(PORT, 's'); /* tell server to send a file */
  wait(PORT); /* wait until server is ready */

  /* get file length */
  send_file_name(fname);

  sport(PORT, '.'); /* acknowledge */
  cnt.c[0] = rport(PORT);
  sport(PORT, '.'); /* acknowledge */
```

```
        cnt.c[1] = rport(PORT);
        sport(PORT, '.'); /* acknowledge */

        for(; cnt.count; cnt.count--) {
          ch = rport(PORT);
          putc(ch, fp);
          if(ferror(fp)) {
            printf("error writing file");
            exit(1);
          }
          sport(PORT, '.'); /* acknowledge */
        }
        fclose(fp);
      }

      /* Send the file name */
      void send_file_name(f)
      char *f;
      {
        do {
          sport(PORT, '?');  /* wait until server is ready */
        } while(!kbhit() && !(check_stat(PORT)&256));
        if(kbhit()) {
          getch();
          exit(1);
        }
        wait(PORT);

        while(*f) {
          sport(PORT, *f++);
          wait(PORT);
        }
        sport(PORT, '\0');  /* null terminator */
        wait(PORT);
      }

      /* Wait for a response. */
      void wait(port)
      int port;
      {
        if(rport(port)!='.') {
          printf("communication error\n");
          exit(1);
        }
      }

      /* Send a character out the serial port */
      void sport(port, c)
      int port; /* i/o port */
      char c; /* character to send */
      {
        union REGS r;

        r.x.dx = port; /* serial port */
        r.h.al = c;
        r.h.ah = 1;  /* send character function */
        int86(0x14, &r, &r);
        if(r.h.ah & 128) {
          printf("send error detected in serial port %d", r.h.ah);
          exit(1);
        }
      }
```

```
/* Read a character from a port */
rport(port)
int port; /* i/o port */
{
  union REGS r;

  /* wait for a character */
  while(!(check_stat(PORT)&256))
    if(kbhit()) {
      getch();
      exit(1);
    }

  r.x.dx = port; /* serial port */
  r.h.ah = 2;  /* read character function */
  int86(0x14, &r, &r);
  if(r.h.ah & 128)
    printf("read error detected in serial port");
  return r.h.al;
}

/* Check the status of the serial port. */
check_stat(port)
int port; /* i/o port */
{
  union REGS r;

  r.x.dx = port; /* serial port */
  r.h.ah = 3;  /* read status */
  int86(0x14, &r, &r);
  return r.x.ax;
}

/* Initialize port to 9600 baud, two stop-bits,
   no parity, 8 data bits.
*/
void port_init(port)
int port;
{
  union REGS r;
  r.x.dx = port; /* serial port */
  r.h.ah = 0;  /* initialize port function */
  r.h.al = 231; /* initialization code - see text for details */
  int86(0x14, &r, &r);
}
```

Storing Files

In many networks, files may not only be downloaded but also uploaded onto the file server for storage. To support this, the program PUT is created. PUT is run by the workstation to transfer a file to a file server. Its usage is exactly like GET, with its general form being

PUT <*filename*>

Its operation is virtually identical to the file transfer program.
The entire code for the PUT program is shown here.

```c
/* Store a file on the file server.
*/

#define PORT 0

#include "dos.h"
#include "stdio.h"

unsigned int filesize();
void sport(), send_file(),  send_file_name();
void  port_init(), wait();

main(argc,argv)
int argc;
char *argv[];
{
  if(argc!=2) {
    printf("Usage: get <filename>");
    exit(1);
  }

  port_init(PORT); /* initialize the serial port */

  send_file(argv[1]);
}

/* Send the specified file. */
void send_file(fname)
char *fname;
{
  FILE *fp;
  char ch;
  union {
    char c[2];
    unsigned int count;
  } cnt;

  if(!(fp=fopen(fname,"rb"))) {
    printf("cannot open input file\n");
    exit(1);
  }
  printf("sending file %s\n", fname);

  /* request service */
  sport(PORT, 'r'); /* request server to receive a file */
  wait(PORT);   /* wait until server is ready */

  send_file_name(fname); /* send the file name */

  if(rport(PORT)!='.') {
    printf("remote file failure\n");
    exit(1);
  }

  /* found out the size of the file */
  cnt.count = filesize(fp);
```

```
/* send size */
sport(PORT, cnt.c[0]);
wait(PORT);
sport(PORT, cnt.c[1]);
do {
  ch = getc(fp);

  if(ferror(fp)) {
    printf("error reading input file");
    break;
  }

  /* wait until receiver is ready */
  if(!feof(fp)) {
    wait(PORT);
    sport(PORT, ch);
  }
} while(!feof(fp));
wait(PORT);/* read the last period from port */
fclose(fp);
}

/* Return the length, in bytes, of a file */
unsigned int filesize(fp)
FILE *fp;
{
  unsigned long int i;

  i = 0;
  do {
    getc(fp);
    i++;
  } while(!feof(fp));
  rewind(fp);
  return i-1; /* don't count the EOF char */
}

/* Send the file name */
void send_file_name(f)
char *f;
{
  do {
    sport(PORT, '?');
  } while(!kbhit() && !(check_stat(PORT)&256));
  if(kbhit()) {
    getch();
    exit(1);
  }
  wait(PORT);

  while(*f) {
    sport(PORT, *f++);
    wait(PORT);
  }
  sport(PORT, '\0'); /* null terminator */
  wait(PORT);
}

/* Wait for a response. */
void wait(port)
int port;
{
```

```
      if(rport(port)!='.') {
        printf("communication error\n");
        exit(1);
      }
    }

    /* Send a character out the serial port */
    void sport(port, c)
    int port; /* i/o port */
    char c; /* character to send */
    {
      union REGS r;

      r.x.dx = port; /* serial port */
      r.h.al = c; /* byte to send */
      r.h.ah = 1;  /* send character function */
      int86(0x14, &r, &r);
      if(r.h.ah & 128) {
        printf("send error detected in serial port %d", r.h.ah);
        exit(1);
      }
    }

    /* Read a character from a port */
    rport(port)
    int port; /* i/o port */
    {
      union REGS r;

      /* wait for a character */
      while(!(check_stat(PORT)&256))
        if(kbhit()) {
          getch();
          exit(1);
        }

      r.x.dx = port; /* serial port */
      r.h.ah = 2;  /* read character function */
      int86(0x14, &r, &r);
      if(r.h.ah & 128)
        printf("read error detected in serial port");
      return r.h.al;
    }

    /* Check the status of the serial port. */
    check_stat(port)
    int port; /* i/o port */
    {
      union REGS r;

      r.x.dx = port; /* serial port */
      r.h.ah = 3;  /* read status */
      int86(0x14, &r, &r);
      return r.x.ax;
    }

    /* Initialize port to 9600 baud, two stop-bits,
       no parity, 8 data bits.
    */
    void port_init(port)
    int port;
    {
      union REGS r;
```

```
r.x.dx = port; /* serial port */
r.h.ah = 0;   /* initialize port function */
r.h.al = 231; /* initialization code - see text for details */
int86(0x14, &r, &r);
}
```

Using the LAN

To use the LAN run the file server on the central computer. Put the files GET.EXE and PUT.EXE on each workstation. When a file is needed, use the GET command. To store a file use the PUT command.

Improving the LAN

One of the first improvements to make is to add the ability for a workstation to request a directory listing from the central computer. To do this, add the 'd' (directory) command to the main loop and then transmit the directory listing as if it were a file when the command is received. At the workstation end, you would simply display the directory on the screen.

A very challenging enhancement would be adding a RUN command that would automatically download an executable file, place it in the workstation's memory, and begin execution.

Electronic mail, whereby users can leave messages for each other via the network, is an easier feature to add.

Finally, you might want to prohibit the system from uploading certain files in order to protect their contents.

7: Language
Interpreters

Have you ever wanted to create your own computer language? Most programmers find the idea of creating, controlling, enhancing, and modifying their own computer language very appealing. Few programmers, however, realize how easy and enjoyable the creation of a computer language can be. Developing a full-featured compiler is certainly a major undertaking, but creating a language interpreter is a much simpler task. Unfortunately, the methods used to create language interpreters are rarely taught in computer science classes, or they are taught only as abstractions. In this chapter, you will learn the secrets of language interpretation and expression parsing by developing a working, practical example.

Language interpreters are important for three very different reasons. First, they can provide a truly interactive environment, as evidenced by the standard BASIC interpreter that comes with most microcomputers. Many novice users find an interactive environment easier to use than a compiler. Second, language interpreters can provide excellent interactive debugging facilities. Even veteran programmers sometimes resort to debugging a misbehaving routine with an interpreter because it is possible to dynamically set the value of variables and conditions. Third, most database management programs interpret the query language accepted by the database.

In this chapter, an interpreter for a subset of BASIC, hereafter referred to as "Small BASIC," will be developed. BASIC is chosen over C because BASIC, by design, is much easier to interpret than C or any other structured language. An interpreter for a structured language, such as C, is more difficult than one for BASIC because of the stand-alone functions with local variables; they add significant complexity to an interpreter. However, the same principles used to interpret BASIC also apply to any other language, and you can use the routines developed here as a starting point. Just as you must learn to crawl before you walk, it is necessary to learn the essentials of language interpretation before tackling the interpretation of a language as complex as C. If you don't know BASIC, don't worry. The commands used in Small BASIC are very easy to understand.

We begin with the heart of any interpreter: the expression parser.

EXPRESSION PARSING

The most important part of a language interpreter is the *expression parser*, which transforms numeric expressions, such as $(10-X)/23$, into a form that the computer can understand and evaluate. In my book, *C: The Complete Reference* (Osborne/McGraw-Hill, 1987), an entire chapter is devoted to expression parsing, and the parser developed there will be used here, with slight modifications, as support for the Small BASIC interpreter. (As such, this chapter presents only a brief explanation of expression parsing; for a detailed discussion, refer to *C: The Complete Reference.*)

Expression parsing is similar to other programming tasks but in some ways easier because it works with the very strict rules of algebra. The expression parser developed in this chapter is commonly referred to as a *recursive descent parser.* Before developing the actual parser, you should first understand how to think about expressions.

Expressions

Although expressions can be composed of all types of information, this chapter deals only with *numeric expressions*. For our purposes, numeric expressions can be made up of the following items:

- Numbers
- The operators $+ - / * \wedge \% = (\,) < > ; ,$
- Parentheses
- Variables

The $\wedge$ indicates exponentiation. The $=$ is used as the assignment operator and for equality. These items can be combined in expressions according to the rules of algebra. Here are some examples:

```
7-8
(100-5) * 14/6
a+b-c
10^5
a=7-b
```

Although the $=, >, <$, comma, and semicolon are operators, the way BASIC treats them, they do not fit easily into the expression parser and are instead handled explicitly by the specific functions that process the IF, PRINT, and assignment statements. (A C language parser would contain these operators.) As far as BASIC is concerned, the precedence of these operators is not defined. (Or you can also think of them as having the highest precedence.) For the operators that are actually processed by the parser, assume this precedence:

```
highest          ()
                 ^

                 * / %
                 + -
lowest           =
```

Operators of equal precedence evaluate from left to right.

Small BASIC assumes that all variables are single letters; this means that 26 variables (the letters A through Z) are available for use. Although most BASIC interpreters support more variables by allowing a number to follow a letter, such as X27, for simplicity the Small BASIC interpreter developed here does not. The variables are not case-sensitive; *a* and *A* are treated as the same variable. All numbers are integers, although you could easily write the routines to handle other types of numbers. Finally, no string variables are supported, although quoted string constants can be used for writing messages to the screen. These assumptions are built into the parser.

Tokens

Before you can develop a parser to evaluate expressions, you must have some way to decompose the string that contains the expression into its components. For example, the expression

A*B−(W+10)

has the components A, *, B, −, (, W, +, 10, and). Each component represents an indivisible unit of the expression. Formally, each component or indivisible piece of an expression is called a *token*. In general, the function that breaks an expression into its component parts must do four tasks: (1) ignore spaces and tabs, (2) extract each token, (3) convert the token into an internal format, if necessary, and (4) determine the type of the token.

Each token has two formats: external and internal. The *external format* is the string form that you use when writing a program. For example, PRINT is the external form of the BASIC PRINT command. Although it is possible for an interpreter to be designed in such a way that each token is used in its external string format, this is seldom (if ever) done because it is horribly inefficient. Instead, the *internal format* of a token, which is simply an integer, is used. For example, the PRINT command might be represented by a 1, the INPUT command by a 2, and so on. The advantage of the internal representation is that much faster routines can be written using integers rather than strings. It is the job of the function that returns the next token to convert the token from its external format into its internal format. Keep in mind that not all tokens have different formats. For example, there is no advantage to converting the operators, because they can be treated as characters or integers in their external form.

It is important to know what type of token is being returned. For example, the expression parser needs to know whether the next token is a number, an operator, or a variable. The importance of the token type will become evident as the interpreter is developed.

The function that returns the next token in the expression is called **get_token( )**. In Small BASIC, the program is stored as one null terminated string. The **get_token( )** function progresses through the program one character at a time. A global character pointer points to the next character to be read. In the version of **get_token( )** shown here, this pointer is called **prog**. The reason that **prog** is global is that it must maintain its value between calls to **get_token( )** and allow other functions to use it. The parser developed in this chapter uses six types: DELIMITER, VARIABLE, NUMBER, COMMAND, STRING, and QUOTE. DELIMITER is used for both operators and parentheses. VARIABLE is used when a variable is encountered. NUMBER is for numbers. COMMAND is assigned when a BASIC command is found. STRING is used temporarily inside **get_token( )** until a determination is made about a token. QUOTE is for quoted strings. The global variable **token_type** holds the token type. The internal representation of the token is placed into the global variable **tok**.

Here is **get_token( )**. Its necessary support functions are shown in the listing of the entire parser presented later in the chapter.

```
#define DELIMITER  1
#define VARIABLE   2
#define NUMBER     3
#define COMMAND    4
#define STRING     5
#define QUOTE      6
```

```
external int tok, token_type;
extern char *prog;  /* holds expression to be analyzed */

/* Get a token. */
get_token()
{
  register char *temp;

  token_type=0; tok=0;
  temp=token;

  if(*prog=='\0') { /* end of file */
    *token=0;
    tok = FINISHED;
    return(token_type=DELIMITER);
  }

  while(iswhite(*prog)) ++prog;  /* skip over white space */

  if(*prog=='\r') { /* crlf */
    ++prog; ++prog;
    tok = EOL; *token='\r';
    token[1]='\n'; token[2]=0;
    return (token_type = DELIMITER);
  }

  if(strchr("+-*^/%=;(),><", *prog)){ /* delimiter */
    *temp=*prog;
    prog++; /* advance to next position */
    temp++;
    *temp=0;
    return (token_type=DELIMITER);
  }

  if(*prog=='"') { /* quoted string */
    prog++;
    while(*prog!='"'&& *prog!='\r') *temp++=*prog++;
    if(*prog=='\r') serror(1);
    prog++;*temp=0;
    return(token_type=QUOTE);
  }

  if(isdigit(*prog)) { /* number */
    while(!isdelim(*prog)) *temp++=*prog++;
    *temp = '\0';
    return(token_type = NUMBER);
  }

  if(isalpha(*prog)) { /* var or command */
    while(!isdelim(*prog)) *temp++=*prog++;
    token_type=STRING;
  }

  *temp = '\0';

  /* see if a string is a command or a variable */
  if(token_type==STRING) {
    tok=look_up(token); /* convert to internal rep */
    if(!tok) token_type = VARIABLE;
    else token_type = COMMAND; /* is a command */
  }
  return token_type;
}
```

Look closely at **get_token( )**. Because many programmers like to put spaces into expressions to add clarity, leading spaces are skipped over using the function **iswhite( )**, which returns "true" if its argument is a space or tab. Once the spaces have been skipped, **prog** points to either a number, a variable, a command, a carriage return (linefeed), an operator, or a null if trailing spaces end the expression. If a carriage return is next, EOL is returned. If the next character is an operator, it is returned as a string in the global variable **token**, and DELIMITER is placed in **token_type**. Otherwise, a quoted string is checked for. After that, the function sees if the next token is a number. If, instead, the next character is a letter, either a variable or a command is indicated. The function **look_up( )** compares the token against strings in a table and, if it finds a match, returns the appropriate internal representation. (The **look_up( )** function will be discussed later.) If a match is not found, the token is assumed to be a variable. Finally, if the character is none of the above, it is assumed that the end of the expression has been reached and **token** is null, signaling the end of the expression.

To understand better how **get_token( )** works, study the type that the function returns for each token in the following expression.

PRINT A + 100 −(B∗C)/2

Token	Token type
PRINT	COMMAND
A	VARIABLE
+	DELIMITER
100	NUMBER
−	DELIMITER
(	DELIMITER
B	VARIABLE
∗	DELIMITER
C	VARIABLE
)	DELIMITER
/	DELIMITER
2	NUMBER
null	DELIMITER

Remember that **token** always holds a null terminated string even if it contains just a single character.

Some of the functions in the interpreter need to look ahead one token to determine its next course of action. In some of these cases, the token must be returned to the input stream if it is not needed by the routine. The function **putback( )** performs this task.

```
/* Return a token to input stream. */
void putback()
{

  char *t;

  t = token;
  for(; *t; t++) prog--;
}
```

How Expressions Are Constructed

There are a number of ways to parse and evaluate an expression. For use with a recursive descent parser, you should think of expressions as *recursive data structures,* that is, expressions defined in terms of themselves. If, for the moment, expressions are restricted to using only $+$, $-$, $*$, $/$, and parentheses, then all expressions can be defined using the following rules.

Expression $=>$ Term [+ Term] [− Term]
Term $\quad\quad => $ Factor [* Factor] [/ Factor]
Factor $\quad\quad => $ Variable, Number or (Expression)
Any part of the above can be null.

The square brackets mean "optional" and $=>$ means "produces." In fact, the above rules are usually called the *production rules* of the expression. Therefore, you can say "Term produces factor times factor or factor divided by factor" for the definition of *term.* You should notice that the precedence of the operators is implicit in the way an expression is defined, that is, "deeper/lower" elements involve operators with higher precedence.

The expression

10+5*B

has two terms: 10 and 5*B. It has three factors: 10, 5, and B, consisting of two numbers and one variable.

On the other hand, the expression

14*(7—C)

has two factors, 14 and (7—C), consisting of one number and one parenthetical expression. The parenthetical expression evaluates to one number and one variable.

You can transform the production rules for expressions into a set of mutually recursive chain-like functions that form a recursive descent parser. At each appropriate step the parser performs the specified operations in the algebraically correct sequence. To see how this process works, parse the following expression and perform the arithmetic operations at the right time.

input expression: 9/3—(100+56)

1. Get first term: 9/3

2. Get each factor and divide integers. The value is 3.

3. Get second term: (100+56). At this point, start recursively analyzing the second expression.

4. Get each factor and add. The value is 156.

5. Return from recursive call and subtract 156 from 3, yielding answer of −153.

If you are a little confused at this point, don't feel bad! This complex concept takes some getting used to. You should remember two basic ideas about this recursive view of expressions: (1) the precedence of the operators is *implicit* in the way the production rules are defined and (2) this method of parsing and evaluating expressions is very similar to the way people do the same operations.

Expression Parser

Here is the entire simple recursive descent parser for integer expressions along with some support functions. You should put this code into its own file. (The code to the parser and the interpreter when combined make a fairly large file, so two separately compiled files are recommended.) The meaning and use of the external variables will be described shortly, when the interpreter is discussed.

```
/* recursive descent parser for integer expressions
   which may include variables  */
#include "setjmp.h"
#include "math.h"
#include "ctype.h"
#include "stdlib.h"

#define DELIMITER  1
#define VARIABLE   2
#define NUMBER     3
#define COMMAND    4
#define STRING     5
#define QUOTE      6

#define EOL    9
#define FINISHED   10

extern char *prog;  /* holds expression to be analyzed */
extern jmp_buf e_buf; /* hold environment for longjmp() */
extern int variables[26]; /* variables */
extern struct commands {
  char command[20];
  char tok;
} table[];

extern char token[80]; /* holds string representation of token */
extern char token_type; /* contains type of token */
extern char tok; /* holds the internal representation of token */

void get_exp(),level2(), level3(), level4(), level5();
void level6(), primitive(), arith(), unary();
void serror(), putback();

/* Entry point into parser. */
void get_exp(result)
int *result;
{
  get_token();
  if(!*token) {
    serror(2);
```

```
    return;
  }
  level2(result);
  putback(); /* return last token read to input stream */
}

/*  Add or subtract two terms. */
void level2(result)
int *result;
{
  register char  op;
  int hold;

  level3(result);
  while((op = *token) == '+' || op == '-') {
    get_token();
    level3(&hold);
    arith(op, result, &hold);
  }
}


/* Multiply or divide two factors. */
void level3(result)
int *result;
{
  register char  op;
  int hold;

  level4(result);
  while((op = *token) == '*' || op == '/' || op == '%') {
    get_token();
    level4(&hold);
    arith(op, result, &hold);
  }
}

/* Process integer exponent. */
void level4(result)
int *result;
{
  int hold;

  level5(result);
  if(*token== '^') {
    get_token();
    level4(&hold);
    arith('^', result, &hold);
  }
}

/* Is a unary + or -. */
void level5(result)
int *result;
{
  register char  op;

  op = 0;
  if((token_type==DELIMITER) && *token=='+' || *token=='-') {
    op = *token;
    get_token();
  }
  level6(result);
  if(op)
    unary(op, result);
}
```

```
/* Process parenthesized expression. */
void level6(result)
int *result;
{
  if((*token == '(') && (token_type == DELIMITER)) {
    get_token();
    level2(result);
    if(*token != ')')
      serror(1);
    get_token();

  }
  else
    primitive(result);
}

/* Find value of number or variable. */
void primitive(result)
int *result;
{

  switch(token_type) {
  case VARIABLE:
    *result = find_var(token);
    get_token();
    return;
  case NUMBER:
    *result = atoi(token);
    get_token();
    return;
  default:
    serror(0);
  }
}

/* Perform the specified arithmetic. */
void arith(o, r, h)
char o;
int *r, *h;
{
  register int t, ex;

  switch(o) {
    case '-':
      *r = *r-*h;
      break;
    case '+':
      *r = *r+*h;
      break;
    case '*':
      *r = *r * *h;
      break;
    case '/':
      *r = (*r)/(*h);
      break;
    case '%':
      t = (*r)/(*h);
      *r = *r-(t*(*h));
      break;
    case '^':
      ex = *r;
      if(*h==0) {
        *r = 1;
        break;
      }
      for(t=*h-1; t>0; --t) *r = (*r) * ex;
```

```
      break;
    }
}

/* Reverse the sign. */
void unary(o, r)
char o;
int *r;
{
  if(o=='-') *r = -(*r);
}

/* Find the value of a variable. */
int find_var(s)
char *s;
{
  if(!isalpha(*s)){
    serror(4); /* not a variable */
    return 0;
  }
  return variables[toupper(*token)-'A'];
}

/* display an error message */
void serror(error)
int error;
{
  static char *e[]= {
    "syntax error",
    "unbalanced parentheses",
    "no expression present",
    "equals sign expected",
    "not a variable",
    "Label table full",
    "duplicate label",
    "undefined label",
    "THEN expected",
    "TO expected",
    "too many nested FOR loops",
    "NEXT without FOR",
    "too many nested GOSUBs",
    "RETURN without GOSUB"
  };
  printf("%s\n", e[error]);
  longjmp(e_buf, 1); /* return to save point */
}

/* Get a token. */
get_token()
{

  register char *temp;

  token_type=0; tok=0;
  temp=token;
  if(*prog=='\0') { /* end of file */
    *token=0;
    tok = FINISHED;
    return(token_type=DELIMITER);
  }

  while(iswhite(*prog)) ++prog;  /* skip over white space */

  if(*prog=='\r') { /* crlf */
    ++prog; ++prog;
```

```
    tok = EOL; *token='\r';
    token[1]='\n'; token[2]=0;
    return (token_type = DELIMITER);
  }

  if(strchr("+-*^/%=;(),><", *prog)){ /* delimiter */
    *temp=*prog;
    prog++; /* advance to next position */
    temp++;
    *temp=0;
    return (token_type=DELIMITER);
  }

  if(*prog=='"') { /* quoted string */
    prog++;
    while(*prog!='"'&& *prog!='\r') *temp++=*prog++;
    if(*prog=='\r') serror(1);
    prog++;*temp=0;
    return(token_type=QUOTE);
  }

  if(isdigit(*prog)) { /* number */
    while(!isdelim(*prog)) *temp++=*prog++;
    *temp = '\0';
    return(token_type = NUMBER);
  }

  if(isalpha(*prog)) { /* var or command */
    while(!isdelim(*prog)) *temp++=*prog++;
    token_type=STRING;
  }

  *temp = '\0';

  /* see if a string is a command or a variable */
  if(token_type==STRING) {
    tok=look_up(token); /* convert to internal rep */
    if(!tok) token_type = VARIABLE;
    else token_type = COMMAND; /* is a command */
  }
  return token_type;
}

/* Return a token to input stream. */
void putback()
{

  char *t;

  t = token;
  for(; *t; t++) prog--;
}

/* Look up a token's internal representation in the
   token table.
*/
look_up(s)
char *s;
{
  register int i,j;
  char *p;

  /* convert to lowercase */
  p = s;
  while(*p){ *p = tolower(*p); p++; }
```

```
/* see if token is in table */
for(i=0; *table[i].command; i++)
    if(!strcmp(table[i].command, s)) return table[i].tok;
return 0; /* unknown command */
}

/* Return true if c is a delimiter. */
isdelim(c)
char c;
{
  if(strchr(" ;,+-<>/*%^=()", c) || c==9 || c=='\r' || c==0)
    return 1;
  return 0;
}

/* Return 1 if c is space or tab. */
iswhite(c)
char c;
{
  if(c==' ' || c=='\t') return 1;
  else return 0;
}
```

The parser as shown can handle the following operators: $+, -, *, /,$ %, integer exponentiation ($^\wedge$), and the unary minus. It also deals with parentheses correctly. You should notice that it has six levels as well as the **primitive( )** function, which returns the value of a number. Also included are routines for performing the various arithmetic operations, **arith( )** and **unary( )**, as well as the **get_token( )** code.

To evaluate an expression, set **prog** to point to the beginning of the string that holds the expression and call **get_exp( )** with the address of the variable you want to hold the result.

You should pay special attention to the **serror( )** function, which is used to report errors. When a syntax error is detected, **serror( )** is called with the number of the error. Error 0, which displays the message *syntax error,* is a sort of catchall message used when nothing else applies. Otherwise, the specific error is reported. Notice that **serror( )** ends with a call to **longjmp( )**. The **longjmp( )** function performs a nonlocal goto, returning to the point defined by its companion function **setjmp( )** — presumably a safe place. (The **setjmp( )** function is found in the interpreter code, not the parser code.) The first argument in **longjmp( )** is an environment buffer that is initialized by **setjmp( )** and resets the state of the computer to what it was at the time of the **setjmp( )** call. The second argument is a value that appears to be "returned" by **setjmp( )**. You will see how it is used later. The use of

longjmp( ) simplifies error handling because the parser routines do not
have to abort explicitly when errors occur. If your compiler does not
support **setjmp( )** and **longjmp( )**, each function will have to return
manually when an error occurs.

How the Parser Handles Variables

As stated earlier, the Small BASIC interpreter only recognizes the
variables A through Z. Each variable uses one array location in a
26-element array of integers called **variables**. This array is defined in the
interpreter code (shown here) with each variable initialized to 0.

```
int variables[26]= {      /* 26 user variables,  A-Z */
  0, 0, 0, 0, 0, 0, 0, 0, 0, 0,
  0, 0, 0, 0, 0, 0, 0, 0, 0, 0,
  0, 0, 0, 0, 0, 0
};
```

Because the variable names are the letters A through Z, they can
easily be used to index the array **variables** by subtracting the ASCII value
for A from the variable name. The function **find__var( )**, which finds a
variable's value, is shown here.

```
/* Find the value of a variable. */
int find_var(s)
char *s;
{
  if(!isalpha(*s)){
    serror(4); /* not a variable */
    return 0;
  }
  return variables[toupper(*token)-'A'];
}
```

As this function is written, it actually accepts long variable names,
but only the first letter is significant. You can modify it to enforce
single-letter variable names if you like.

THE SMALL BASIC INTERPRETER

Once expressions can be parsed and evaluated, it is time to develop the Small BASIC interpreter. The interpreter will recognize the following BASIC keywords:

PRINT
INPUT
IF
THEN
FOR
NEXT
TO
GOTO
GOSUB
RETURN
END

The internal representation of these commands (plus EOL for end-of-line and FINISHED for signaling end-of-program) are defined as shown here.

```
#define PRINT 1
#define INPUT 2
#define IF    3
#define THEN  4
#define FOR   5
#define NEXT  6
#define TO    7
#define GOTO  8
#define EOL   9
#define FINISHED  10
#define GOSUB 11
#define RETURN 12
#define END 13
```

In order for the external representation of a token to be converted into the internal representation, both the external and internal formats are held in a table of structures called **table,** shown here.

```
struct commands { /* keyword lookup table */
  char command[20];
  char tok;
} table[] = { /* Commands must be entered lowercase */
  "print", PRINT, /* in this table. */
  "input", INPUT,
  "if", IF,
  "then", THEN,
  "goto", GOTO,
  "for", FOR,
  "next", NEXT,
  "to", TO,
  "gosub", GOSUB,
  "return", RETURN,
  "end", END,
  "", END  /* mark end of table */
};
```

Notice that a null string marks the end of the table.

The function **look—up**( ), shown here, returns either a token's internal representation or a null if no match is found.

```
/* Look up a a token's internal representation in the
   token table.
*/
look_up(s)
char *s;
{
  register int i,j;
  char *p;

  /* convert to lowercase */
  p = s;
  while(*p){ *p = tolower(*p); p++; }

  /* see if token is in table */
  for(i=0; *table[i].command; i++)
      if(!strcmp(table[i].command, s)) return table[i].tok;
  return 0; /* unknown command */
}
```

The Small BASIC interpreter does not support an integral editor. Instead, you must create a BASIC program using a standard text editor. The program is then read in and executed by the interpreter. The function that loads the program is called **load—program**( ) and is shown here.

```
/* Load a program. */
load_program(p, fname)
char *p;
char *fname;
{
  FILE *fp;
  int i=0;
```

```
if(!(fp=fopen(fname, "rb"))) return 0;

i = 0;
  do {
    *p = getc(fp);
    p++; i++;
  } while(!feof(fp) && i<PROG_SIZE);
  *(p-2) = '\0'; /* null terminate the program */
  fclose(fp);
  return 1;
}
```

The Main Loop

All interpreters are driven by a top-level loop that operates by reading
the next token from the program and selecting the right function to
process it. The main loop for the Small BASIC interpreter looks like
this:

```
do {
  token_type = get_token();
  /* check for assignment statement */
  if(token_type==VARIABLE) {
    putback(); /* return the var to the input stream */
    assignment(); /* must be assignment statement */
  }
  else /* is command */
    switch(tok) {
      case PRINT:
        print();
        break;
      case GOTO:
        exec_goto();
        break;
      case IF:
        exec_if();
        break;
      case FOR:
        exec_for();
        break;
      case NEXT:
        next();
        break;
      case INPUT:
        input();
        break;
      case GOSUB:
        gosub();
        break;
      case RETURN:
        greturn();
        break;
      case END:
        exit(0);
    }
} while (tok != FINISHED);
```

First, a token is read from the program. For reasons that will become clear, that token is always the first token on each line. Assuming no syntax errors have been made, if the token is a variable, an assignment statement is occurring. (The Small BASIC interpreter does not support the antiquated LET command.) Otherwise, the token must be a command and the appropriate **case** statement is selected based on the value of **tok**. Let's see how each of these commands works.

The Assignment Function

In BASIC, the general form of an assignment statement is

<var-name> = <expression>

The **assignment( )** function that is shown here supports this type of assignment.

```
/* Assign a variable a value. */
assignment()
{
  int var, value;

  /* get the variable name */
  get_token();
  if(!isalpha(*token)) {
    serror(4); /* not a variable */
    return;
  }

  /* find the index of the variable */
  var = toupper(*token)-'A';

  /* get the equals sign */
  get_token();
  if(*token!='=') {
    serror(3);
    return;
  }

  /* get the value to assign to var */
  get_exp(&value);

  /* assign the value */
  variables[var] = value;
}
```

First, **assignment( )** reads a token from the program. This token is the variable that has its value assigned. If it is not a valid variable, an error is reported. Next, the equal sign is read. Next, **get_exp( )** is called so that the value to assign the variable can be computed. Finally, the value is assigned to the variable. The function is surprisingly simple and uncluttered because the expression parser and the **get_token( )** function do much of the "messy" work.

The PRINT Command

The standard BASIC PRINT command is quite powerful and flexible, especially when PRINT USING is employed. Although it is beyond the scope of this chapter to create a function that supports all the functionality of the PRINT command, the one developed here embodies its most important functions. The general form of the Small BASIC PRINT command is

PRINT *<arg-list>*

where *arg-list* is a list of variables or quoted strings separated by commas or semicolons. The function **print( )**, shown here, executes a BASIC PRINT command. Notice that the *DO-WHILE* loop allows a comma- or semicolon-separated list of arguments to be printed.

```
/* Execute a simple version of the BASIC PRINT statement */
void print()
{
  int answer;
  int len=0, spaces;
  char last_delim;

  do {
    get_token(); /* get next list item */
    if(tok==EOL || tok==FINISHED) break;
    if(token_type==QUOTE) { /* is string */
      printf(token);
      len += strlen(token);
      get_token();
    }
    else { /* is expression */
      putback();
      get_exp(&answer);
      get_token();
      len += printf("%d", answer);
    }
    last_delim = *token;

    if(*token==';') {
```

```
    /* compute number of spaces to move to next tab */
    spaces = 8 - (len % 8);
    len += spaces; /* add in the tabbing position */
    while(spaces) {
      printf(" ");
        spaces--;
    }
  }
  else if(*token==',') /* do nothing */;
  else if(tok!=EOL && tok!=FINISHED) serror(0);
} while (*token==';' || *token==',');

if(tok==EOL || tok==FINISHED) {
  if(last_delim != ';' && last_delim!=',') printf("\n");
}
else serror(0); /* error is not , or ; */

}
```

The PRINT command can be used to print a list of variables and quoted strings on the screen. If two items are separated by a comma, no space is printed between them. If two items are separated by a semi-colon, the second item is displayed beginning with the next tab position. If the list ends in a comma or semicolon then no new line is issued. Here are some examples of valid PRINT statements. The last example simply prints a new line.

```
PRINT X; Y; "THIS IS A STRING"
PRINT 10 / 4
PRINT
```

Notice that **print( )** makes use of the **putback( )** function to return a token to the input stream. The reason for this is that **print( )** must look ahead to see whether the next item to be printed is a quoted string or a numeric expression. If it is an expression, the first term in the expression must be placed back on the input stream so that the expression parser can correctly compute the value of the expression.

The INPUT Command

In BASIC, the INPUT command is used to read information from the keyboard into a variable. It has two general forms. The first is

INPUT <*var-name*>

which displays a question mark and waits for input. The second is

INPUT "<*prompt-string*>", <*var-name*>

which displays a prompting message and waits for input. The function
input( ), shown here, implements the BASIC INPUT command.

```
/* Execute a simple form of the BASIC INPUT command */
void input()
{
  char str[80], var;
  int i;

  get_token(); /* see if prompt string is present */
  if(token_type==QUOTE) {
    printf(token); /* if so, print it and check for comma */
    get_token();
    if(*token!=',') serror(1);
    get_token();
  }
  else printf("? "); /* otherwise, prompt with ? */

  var = toupper(*token)-'A'; /* get the input var */

  scanf("%d", &i); /* read input */

  variables[var] = i; /* store it */
}
```

The operation of this function is straightforward and should be clear
after reading the comments.

The GOTO Command

Now that you have seen how a few simple commands work, it is time to
develop a more difficult command. In BASIC, the most important form
of program control is the lowly GOTO. In standard BASIC, the object of
a GOTO must be a line number, and this traditional approach is
preserved in Small BASIC. However, Small BASIC does not require a
line number for each line; a number is needed only if that line is the
target of a GOTO. The general form of the GOTO is

GOTO <*line-number*>

The main complexity associated with GOTO is that both forward and backward jumps must be allowed. To satisfy this constraint in an efficient manner requires the entire program to be scanned prior to execution and the location of each label to be placed in a table that holds both the label name and a pointer to its location in the program. Then, each time a GOTO is executed, the location of the target line can be looked up and program control transferred to that point. The table that holds the labels is declared as shown here.

```
struct label {
  char name[LAB_LEN]; /* name of label */
  char *p;  /* points to place of label in source file*/
};
struct label label_table[NUM_LAB];
```

The routine that scans the program and puts each label's location in the table is called **scan_labels( )** and is shown here along with several of its support functions.

```
/* Find all labels. */
void scan_labels()
{
  register int loc;
  char *temp;

  label_init(); /* zero all labels */
  temp = prog;   /* save pointer to top of program */

  /* if the first token in the file is a label */
  get_token();
  if(token_type==NUMBER) {
    strcpy(label_table[0].name,token);
    label_table[0].p=prog;
  }

  find_eol();
  do {
    get_token();
    if(token_type==NUMBER) {
      loc=get_next_label(token);
      if(loc==-1||loc==-2) {
          (loc==-1) ?serror(5):serror(6);
      }
      strcpy(label_table[loc].name, token);
      label_table[loc].p = prog;  /* current point in program */
    }
    /* if not on a blank line, find next line */
    if(tok!=EOL) find_eol();
  } while(tok!=FINISHED);
  prog = temp;  /* restore to original */
}

/* Initialize the array that holds the labels.
   By convention, a null label name indicates that
   array position is unused.
```

```
*/
void label_init()
{
  register int t;

  for(t=0;t<NUM_LAB;++t) label_table[t].name[0]='\0';
}

/* Find the start of the next line. */
void find_eol()
{
  while(*prog!='\n'  && *prog!='\0') ++prog;
  if(*prog) prog++;
}

/* Return index of next free position in label array.
   A -1 is returned if the array is full.
   A -2 is returned if a duplicate label is found.
*/
get_next_label(s)
char *s;
{
  register int t;

  for(t=0;t<NUM_LAB;++t) {
    if(label_table[t].name[0]==0) return t;
    if(!strcmp(label_table[t].name,s)) return -2; /* dup */
  }

  return -1;
}
```

Two types of errors are reported by **scan__labels( )**. The first is duplicate labels. In BASIC (and most other languages) no two labels can be the same. Second, a full label table is reported. The table's size is defined by **NUM__LAB**, which you can set to any size you desire.

Once the label table has been built, it is quite easy to execute a GOTO instruction with **exec__goto( )**, shown here.

```
/* Execute a GOTO statement. */
void exec_goto()
{

  char *loc;

  get_token(); /* get label to go to */
  /* find the location of the label */
  loc = find_label(token);
  if(loc=='\0')
    serror(7); /* label not defined */

  else prog=loc;  /* start program running at that loc */
}

/* Find location of given label.  A null is returned if
   label is not found; otherwise a pointer to the position
   of the label is returned.
```

```
*/
char *find_label(s)
char *s;
{
  register int t;

  for(t=0;t<NUM_LAB;++t)
    if(!strcmp(label_table[t].name,s)) return label_table[t].p;
  return '\0'; /* error condition */
}
```

The support function **find—label**( ) looks a label up in the label table and returns a pointer to it. If the label is not found, a null — which can never be a valid pointer — is returned. If the address is not null, it is assigned to the global **prog**, causing execution to resume at the location of the label. (Remember, **prog** is the pointer that keeps track of where the program is currently being read.) If the label is not found, an undefined label message is issued.

The IF Statement

The Small BASIC interpreter executes a subset of the standard BASIC's IF statement. In Small BASIC, no ELSE is allowed and only the conditions "greater than," "less than," or "equal to" are supported. (However, you will find it easy to enhance the IF once you understand its operation.) The IF statement takes this general form:

IF *<expression> <operator> <expression>* THEN *<statement>*

The statement that follows THEN is executed only if the relational expression is true. The function **exec—if**( ), shown here, executes this form of the IF statement.

```
/* Execute an IF statement. */
void exec_if()
{
  int x , y, cond;
  char op;

  get_exp(&x); /* get left expression */
```

```
get_token(); /* get the operator */
if(!strchr("=<>", *token)) {
  serror(0); /* not a legal operator */
  return;
}
op=*token;

get_exp(&y); /* get right expression */

/* determine the outcome */
cond=0;
switch(op) {
    case '=':
  if(x==y) cond=1;
  break;
    case '<':
  if(x<y) cond=1;
  break;
    case '>':
  if(x>y) cond=1;
  break;
}
if(cond) { /* is true so process target of IF */
  get_token();
  if(tok!=THEN) {
    serror(8);
    return;
  }/* else prog exec starts on next line */
}
  else find_eol(); /* find start of next line */
}
```

The **exec_if( )** function operates as follows:

1. The value of the left expression is computed.

2. The operator is read.

3. The value of the right expression is computed.

4. The relational operation is evaluated.

5. If the condition is true, the target of the THEN is executed; other-
    wise, **find_eol( )** finds the start of the next line.

The FOR Loop

The implementation of the BASIC FOR loop presents a challenging
problem that lends itself to a rather elegant solution. The general form
of the FOR loop is

FOR <*control var-name*> = <*initial value*> TO <*target value*>

.

.

.

statement sequence

.

.

.

NEXT

The Small BASIC version of the FOR allows only positively running loops that increment the control variable by one for each iteration. The STEP command is not supported.

In BASIC, as in C, FOR loops may be nested to several levels. The main challenge this presents is keeping track of the information associated with each loop. By giving this a little thought, you will see that a FOR loop is a stack-based construct, which works like this: At the top of the loop, information about the status of the control variable, the target value, and the location of the top of the loop in the program is pushed onto a stack. Each time the NEXT is encountered, this information is popped, the control variable updated, and its value checked against the target value. If the control value exceeds the target, the loop stops and execution continues with the next line following the NEXT statement. Otherwise, the updated information is placed on the stack, and execution resumes at the top of the loop. Implementing a FOR loop in this way works not only for a single loop but also for loops nested to any level. The stack-like nature of the loop causes each NEXT to be associated with the proper FOR.

To support the FOR loop, a stack that holds the loop information must be created, as shown here.

```
struct for_stack {
  int var;  /* counter variable */
  int target;  /* target value */
  char *loc;
} fstack[FOR_NEST]; /* stack for FOR/NEXT loop */
int ftos;  /* index to top of FOR stack */
```

The value of FOR—NEST defines how deeply nested the FOR loops may be. (Twenty-five levels is generally more than adequate.) The **ftos** variable holds the index to the top of the stack.

You will need two stack routines called **fpush( )** and **fpop( )**, both of which are shown here.

```
/* Push function for the FOR stack. */
void fpush(i)
struct for_stack i;
{
   if(ftos>FOR_NEST)
     serror(10);

  fstack[ftos]=i;
  ftos++;
}

struct for_stack fpop()
{
   ftos--;
   if(ftos<0) serror(11);
   return(fstack[ftos]);
}
```

Now that the necessary support is in place, the functions that execute the FOR and NEXT statements can be developed as shown here.

```
/* Execute a FOR loop. */
void exec_for()
{
  struct for_stack i;
  int value;

  get_token(); /* read the control variable */
  if(!isalpha(*token)) {
    serror(4);
    return;
  }

  i.var=toupper(*token)-'A'; /* save its index */

  get_token(); /* read the equals sign */
  if(*token!='=') {
    serror(3);
    return;
  }

  get_exp(&value); /* get initial value */

  variables[i.var]=value;
```

```
    get_token();
    if(tok!=TO) serror(9); /* read and discard the TO */

    get_exp(&i.target); /* get target value */

    /* if loop can execute at least once, push info on stack */
    if(value>=variables[i.var]) {
      i.loc = prog;
      fpush(i);
    }
    else { /* otherwise, skip loop code altogether */
      while(tok!=NEXT) get_token();
    }
}


/* Execute a NEXT statement. */
void next()
{
  struct for_stack i;

  i = fpop(); /* read the loop info */

  variables[i.var]++; /* increment control variable */
  if(variables[i.var]>i.target) return;  /* all done */
  fpush(i);  /* otherwise, restore the info */
  prog = i.loc;  /* loop */
}
```

You should be able to follow the operation of these routines by reading the comments. As the code is written, it does not prevent a GOTO out of a FOR loop. However, doing so will corrupt the FOR stack and should be avoided.

The stack-based solution to the FOR loop problem can be generalized to all loops. Although Small BASIC does not implement any other types of loops, you can apply the same sort of procedure to WHILE and DO-WHILE loops. As you will see in the next section, the stack-based solution can also be applied to any language element that may be nested, including calling subroutines.

The GOSUB Statement

Although BASIC does not support true stand-alone subroutines, it does allow portions of a program to be called and returned from using the GOSUB and RETURN statements. The general form of a GOSUB-RETURN is

GOSUB <*line-num*>

    .
    .
    .

<*line-num*>

    .
    . *subroutine code*
    .

RETURN

Calling a subroutine, even as simply as subroutines are implemented in BASIC, requires the use of a stack. The reason for this is similar to that given for the FOR statement. Because it is possible to have one subroutine call another, a stack is required to insure that a RETURN statement is associated with the proper GOSUB. The definition of a GOSUB stack is shown here.

```
char *gstack[SUB_NEST]; /* stack for gosub */

int gtos;  /* index to top of GOSUB stack */
```

The function **gosub( )** and its support routines are shown here.

```
/* Execute a GOSUB command. */
void gosub()
{
  char *loc;

  get_token();
  /* find the label to call */
  loc = find_label(token);
  if(loc=='\0')
    serror(7); /* label not defined */
  else {
    gpush(prog); /* save place to return to */
    prog = loc;  /* start program running at that loc */
  }
}

/* Return from GOSUB. */
void greturn()
{
  prog = gpop();
}

/* GOSUB stack push function. */
void gpush(s)
char *s;
```

```
{
  gtos++;

  if(gtos==SUB_NEST) {
    serror(12);
    return;
  }

  gstack[gtos]=s;

}
/* GOSUb stack pop function. */
char *gpop()
{
  if(gtos==0) {
    serror(13);
    return 0;
  }

  return(gstack[gtos--]);
}
```

The GOSUB command works like this. A current value of **prog** is pushed on the GOSUB stack. The line number that begins the subroutine is looked up and its address is assigned to **prog**. This causes program execution to resume at the start of the subroutine. When a RETURN is encountered, the GOSUB stack is popped and this value is assigned to **prog**, causing execution to continue on the next line after the GOSUB statement. The process allows GOSUBs to be nested to any depth.

The Entire Interpreter File

All the code for the Small BASIC interpreter, except those routines found in the expression parser file, is shown here. Once you have entered it into your computer you should compile both the interpreter and the parser files and link them together.

```
/* A tiny BASIC interpreter */

#include "stdio.h"
#include "setjmp.h"
#include "math.h"
#include "ctype.h"
#include "stdlib.h"

#define NUM_LAB 100
#define LAB_LEN 10
#define FOR_NEST 25
#define SUB_NEST 25
#define PROG_SIZE 10000
```

```
#define DELIMITER  1
#define VARIABLE   2
#define NUMBER     3
#define COMMAND    4
#define STRING     5
#define QUOTE      6

#define PRINT 1
#define INPUT 2
#define IF       3
#define THEN  4
#define FOR   5
#define NEXT  6
#define TO       7
#define GOTO  8
#define EOL   9
#define FINISHED   10
#define GOSUB 11
#define RETURN 12
#define END 13

char *prog;  /* holds expression to be analyzed */
jmp_buf e_buf; /* hold environment for longjmp() */

int variables[26]= {     /* 26 user variables,  A-Z */
  0, 0, 0, 0, 0, 0, 0, 0, 0, 0,
  0, 0, 0, 0, 0, 0, 0, 0, 0, 0,
  0, 0, 0, 0, 0, 0
};

struct commands { /* keyword lookup table */
  char command[20];
  char tok;
} table[] = { /* Commands must be entered lowercase */
  "print", PRINT, /* in this table. */
  "input", INPUT,
  "if", IF,
  "then", THEN,
  "goto", GOTO,
  "for", FOR,
  "next", NEXT,
  "to", TO,
  "gosub", GOSUB,
  "return", RETURN,
  "end", END,
  "", END  /* mark end of table */
};

char token[80];
char token_type, tok;

struct label {
  char name[LAB_LEN];
  char *p;  /* points to place to go in source file*/
};
struct label label_table[NUM_LAB];

char *find_label(), *gpop();

struct for_stack {
  int var; /* counter variable */
  int target;  /* target value */
  char *loc;
} fstack[FOR_NEST]; /* stack for FOR/NEXT loop */
struct for_stack fpop();

char *gstack[SUB_NEST]; /* stack for gosub */
```

```
int ftos; /* index to top of FOR stack */
int gtos; /* index to top of GOSUB stack */

void print(), scan_labels(), find_eol(), exec_goto();
void exec_if(), exec_for(), next(), fpush(), input();
void gosub(), greturn(), gpush(), label_init();

main(argc, argv)
int argc;
char *argv[];
{
  char in[80];
  int answer;
  char *p_buf;
  char *t;

  if(argc!=2) {
    printf("usage: run <filename>\n");
    exit(1);
  }

  /* allocate memory for the program */
  if(!(p_buf=(char *) malloc(PROG_SIZE))) {
    printf("allocation failure");
    exit(1);
  }

  /* load the program to execute */
  if(!load_program(p_buf,argv[1])) exit(1);

  if(setjmp(e_buf)) exit(1); /* initialize the long jump buffer */

  prog = p_buf;
  scan_labels(); /* find the labels in the program */
  ftos = 0; /* initialize the FOR stack index */
  gtos = 0; /* initialize the GOSUB stack index */
  do {
    token_type = get_token();
    /* check for assignment statement */
    if(token_type==VARIABLE) {
      putback(); /* return the var to the input stream */
      assignment(); /* must be assignment statement */
    }
    else /* is command */
      switch(tok) {
        case PRINT:
          print();
          break;
        case GOTO:
          exec_goto();
          break;
        case IF:
          exec_if();
          break;
        case FOR:
          exec_for();
          break;
        case NEXT:
          next();
          break;
        case INPUT:
          input();
          break;
        case GOSUB:
          gosub();
          break;
```

```
        case RETURN:
          greturn();
          break;
        case END:
          exit(0);
    }
  } while (tok != FINISHED);
}

/* Load a program. */
load_program(p, fname)
char *p;
char *fname;
{
  FILE *fp;
  int i=0;

  if(!(fp=fopen(fname, "rb"))) return 0;

  i = 0;
  do {
    *p = getc(fp);
    p++; i++;
  } while(!feof(fp) && i<PROG_SIZE);
  *(p-2) = '\0'; /* null terminate the program */
  fclose(fp);
  return 1;
}

/* Assign a variable a value. */
assignment()
{
  int var, value;

  /* get the variable name */
  get_token();
  if(!isalpha(*token)) {
    serror(4);
    return;
  }

  var = toupper(*token)-'A';

  /* get the equals sign */
  get_token();
  if(*token!='=') {
    serror(3);
    return;
  }

  /* get the value to assign to var */
  get_exp(&value);

  /* assign the value */
  variables[var] = value;
}

/* Execute a simple version of the BASIC PRINT statement */
void print()
{
  int answer;
  int len=0, spaces;
  char last_delim;

  do {
    get_token(); /* get next list item */
```

```
        if(tok==EOL || tok==FINISHED) break;
        if(token_type==QUOTE) { /* is string */
          printf(token);
          len += strlen(token);
          get_token();
        }
        else { /* is expression */
          putback();
          get_exp(&answer);
          get_token();
          len += printf("%d", answer);
        }
        last_delim = *token;

        if(*token==';') {
          /* compute number of spaces to move to next tab */
          spaces = 8 - (len % 8);
          len += spaces; /* add in the tabbing position */
          while(spaces) {
            printf(" ");
            spaces--;
          }
        }
        else if(*token==',') /* do nothing */;
        else if(tok!=EOL && tok!=FINISHED) serror(0);
      } while (*token==';' || *token==',');

      if(tok==EOL || tok==FINISHED) {
        if(last_delim != ';' && last_delim!=',') printf("\n");
      }
      else serror(0); /* error is not , or ; */
}

/* Find all labels. */
void scan_labels()
{
  int addr;
  char *temp;

  label_init(); /* zero all labels */
  temp = prog;   /* save pointer to top of program */

  /* if the first token in the file is a label */
  get_token();
  if(token_type==NUMBER) {
    strcpy(label_table[0].name,token);
    label_table[0].p=prog;
  }

  find_eol();
  do {
    get_token();
    if(token_type==NUMBER) {
      addr = get_next_label(token);
      if(addr==-1 || addr==-2) {
          (addr==-1) ?serror(5):serror(6);
      }
      strcpy(label_table[addr].name, token);
      label_table[addr].p = prog;  /* current point in program */
    }
    /* if not on a blank line, find next line */
    if(tok!=EOL) find_eol();
  } while(tok!=FINISHED);
  prog = temp;  /* restore to original */
}
```

```
/* Find the start of the next line. */
void find_eol()
{
  while(*prog!='\n'  && *prog!='\0') ++prog;
  if(*prog) prog++;
}


/* Return index of next free position in label array.
   A -1 is returned if the array is full.
   A -2 is returned when duplicate label is found.
*/
get_next_label(s)
char *s;
{
  register int t;

  for(t=0;t<NUM_LAB;++t) {
    if(label_table[t].name[0]==0) return t;
    if(!strcmp(label_table[t].name,s)) return -2; /* dup */

  }

  return -1;
}

/* Find location of given label.  A null is returned if
   label is not found; otherwise a pointer to the position
   of the label is returned.
*/
char *find_label(s)
char *s;
{
  register int t;

  for(t=0; t<NUM_LAB; ++t)
    if(!strcmp(label_table[t].name,s)) return label_table[t].p;
  return '\0'; /* error condition */
}


/* Execute a GOTO statement. */
void exec_goto()
{

  char *loc;

  get_token(); /* get label to go to */
  /* find the location of the label */
  loc = find_label(token);
  if(loc=='\0')
    serror(7); /* label not defined */

  else prog=loc;  /* start program running at that loc */
}


/* Initialize the array that holds the labels.
   By convention, a null label name indicates that
   array position is unused.
*/
void label_init()
{
  register int t;

  for(t=0; t<NUM_LAB; ++t) label_table[t].name[0]='\0';
}
```

```
/* Execute an IF statement. */
void exec_if()
{
  int x , y, cond;
  char op;

  get_exp(&x); /* get left expression */

  get_token(); /* get the operator */
  if(!strchr("=<>", *token)) {
     serror(0); /* not a legal operator */
     return;
  }
  op=*token;

  get_exp(&y); /* get right expression */

  /* determine the outcome */
  cond = 0;
  switch(op) {
     case '<':
       if(x<y) cond=1;
       break;
     case '>':
       if(x>y) cond=1;
       break;
     case '=':
       if(x==y) cond=1;
       break;
  }
  if(cond) { /* is true so process target of IF */
     get_token();
     if(tok!=THEN) {
        serror(8);
        return;
     }/* else program execution starts on next line */
  }
  else find_eol(); /* find start of next line */
}

/* Execute a FOR loop. */
void exec_for()
{
  struct for_stack i;
  int value;

  get_token(); /* read the control variable */
  if(!isalpha(*token)) {
     serror(4);
     return;
  }

  i.var=toupper(*token)-'A'; /* save its index */

  get_token(); /* read the equals sign */
  if(*token!='=') {
     serror(3);
     return;
  }

  get_exp(&value); /* get initial value */

  variables[i.var]=value;

  get_token();
```

```
    if(tok!=TO) serror(9); /* read and discard the TO */

    get_exp(&i.target); /* get target value */

    /* if loop can execute at least once, push info on stack */
    if(value>=variables[i.var]) {
      i.loc = prog;
      fpush(i);
    }
    else  /* otherwise, skip loop code altogether */
      while(tok!=NEXT) get_token();
}

/* Execute a NEXT statement. */
void next()
{
  struct for_stack i;

  i = fpop(); /* read the loop info */

  variables[i.var]++; /* increment control variable */
  if(variables[i.var]>i.target) return;  /* all done */
  fpush(i);  /* otherwise, restore the info */
  prog = i.loc;  /* loop */
}

/* Push function for the FOR stack. */
void fpush(i)
struct for_stack i;
{
   if(ftos>FOR_NEST)
    serror(10);

  fstack[ftos]=i;
  ftos++;
}

struct for_stack fpop()
{
  ftos--;
  if(ftos<0) serror(11);
  return(fstack[ftos]);
}

/* Execute a simple form of the BASIC INPUT command */
void input()
{
  char str[80], var;
  int i;

  get_token(); /* see if prompt string is present */
  if(token_type==QUOTE) {
    printf(token); /* if so, print it and check for comma */
    get_token();
    if(*token!=',') serror(1);
    get_token();
  }
  else printf("? "); /* otherwise, prompt with / */
  var = toupper(*token)-'A'; /* get the input var */

  scanf("%d", &i); /* read input */

  variables[var] = i; /* store it */
}
```

```c
/* Execute a GOSUB command. */
void gosub()
{
  char *loc;

  get_token();
  /* find the label to call */
  loc = find_label(token);
  if(loc=='\0')
    serror(7); /* label not defined */
  else {
    gpush(prog); /* save place to return to */
    prog = loc;  /* start program running at that loc */
  }
}

/* Return from GOSUB. */
void greturn()
{
   prog = gpop();
}

/* GOSUB stack push function. */
void gpush(s)
char *s;
{
  gtos++;

  if(gtos==SUB_NEST) {
    serror(12);
    return;
  }

  gstack[gtos]=s;

}

/* GOSUB stack pop function. */
char *gpop()
{
  if(gtos==0) {
    serror(13);
    return 0;
  }

   return(gstack[gtos--]);
}
```

Using Small BASIC

Here are some sample programs that Small BASIC will execute. Notice that both upper- and lowercase letters are supported.

```
PRINT "This program demostrates all commands."
FOR X = 1 TO 100
PRINT X, X/2; X, X*X
NEXT
GOSUB 300
PRINT "hello"
INPUT H
IF H<11 THEN GOTO 200
PRINT 12-4/2
PRINT 100
200 A = 100/2
IF A>10 THEN PRINT "this is ok"
PRINT A
PRINT A+34
INPUT H
PRINT H
INPUT "this is as test ",y
PRINT H+Y
END
300 PRINT "this is a subroutine"
    RETURN



PRINT "This program demonstrates nested GOSUBs."
INPUT "enter a number: ", I
GOSUB 100

END

100 FOR T = 1 TO I
  X = X + I
  GOSUB 150
NEXT
RETURN

150 PRINT X;
    RETURN




print "This program computes the volume of a cube."
input "Enter length of first side ", l
input "Enter length of second side ", w
input "Enter length of third side ", d
t = l * w * d
print "Volume is ",t




PRINT "This program demostrates nested FOR loops."
FOR X = 1 TO 100
  FOR Y = 1 TO 10
    PRINT X; Y; X*Y
  NEXT
NEXT
```

ENHANCING AND EXPANDING
THE INTERPRETER

The most important point about expanding or enhancing the interpreter is that you are not limited to the BASIC language. The same techniques described in this chapter will work on any procedural language. You can even invent your own language, which reflects your own programming style and personality.

To add commands, follow the general format taken by the ones presented in the chapter. To add different variable types you must use an array of structures to hold the variables; one field in the structure should indicate the type of the variable and the other field should hold the value. To add strings, you need to establish a string table. The easiest approach is to require fixed-length strings where each string is allocated 255 bytes of storage.

One final thought: The types of statements that you can interpret are bounded only by your imagination.

8: Of Screens
and Speakers

Throughout this book we have been exploring those aspects of C that add professional appeal to programs. Because the user's opinion of your program is often determined by the user interface, this chapter will take a final, close look at screen manipulation, with special emphasis on displaying text in different colors. In addition, some other screen-related topics are covered: how to change the size of the cursor, how to scroll part of the screen, and how to save what is on the screen to a disk file. Since the tasteful use of sound can dramatically enhance your work, the chapter concludes with a section on using the speaker to generate tones and special effects.

The routines in this chapter are hardware-dependent. They will work with IBM PCs, XTs, ATs, PS/2s, and compatibles. Some of the functions require that the computer support a color display. If you have a different computer, you will have to modify the functions.

USING COLOR IN TEXT MODE

It is rare to see a professionally written program that does not take full advantage of color. As you learned in Chapter 1, the PC family of computers supports a variety of video modes. If you have a color adapter, the default mode is 3, which specifies 80×25 color text. By default, the color of the text that appears on the screen is white, but it is possible to display text in other colors.

The Attribute Byte in Text Mode

Each character displayed on the screen is associated with an attribute byte that defines the way the character is displayed (see Chapter 1). When the computer is in video mode 3, the attribute byte that is associated with each character determines the color of the character, the background color, the intensity of the character, and whether it is blinking or nonblinking. The attribute byte is organized as shown in Table 8-1.

Bits 0, 1, and 2 of the attribute byte determine the foreground color component of the character associated with the attribute. For example, setting bit 0 causes the character to appear blue. If all bits are off, the character is not displayed. Keep in mind that the colors are additive. When all three bits are on, the character is displayed as white. If you set two of the bits, then either magenta or cyan is produced. The same conditions apply to the background colors. When bits 4 through 6 are off, the background is black; otherwise the background appears in the color specified.

In the early days of microcomputers, the default operation of the video system displayed characters in full intensity, and gave you the option of displaying in low intensity. When the IBM PC was released, it worked the opposite way: the default video operation of the PC line is in "normal" intensity, but you can display characters in high intensity by setting the high-intensity bit. In addition, you can cause a character to blink by setting the blinking bit.

Table 8-1.

The Attribute Byte Organization
in Video Mode 3

Bit	Meaning When Set
0	foreground blue
1	foreground green
2	foreground red
3	high intensity
4	background blue
5	background green
6	background red
7	blinking character

Previous chapters developed functions that wrote characters to the screen using both BIOS calls and direct video RAM access. Direct video RAM accessing was necessary in the context of pop-up or pull-down menus or windows for speed of execution. However, direct accessing of the video RAM reduces the portability of the code and can interfere with multitasking operating systems like the OS/2. The functions developed in this chapter use ROM-BIOS calls because the code is more portable, and extremely fast execution is not usually required for normal display output. However, feel free to use the direct video RAM routines if you prefer.

Writing a String in Color

Writing a string in color is not quite as simple as you might think because of the way the ROM-BIOS write-character function operates. The ROM-BIOS interrupt 10H, function 9 writes one character and its attribute to the current cursor location. The problem is that it does not advance the cursor location; this must be done by your routine. In order to accomplish this, it is first necessary to determine the current cursor position. The function **read_cursor_xy( )**, shown here, uses ROM-BIOS interrupt 10H, function 3 to read the cursor's current X, Y position. This position is returned in the arguments to the function.

```
/* Read the current cursor position. */
void read_cursor_xy(x, y)
char *x, *y;
{
  union REGS r;

  r.h.ah = 3; /* read cursor position */
  r.h.bh = 0; /* video page */
  int86(0x10, &r, &r);
  *y = r.h.dl;
  *x = r.h.dh;
}
```

Once the position of the cursor is known, the function that prints a string must manually advance the cursor with each character written using the **goto_xy( )** routine developed earlier and repeated here for your convenience.

```
/* Send the cursor to the specified X,Y position. */
void goto_xy(x, y)
int x, y;
{
  union REGS r;

  r.h.ah = 2; /* cursor addressing function */
  r.h.dl = x; /* column coordinate */
  r.h.dh = y; /* row coordinate */
  r.h.bh = 0; /* video page */
  int86(0x10, &r, &r);
}
```

The function **color_puts( )**, shown here, displays the specified string in the specified color.

```
/* Print a string in color. */
void color_puts(s, color)
char *s; /* string */
char color; /* color of string */
{
  union REGS r;
  char x, y;
```

```
read_cursor_xy(&x, &y); /* get current cursor position
while(*s) {
if(*s=='\n') { /* process a newline */
  printf("\n");
  s++;
  x = 0; y++; /* advance to next line */
  continue;
}

r.h.ah = 9; /* write character and attribute */
r.h.al = *s++; /* character to write */
r.h.bl = color; /* color attribute */
r.h.bh = 0; /* video page 0 */
r.x.cx = 1; /* write it one time */
int86(0x10, &r, &r);
x++;
goto_xy(x, y); /* advance the cursor */
  }
}
```

As you can see, the character is placed in AL, the color attribute in BL, the video page in BH, and the number of times to write the character in CX. Notice that the function properly processes a newline character. You might also want it to process tabs, double quotes, and other special characters.

To use the **color—puts( )** function, define the macros shown here at the top of your program.

```
#define BLUE        1
#define GREEN       2
#define RED         4
#define INTENSE     8
#define BLUE_BACK   16
#define GREEN_BACK  32
#define RED_BACK    64
#define BLINK       128
```

Using these macros, you can print a string with any foreground or background color that you desire. You can also control whether the string blinks or is in high intensity. To combine colors, blinking, or high intensity, simply OR together the characteristics that you want to appear. For example, the following code prints the string "this is a test" in high intensity cyan:

```
color_puts("this is a test", GREEN | RED | INTENSE);
```

Using Color

The effective use of multicolored text is more art than science, but a few general suggestions can be offered.

- Do not over use color. It is generally best to use the standard white characters on black background for most of the screen, relying on different colored text to highlight a relatively few bits of important information.

- A colored border around a screen or window can be a very effective use of color.

- In some situations it is helpful to display negative dollar amounts in red.

- Displaying the active line (or partial line) in a different color can be an excellent way to indicate the user's current position on the screen.

CHANGING THE SIZE OF THE CURSOR

Many users aren't aware that the IBM PC and derivatives allow you to change the size of the cursor. In its default size, the cursor appears as one short blinking line, but you can vary the size of the cursor from one scan line to the full height of a character. In color text modes, the cursor can be from 0 to 8 scan lines tall. (In monochrome, the cursor can be from 0 to 14 scan lines, but here we are concerned only with color modes.) The lowest scan line is number 0. It is best to build from scan line 0 upward because the results of using another method differ widely among computers. (It's all right to try other methods, but remember that the cursor may not look the same from one machine to another.) Should you build upward from scan line 0, the cursor might look like those shown in Figure 8-1.

To set the size of the cursor, you will need to use the ROM-BIOS interrupt 10H, function 1, which sets the cursor size. Place the starting scan line of the cursor in CH and the ending scan line in CL. The

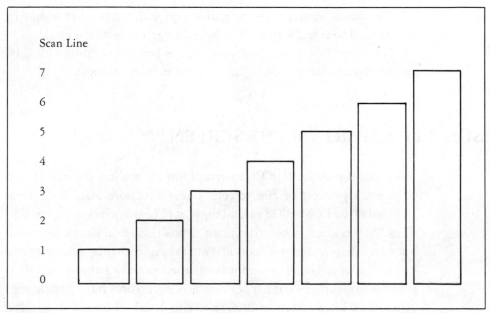

Scan Line

Figure 8-1.

The possible shapes for the cursor
in color mode

function **size—cursor**( ), shown here, sets the size of the cursor.

```
/* Set the size of the cursor */
void size_cursor(start, end)
char start, end; /* starting and ending scan lines */
{
  union REGS r;

  r.h.ah = 1; /* cursor addressing function */
  r.h.ch = start;
  r.h.cl = end;
  int86(0x10, &r, &r);
}
```

To use **size—cursor**( ), call the function with the beginning and
ending scan lines of the cursor size you want. For example, the following
constructs a cursor three scan lines tall:

```
size_cursor(0,2);
```

The cursor remains the specified size until it is reset either by another call to **size—cursor( )** or by a change in the video mode.

The use of different cursors can give any program a custom look. Be careful though; large blinking cursors can be very annoying.

SCROLLING PART OF THE SCREEN

Two seldom-used ROM-BIOS interrupt functions allow you to scroll up or down a portion of the screen. These functions may have been included in the ROM-BIOS to lend support to future windowing applications. As you know, when the cursor is positioned on the twenty-fifth line of the display and you press ENTER, the entire display scrolls up one line and a new, blank line appears at the bottom of the screen. It is possible to make this same type of scroll occur on only part of the screen using ROM-BIOS interrupt 10H, functions 6 and 7. Function 6 scrolls a window up; function 7 scrolls it down.

Both functions are called using the register assignments that follow. Put the number of lines to scroll in the AL register. Put the upper-left row number in CH, the upper-left column number in CL. Put the lower-left row number into DH, and the lower-right column number into DL. Finally, put the display attribute, which determines how the scrolled-in blank lines appear, into BH. The **scroll—window( )** function is shown here.

```
/* Scroll a window up or down. */
void scroll_window(startx, starty, endx, endy, lines, direct)
char startx, starty; /* upper left corner */
char endx, endy; /* lower right corner */
char lines; /* number of lines to scroll */
char direct; /* up or down */
{
  union REGS r;

  if(direct==UP) r.h.ah = 6; /* scroll up */
  else r.h.ah = 7; /* scroll down */

  r.h.al = lines;
  r.h.ch = starty;
  r.h.cl = startx;
```

```
   r.h.dh = endy;
   r.h.dl = endx;
   r.h.bh = 0; /* display attribute */
   int86(0x10, &r, &r);
}
```

You can define the macro UP as having any value. You should also define another macro called DOWN that has a different value than UP and use it to call **scroll__window( )** when you want to scroll a window down. The **scroll__window( )** function assigns the attribute 0 to BH to insure a blank line, but you can change this if you wish.

A SIMPLE DEMONSTRATION PROGRAM

The program shown here demonstrates the functions developed so far in this chapter: changing the size of the cursor; outputting a message in color; and scrolling a portion of the screen. . Its output is shown in Figure 8-2.

```
/* Demonstration program for printing text in color,
   sizing the cursor, and scrolling a window.
*/
#include "dos.h"

#define BLUE        1
#define GREEN       2
#define RED         4
#define INTENSE     8
#define BLUE_BACK   16
#define GREEN_BACK  32
#define RED_BACK    64
#define BLINK       128

#define UP    0
#define DOWN  1

void mode(), color_puts(), palette(), read_cursor_xy();
void goto_xy(), size_cursor(), scroll_window();

main()
{
  int i, j;

  mode(3); /* color text */

  size_cursor(0, 3);
  goto_xy(0, 0);
  color_puts("this is a test\n", BLUE | RED | INTENSE);
```

a)

```
this is a test
aaaaaaaaaaaaaaaaaaaaaaaaaaaaaaaaaaaaaaaaaaaaaaaaaaaaaaaaaaaaaaaaaaaaaaaaaaaaaaaaa
bbbbbbbbbbbbbbbbbbbbbbbbbbbbbbbbbbbbbbbbbbbbbbbbbbbbbbbbbbbbbbbbbbbbbbbbbbbbbbbbbb
cccccccccccccccccccccccccccccccccccccccccccccccccccccccccccccccccccccccccccccccccc
dddddddddddddddddddddddddddddddddddddddddddddddddddddddddddddddddddddddddddddddddd
eeeeeeeeeeeeeeeeeeeeeeeeeeeeeeeeeeeeeeeeeeeeeeeeeeeeeeeeeeeeeeeeeeeeeeeeeeeeeeeeeee
fffffffffffffffffffffffffffffffffffffffffffffffffffffffffffffffffffffffffffffff,f
gggggggggggggggggggggggggggggggggggggggggggggggggggggggggggggggggggggggggggggggggg
hhhhhhhhhhhhhhhhhhhhhhhhhhhhhhhhhhhhhhhhhhhhhhhhhhhhhhhhhhhhhhhhhhhhhhhhhhhhhhhhhh
iiiiiiiiiiiiiiiiiiiiiiiiiiiiiiiiiiiiiiiiiiiiiiiiiiiiiiiiiiiiiiiiiiiiiiiiiiiiiiiiii
jjjjjjjjjjjjjjjjjjjjjjjjjjjjjjjjjjjjjjjjjjjjjjjjjjjjjjjjjjjjjjjjjjjjjjjjjjjjjjjjjjj
kkkkkkkkkkkkkkkkkkkkkkkkkkkkkkkkkkkkkkkkkkkkkkkkkkkkkkkkkkkkkkkkkkkkkkkkkkkkkkkkkkk
lllllllllllllllllllllllllllllllllllllllllllllllllllllllllllllllllllllllllllllll11
mmmmmmmmmmmmmmmmmmmmmmmmmmmmmmmmmmmmmmmmmmmmmmmmmmmmmmmmmmmmmmmmmmmmmmmmmmmmmmmmmmm
nnnnnnnnnnnnnnnnnnnnnnnnnnnnnnnnnnnnnnnnnnnnnnnnnnnnnnnnnnnnnnnnnnnnnnnnnnnnnnnnnn
oooooooooooooooooooooooooooooooooooooooooooooooooooooooooooooooooooooooooooooooooo
pppppppppppppppppppppppppppppppppppppppppppppppppppppppppppppppppppppppppppppppppp
qqqqqqqqqqqqqqqqqqqqqqqqqqqqqqqqqqqqqqqqqqqqqqqqqqqqqqqqqqqqqqqqqqqqqqqqqqqqqqqqqqq
rrrrrrrrrrrrrrrrrrrrrrrrrrrrrrrrrrrrrrrrrrrrrrrrrrrrrrrrrrrrrrrrrrrrrrrrrrrrrrrrrrr
sssssssssssssssssssssssssssssssssssssssssssssssssssssssssssssssssssssssssssssssssss
ttttttttttttttttttttttttttttttttttttttttttttttttttttttttttttttttttttttttttttttttt
uuuuuuuuuuuuuuuuuuuuuuuuuuuuuuuuuuuuuuuuuuuuuuuuuuuuuuuuuuuuuuuuuuuuuuuuuuuuuuuuuuu
vvvvvvvvvvvvvvvvvvvvvvvvvvvvvvvvvvvvvvvvvvvvvvvvvvvvvvvvvvvvvvvvvvvvvvvvvvvvvvvvvvvv
```

b)

```
this is a test
aaaaaaaaaaaaaaaaaaaaaaaaaaaaaaaaaaaaaaaaaaaaaaaaaaaaaaaaaaaaaaaaaaaaaaaaaaaaaaaaa
bbbbbbbbbbbbbbbbbbbbbbbbbbbbbbbbbbbbbbbbbbbbbbbbbbbbbbbbbbbbbbbbbbbbbbbbbbbbbbbbbb
cccccccccccccccccccccccccccccccccccccccccccccccccccccccccccccccccccccccccccccccccc
dddddddddddddddddddddddddddddddddddddddddddddddddddddddddddddddddddddddddddddddddd
eeeeeeeeeeeeeeeeeeeeeeeeeeeeeeeeeeeeeeeeeeeeeeeeeeeeeeeeeeeeeeeeeeeeeeeeeeeeeeeeeee
fffffffffffffffffffffffffffffffffffffffffffffffffffffffffffffffffffffffffffffffff
gggggggggggggggggggggggggggggggggggggggggggggggggggggggggggggggggggggggggggggggggg
hhhhhhhhhhhhhhhhhhhhhhhhhhhhhhhhhhhhhhhhhhhhhhhhhhhhhhhhhhhhhhhhhhhhhhhhhhhhhhhhhh
iiiiiiiiiiiiiiiiiiiiiiiiiiiiiiiiiiiiiiiiiiiiiiiiiiiiiiiiiiiiiiiiiiiiiiiiiiiiiiiiii
jjjjjjjjjjj                                  jjjjjjjjjjjjjjjjjjjjjjjjjjjjjjjj
kkkkkkkkkkk                                  kkkkkkkkkkkkkkkkkkkkkkkkkkkkkkkk
lllllllllll                                  lllllllllllllllllllllllllllllll
mmmmmmmmmmmjjjjjjjjjjjjjjjjjjjjjjjjjjjjjjjjjjjjjjjjjjjjjjjjjjjjmmmmmmmmmmmmmmmmmmmm
nnnnnnnnnnnkkkkkkkkkkkkkkkkkkkkkkkkkkkkkkkkkkkkkkkkkkkkkkkknnnnnnnnnnnnnnnnnnnnnnnn
ooooooooooollllllllllllllllllllllllllllllllllllllllllllllllllooooooooooooooooooooo
pppppppppppppppppppppppppppppppppppppppppppppppppppppppppppppppppppppppppppppppppp
qqqqqqqqqqqqqqqqqqqqqqqqqqqqqqqqqqqqqqqqqqqqqqqqqqqqqqqqqqqqqqqqqqqqqqqqqqqqqqqqqqq
rrrrrrrrrrrrrrrrrrrrrrrrrrrrrrrrrrrrrrrrrrrrrrrrrrrrrrrrrrrrrrrrrrrrrrrrrrrrrrrrrrr
ssssssssssssssssssssssssssssssssssssssssssssssssssssssssssssssssssssssssssssssssss
ttttttttttttttttttttttttttttttttttttttttttttttttttttttttttttttttttttttttttttttttt
uuuuuuuuuuuuuuuuuuuuuuuuuuuuuuuuuuuuuuuuuuuuuuuuuuuuuuuuuuuuuuuuuuuuuuuuuuuuuuuuuuu
vvvvvvvvvvvvvvvvvvvvvvvvvvvvvvvvvvvvvvvvvvvvvvvvvvvvvvvvvvvvvvvvvvvvvvvvvvvvvvvvvvvv
```

Figure 8-2.

Output from the screen
demonstration program

```
    for(i=0; i<22; i++ ) {
      for(j=0; j<79; j++)
        printf("%c", i+'a');
      printf("\n");
    }
    getche();
    scroll_window(10, 10, 50, 15, 3, DOWN);
    getche();
}

/* Print a string in color. */
void color_puts(s, color)
char *s; /* string */
char color; /* color of string */
{
  union REGS r;
  char x, y;

  read_cursor_xy(&x, &y); /* get current cursor position */
  while(*s) {
    if(*s=='\n') { /* process a newline */
      printf("\n");
      s++;
      x = 0; y++; /* advance to next line */
      continue;
    }

    r.h.ah = 9; /* write character and attribute */
    r.h.al = *s++; /* character to write */
    r.h.bl = color; /* color attribute */
    r.h.bh = 0; /* video page 0 */
    r.x.cx = 1; /* write it one time */
    int86(0x10, &r, &r);
    x++;
    goto_xy(x, y); /* advance the cursor */
  }
}

/* Read the current cursor position. */
void read_cursor_xy(x, y)
char *x, *y;
{
  union REGS r;

  r.h.ah = 3; /* read cursor position */
  r.h.bh = 0; /* video page */
  int86(0x10, &r, &r);
  *y = r.h.dl;
  *x = r.h.dh;
}

/* Set the palette. */
void palette(pnum)
int pnum;
{
  union REGS r;

  r.h.bh = 1;    /* code for mode 4 graphics */
  r.h.bl = pnum;
  r.h.ah = 11;   /* set palette function */
  int86(0x10, &r, &r);
}
```

```
/* Set the video mode. */
void mode(mode_code)
int mode_code;
{
  union REGS r;

  r.h.al = mode_code;
  r.h.ah = 0;
  int86(0x10, &r, &r);
}

/* Send the cursor to the specified X,Y position. */
void goto_xy(x, y)
int x, y;
{
  union REGS r;

  r.h.ah = 2; /* cursor addressing function */
  r.h.dl = x; /* column coordinate */
  r.h.dh = y; /* row coordinate */
  r.h.bh = 0; /* video page */
  int86(0x10, &r, &r);
}


/* Set the size of the cursor */
void size_cursor(start, end)
char start, end; /* starting and ending scan lines */
{
  union REGS r;

  r.h.ah = 1; /* cursor addressing function */
  r.h.ch = start;
  r.h.cl = end;
  int86(0x10, &r, &r);
}

/* Scroll a window up or down. */
void scroll_window(startx, starty, endx, endy, lines, direct)
char startx, starty; /* upper left corner */
char endx, endy; /* lower right corner */
char lines; /* number of lines to scroll */
char direct; /* up or down */
{
  union REGS r;

  if(direct==UP) r.h.ah = 6; /* scroll up */
  else r.h.ah = 7; /* scroll down */

  r.h.al = lines;
  r.h.ch = starty;
  r.h.cl = startx;
  r.h.dh = endy;
  r.h.dl = endx;
  r.h.bh = 0; /* display attribute */
  int86(0x10, &r, &r);
}
```

SAVING THE SCREEN TO A DISK FILE

Neither DOS nor OS/2 provides a utility similar to the print screen command, which saves the current contents of the screen to a disk file. In this section, you'll find out how to create a program that performs this function.

The program works by using ROM-BIOS interrupt 10H, function 8 to read the character at the current cursor position. This character is then written to the file. Once again, the function **goto_xy( )** is used to move the cursor around on the screen, beginning with the upper-left corner and stopping at the lower-right corner.

Here, the file name is specified as an argument to the program. Assuming that the program is called **screen**, this line evokes the program and saves the screen in a file called **scr.sav**:

```
C>screen scr.sav
```

This is the **screen** program:

```
/* This program saves what is currently on the video
   display to the disk file specified on the command line.
*/

#include "dos.h"
#include "stdio.h"

void save_screen(), goto_xy();

main(argc, argv)
int argc;
char *argv[];
{
  if(argc!=2) {
    printf("usage: screen <filename>");
    exit(1);
  }
  save_screen(argv[1]);
}

/* Save the contents of the screen to a disk file. */
void save_screen(fname)
char *fname;
```

```
{
  FILE *fp;
  union REGS r;
  register char x, y;

  if(!(fp=fopen(fname, "w"))) {
    printf("cannot open file");
    exit(1);
  }

  for(y=0; y<25; y++)
    for(x=0; x<80; x++) {
      goto_xy(x, y);
      r.h.ah = 8; /* read a character */
      r.h.bh = 0; /* video page */
      int86(0x10, &r, &r);
      putc(r.h.al, fp); /* write the character */
    }
  fclose(fp);
}

/* Send the cursor to the specified X,Y position. */
void goto_xy(x, y)
int x, y;
{
  union REGS r;

  r.h.ah = 2; /* cursor addressing function */
  r.h.dl = x; /* column coordinate */
  r.h.dh = y; /* row coordinate */
  r.h.bh = 0; /* video page */
  int86(0x10, &r, &r);
}
```

The file created is a standard ASCII file, which can be edited or printed like any standard text file. As the program stands, only the characters on the screen are saved, not the attribute associated with each character. However, this addition is easy to make and you might want to try it on your own.

ADDING SOUND

Tastefully applied, sound greatly enhances a program's appeal. Sound can range from a subtle "beep" to music or special effects. In this section, you will learn how to control the pitch and duration of a note produced by your computer's speaker. You will also hear demonstrations of some interesting sound effects.

The 8253 Programmable Timer

Sound is generated on a PC using the 8253 programmable timer, which is used to pulse the speaker on and off at a frequency determined by the contents of various internal registers. These registers are set by writing to certain ports. Port 66 is used to specify a count that the timer uses as an interval between speaker pulses. The timer operates by counting system clock pulses up to the specified count, pulsing the speaker, resetting, and counting again. The value of the count is determined by the formula

count = 1,193,180/desired frequency

where 1,193,180 is the speed at which the system clock oscillates.

The 8253 count register is set using the following sequence:

1. Output to port 67 the value 182 (notice to receive count)

2. Output to port 66 the low-order byte of the integer that contains the count

3. Output to port 66 the high-order byte of the integer that contains the count

The speaker in most PCs is not designed to reproduce the full range of human hearing (20Hz to 18,000 Hz). Instead, it plays some notes better than others and "tops out" at around 12,000 Hz. The speaker's most useful range is between 100 and 5000 Hz.

Although the timer is set, the speaker does not sound because it has not been turned on. The 8253 counts continuously, but the speaker only responds when it is turned on.

Turning on the speaker requires setting bits 0 and 1 of a register in a programmable peripheral interface circuit accessed through port 97.

When these two bits are on, the speaker sounds at the frequency specified by count in the 8253. When the bits are zero, no sound is heard. The other bits in the byte are used by other devices and must be left unaltered. Therefore, to set the speaker bits, the following sequence must be followed:

1. Input the current value at port 97

2. OR that value with 3

3. Output the result to port 97

To turn off the speaker, AND the current value with 253.

The easiest way to read and write a port in C is to use functions that read and write a byte to or from a port. In Turbo C, these functions are called **inportb( )** and **outportb( )**. In Microsoft C, they are called **inp( )** and **outp( )**. They take the following general forms:

```
int inportb(int port);
void outportb(int port, char value);
int inp(unsigned port);
int outp(unsigned port, int value);
```

These functions may not have the same name in every C compiler, but you will almost certainly have similar functions in your library. The code in the remainder of this chapter uses the Turbo C functions.

A Simple Hearing Tester

You can construct a crude but effective hearing tester that may disclose certain types of hearing loss. As mentioned earlier, the speaker in the average PC has an upper limit of about 12,000 Hz. However, a person with acute hearing loss cannot hear frequencies that high. In fact, when you try the tester, you might be surprised at how high-pitched 12,000 Hz is. (*Caution:* This hearing tester is provided only for fun. It is, by no means, an accurate hearing test. If you suspect that you suffer hearing loss, see your doctor.)

The heart of the hearing tester is the function **sound( )**, which generates a specified note of short duration. As it is presented here, this function also shows all the code necessary to produce sound on the speaker.

```
/* Beep the speaker using the specified frequency. */
void sound(freq)
int freq;
{
  unsigned i;
  union {
    long divisor;
    unsigned char c[2];
  } count;

  unsigned char p;

  count.divisor = 1193280 / freq;  /* compute the proper count */
  outportb(67, 182); /* tell 8253 that a count is coming */
  outportb(66, count.c[0]); /* send low-order byte */
  outportb(66, count.c[1]); /* send high-order byte */
  p = inportb(97); /* get existing bit pattern */
  outportb(97, p | 3); /* turn on bits 0 and 1 */

  for(i=0; i<64000; ++i) ; /* delay loop */

  outportb(97, p); /* restore original bits to turn off speaker */
}
```

Notice that the frequency of the note to be reproduced is specified as an argument. The delay loop is necessary; without it you would, at most, hear only a click. You can change the delay to suit the clock rate of the processor in your computer. You could even specify it as a parameter. The **sound( )** function can also be used to supply a custom beep.

The **main( )** function to the hearing tester program is shown here.

```
/* A simple hearing tester. */
#include "dos.h"

void sound();

main()
{
  int freq;

  do {
    printf("enter frequency (0 to exit): ");
    scanf("%d", &freq);
    if(freq) sound(freq);
  } while(freq);
}
```

To use the tester, simply specify increasingly higher pitches until you cannot hear them any more. To exit, enter a value of 0.

Creating a Siren and a "Laser Blast"

You can use the speaker to create sound effects, such as those that might add interest to a video game. The key to most sound effects is to vary the frequency of the sound—often in some unusual way.

For example, to create a siren effect, you vary the frequency of the sound between two end points. The pitch should ascend from low to high, and then descend back to the low pitch. The function **siren( )**, shown here, uses this method to produce a siren-like effect.

```c
#define DELAY 10000

/* Create a siren effect. */
void siren()
{
  unsigned i, freq;
  union {
    long divisor;
    unsigned char c[2];
  } count;

  unsigned char p;

  p = inportb(97); /* get existing bit pattern */
  outportb(97, p | 3); /* turn on bits 0 and 1 */
  /* ascending siren */
  for(freq=1000; freq<3000; freq+=RATE) {
    count.divisor = 1193280 / freq;  /* compute the proper count */
    outportb(67, 182); /* tell 8253 that a count is coming */
    outportb(66, count.c[0]); /* send low-order byte */
    outportb(66, count.c[1]); /* send high-order byte */

    for(i=0; i<DELAY; ++i) ;
  }

  /* descending siren */
  for( ; freq>1000; freq-=RATE) {
    count.divisor = 1193280 / freq;  /* compute the proper count */
    outportb(67, 182); /* tell 8253 that a count is coming */
    outportb(66, count.c[0]); /* send low-order byte */
    outportb(66, count.c[1]); /* send high-order byte */

    for(i=0; i<DELAY; ++i) ;
  }
  outportb(97, p); /* restore original bits to turn off speaker */
}
```

You should define the macro DELAY to match the speed of your system and your personal preference. As shown, **siren( )** produces one full cycle and then returns. To create a continous cycle, simply place the call to **siren( )** in a loop.

To produce the "laser blast" sound effect used by many video games, modify **siren( )** so that only a descending sound is heard. The function **laser( )**, shown here, produces this effect.

```
#define DELAY 10000

/* Create a laser blast effect. */
void siren()
{
  unsigned i, freq;
  union {
    long divisor;
    unsigned char c[2];
  } count;
  unsigned char p;

  p = inportb(97); /* get existing bit pattern */
  outportb(97, p | 3); /* turn on bits 0 and 1 */
  /* laser blast */
  for( ; freq>1000; freq-=RATE) {
    count.divisor = 1193280 / freq;  /* compute the proper count */
    outportb(67, 182); /* tell 8253 that count is coming */
    outportb(66, count.c[0]); /* send low-order byte */
    outportb(66, count.c[1]); /* send high-order byte */

    for(i=0; i<DELAY; ++i) ;
  }
  outportb(97, p); /* restore original bits to turn off speaker */
}
```

With a little ingenuity and experimentation, you can produce a wide range of sound effects. One thing interesting to try is varying the rate of change as an effect is produced.

Making Celestial Music

By connecting the standard C random number function **rand( )** to the **sound( )** function, you can create "celestial music." The sounds produced by the program shown here are reminiscent of "space music" used in old science fiction movies. Although all the tones are generated at random, bits and pieces of melodies emerge from time to time in a most haunting fashion.

```c
/* Celestial Music of the Cosmic Spheres. */

#define DELAY 64000

#include "dos.h"

void sound();

main()
{
  int freq;

  do {
    do {
      freq = rand();
    } while(freq>5000); /* alter to your personal taste */
    sound(freq);
  } while(!kbhit());
}

/* Beep the speaker using the specified frequency. */
void sound(freq)
int freq;
{
  unsigned i;
  union {
    long divisor;
    unsigned char c[2];
  } count;

  unsigned char p;
  count.divisor = 1193280 / freq;  /* compute the proper count */
  outportb(67, 182); /* tell 8253 that count is coming */
  outportb(66, count.c[0]); /* send low-order byte */
  outportb(66, count.c[1]); /* send high-order byte */
  p = inportb(97); /* get existing bit pattern */
  outportb(97, p | 3); /* turn on bits 0 and 1 */

  for(i=0; i<DELAY; ++i) ; /* delay 64000 for 10+ mhz computers
                              32000 for 6 mhz ATs
                              20000 for standard PCs and XTs */

  outportb(97, p); /* restore original bits to turn off speaker */
}
```

The program uses frequencies less than 5000 because higher frequencies are either very soft or are outside the average hearing range.

You might experiment with this program by allowing a random length of time between notes or filtering the values actually sent to **sound( )** in different ways.

9: Interfacing to the Mouse

After the keyboard, the most popular input device for microcomputers is the mouse. Although the mouse and similar technologies, such as the roller ball, have been available for some time, the mouse became popular with the advent of the Apple Lisa, which came with a mouse and an icon interface to its operating system. The Lisa eventually evolved into the Macintosh, which kept the mouse and icon interface. Prior to the advent of the IBM PS/2 line of computers, the mouse had been a third-party add-on to the PC. However, with the introduction of the IBM PS/2 system, which offers a mouse port and mouse, the mouse is certain to find an important place in the PC environment.

The best way to use a mouse is a topic that usually stimulates considerable debate. Not all programmers (or users) like an icon user interface. Because the mouse was first used with an icon-based interface, the mouse became associated with it—a negative association to some people. However, the mouse can be used in many ways. For example, almost everyone agrees that the mouse is particularly useful for interactive graphics.

Several types and brands of mice are available, and some function differently from others. The routines in this chapter use the Microsoft two-button mouse, which is functionally identical to the IBM PS/2 mouse. In order to interface to the Microsoft Mouse you must have the *Microsoft Mouse Programmer's Reference Guide* and companion disk. The disk contains a special library called MOUSE.LIB, which provides the low-level support functions for the mouse. We use these functions as a basis for the mouse routines developed in this chapter. Keep in mind that your compiler must be capable of linking library routines from a Microsoft-compatible library, and that you must also have the device driver MOUSE.SYS.

After covering the basics of mouse interfacing, this chapter expands the "paint" program developed earlier so that it will work with the mouse (though the mouse concepts and routines developed will generally apply to any mouse application).

SOME MOUSE BASICS

Before the mouse can be used its device driver must be installed. For the Microsoft Mouse, the line of code shown here must be placed in the CONFIG.SYS file.

```
device=mouse.sys
```

To install the IBM mouse driver, the program MOUSE.COM is executed. For this mouse, place the line shown here in the AUTO-EXEC.BAT file.

```
mouse
```

Once the mouse driver is in place, whenever you move the mouse or press a button an interrupt 33H is generated. The mouse driver processes the interrupt, setting the appropriate internal variables and returns. Because an interrupt is generated only when the mouse changes state, an idle mouse has no effect on the performance of the computer.

Just as a cursor is associated with the keyboard, a cursor (sometimes called a *pointer*) is associated with the mouse. The routines in the Microsoft Mouse library define a default cursor shape: an arrow in the graphics modes and a solid block in the text modes. The cursor shows the current mouse position on the screen. Like the keyboard cursor, the mouse cursor can be turned on or off. Generally, it is only on when the mouse is actually in use. Otherwise, it is off so that it does not interfere with the application.

Although physically separate, the mouse can be thought of as being linked to the screen because the mouse driver automatically maintains counters that indicate where the mouse cursor is currently located. As you move the mouse, the cursor automatically moves across the screen in the same direction as the mouse.

The distance traveled by the mouse is measured (believe it or not) in "mickeys." One mickey equals 1/200 of an inch. For the most part, however, you will not need to know the actual distance moved by the mouse.

THE VIRTUAL VERSUS THE ACTUAL SCREEN

The Microsoft Mouse library routines operate on a *virtual screen* with pixel dimensions that may be different from the actual physical screen. As the mouse is moved, the cursor location counters are updated. When the cursor is displayed on the screen, the virtual cursor coordinates are mapped onto the actual screen coordinates. In video modes 6, 14, 15, and 16, this is a one-to-one mapping. In modes 4 and 5 only every other point of the virtual horizontal position is mapped to the actual screen. You must keep this fact in mind because the paint program to which the mouse interface will be added uses mode 4 graphics.

MOUSE LIBRARY FUNCTIONS

The routines inside MOUSE.LIB are accessed through a single function using the number of the specific mouse function you wish to call. (This process is somewhat similar to the way you access DOS functions through interrupt 21H using the number of the specific function desired.) The actual name of this mouse function varies depending on the memory model with which you are compiling. Use **cmouses( )** for the small model, **cmousec( )** for the compact model, **cmousem( )** for the medium model, and **cmousel( )** for both the large and huge models. (There is no support for the tiny memory model.) The examples in this chapter use the small model, but you can change that if you like.

The general form of the **cmouses( )** function is

```
void cmouses(fnum, arg2, arg3, arg4);
int *fnum, *arg2, *arg3, *arg4;
```

As indicated, *fnum* is the number of the mouse function you want to call. The other parameters contain whatever information is required by the specific function. Notice that pointers to the arguments are passed—not the actual arguments themselves. The **cmouses( )** function returns results in the parameters and therefore needs the addresses.

Microsoft defines thirty mouse functions, but we only need a few for the paint program. A brief discussion of these functions follows.

Reset and Status

Function 0 resets the mouse. It places the mouse in the center of the screen with the cursor turned off. It returns the number of buttons the mouse has in *arg2*. Upon return, *fnum* will be 0 if the mouse and software are not installed and −1 if they are.

Display Cursor

Function 1 displays the mouse cursor. There are no return values.

Remove Cursor

Function 2 removes the cursor from the screen. There are no return values.

Read Button Status
and Cursor Position

Function 3 returns the status of the buttons in *arg2*. The virtual horizontal cursor position is in *arg3*, and the virtual vertical cursor position is in *arg4*.

The status of the buttons is encoded in *arg2* in bits 0 and 1. When bit 0 is set, the left button is being pressed; when bit 1 is set, the right button is being pressed. When a bit is off, its associated button is not being pressed.

Set Cursor Location

Function 4 sets the mouse cursor location. The value of *arg3* determines the horizontal position, and the value of *arg4* sets the vertical position. You must make sure that only valid values within the range of the virtual screen are used.

Motion Indication

Function 11 returns the vertical and horizontal mickey count since the last call to function 11, that is, the vertical and horizontal distances moved. It also resets its internal counting registers to 0. The vertical count is returned in *arg3* and the horizontal count in *arg4*. This means that if the mouse has not been moved since the last call, both the horizontal and vertical counts will be 0. If either count (or both counts) is any value other than 0, the mouse has moved.

A positive vertical mickey count means that the mouse has moved downward. A negative count indicates that the mouse has moved upward. A positive horizontal count means that the mouse moved to the right. A negative count indicates that the mouse moved to the left.

HIGH-LEVEL MOUSE FUNCTIONS

Using the **cmouses( )** function, you can construct a set of high-level C routines that make programming for the mouse much easier. Let's look at these now.

Resetting the Mouse

The function shown here, **mouse_reset( )**, is used to reset the mouse. Notice it confirms that the proper hardware and software are present and that a two-button mouse is installed.

```
/* Reset the mouse. */
void mouse_reset()
{
  int fnum, arg2, arg3, arg4;

  fnum = 0; /* reset the mouse */
  cmouses(&fnum, &arg2, &arg3, &arg4);
  if(fnum!=-1) {
    printf("mouse hardware or software not installed");
    exit(1);
  }
  if(arg2!=2) {
   printf("two-button mouse required");
   exit(1);
  }
}
```

Displaying and Removing
the Mouse Cursor

The companion functions **cursor_on( )** and **cursor_off( )**, shown here, are used to activate and deactivate the visual mouse cursor.

```
/* Turn on the mouse cursor. */
void cursor_on()
{
  int fnum;

  fnum = 1; /* show the cursor */
  cmouses(&fnum, &fnum, &fnum, &fnum);
}

/* Turn off the mouse cursor. */
void cursor_off()
{
  int fnum;

  fnum = 2; /* erase the cursor */
  cmouses(&fnum, &fnum, &fnum, &fnum);
}
```

Determining if a Button Is Pressed

Another pair of companion functions, **rightb_pressed( )** and **leftb_pressed( )**, shown here, return "True" if the right button or left button is pressed.

```
/* Return true if right button is pressed;
   false otherwise. */
rightb_pressed()
{
  int fnum, arg2, arg3, arg4;

  fnum = 3; /* get position and button status */
  cmouses(&fnum, &arg2, &arg3, &arg4);
  return arg2 & 2;
}

/* Return true if left button is pressed;
   false otherwise. */
leftb_pressed()
{
  int fnum, arg2, arg3, arg4;

  fnum = 3; /* get position and button status */
  cmouses(&fnum, &arg2, &arg3, &arg4);
  return arg2 & 1;
}
```

Detecting Motion

Function 11, which returns the change in the mickey count since the last call, detects mouse motion. The function **mouse__motion( )**, shown here, returns the change in the horizontal and vertical directions in variables pointed to by its arguments. If both **deltax** and **deltay** are 0, no motion has occurred.

```
/* Return the direction of travel. */
void mouse_motion(deltax, deltay)
char *deltax, *deltay;
{
   int fnum, arg2, arg3, arg4;

   fnum = 11; /* get direction of motion */
   cmouses(&fnum, &arg2, &arg3, &arg4);
   if(arg3>0) *deltax = RIGHT;
   else if(arg3<0) *deltax = LEFT;
   else *deltax = NOT_MOVED;

   if(arg4>0) *deltay = DOWN;
   else if(arg4<0) *deltay = UP;
   else *deltay = NOT_MOVED;
}
```

The macros RIGHT, LEFT, UP, DOWN, and NOT__MOVED are defined as shown here:

```
#define NOT_MOVED 0
#define RIGHT     1
#define LEFT      2
#define UP        3
#define DOWN      4
```

Reading and Setting
the Cursor Position

The functions **set__mouse__position( )** and **mouse__position( )**, shown here, are used to set and read the current position of the mouse.

```
/* Set mouse cursor coordinates. */
void set_mouse_position(x, y)
int x, y;
{
   int fnum, arg2;
```

```
      fnum = 4; /* set position */
      cmouses(&fnum, &arg2, &x, &y);
}

/* Return mouse cursor coordinates. */
void mouse_position(x, y)
int *x, *y;
{
      int fnum, arg2, arg3, arg4;

      fnum = 3; /* get position and button status */
      cmouses(&fnum, &arg2, &arg3, &arg4);
      *x = arg3;
      *y = arg4;
}
```

A Simple Demonstration
Program

The program shown here demonstrates the use of the high-level mouse
functions. You should enter it into your computer now.

```
/* Interfacing to the Microsoft/IBM mouse. */

#include "dos.h"

#define NOT_MOVED 0
#define RIGHT     1
#define LEFT      2
#define UP        3
#define DOWN      4

void mouse_position(), mode(), goto_xy(), mouse_motion();
void cursor_on(), cursor_off(), mouse_reset();

main(argc, argv)
int argc;
char *argv[];
{
      char deltax, deltay, x, y;

      if(argc!=2) {
        printf("usage:mouser <video mode>");
        exit(1);
      }

      mode(atoi(argv[1]));

      mouse_reset(); /* initialize the mouse */
      cursor_on(); /* turn on the cursor */

      do {
        goto_xy(0, 0);
        if(leftb_pressed()) printf("left button ");
```

```
      if(rightb_pressed()) {
        printf("right button");
        /* show mouse location */
        mouse_position(&x, &y);
        printf("%d %d - ", x, y);
      }

      /* see if change in position */
      mouse_motion(&deltax, &deltay);
      if(deltax || deltay) {
        printf("moving ");
        switch(deltax) {
          case NOT_MOVED: break;
          case RIGHT: printf("right ");
            break;
          case LEFT: printf("left  ");
            break;
        }
        switch(deltay) {
          case NOT_MOVED: break;
          case UP: printf("up    ");
            break;
          case DOWN: printf("down  ");
            break;
        }
      }
    /* loop until both buttons are pressed at the same time */
    } while(!(leftb_pressed() && rightb_pressed()));
    mode(3);
}

/* Set the video mode. */
void mode(mode_code)
int mode_code;
{
  union REGS r;

  r.h.al = mode_code;
  r.h.ah = 0;
  int86(0x10, &r, &r);
}

/* Send the cursor to the specified X,Y position. */
void goto_xy(x, y)
int x, y;
{
  union REGS r;

  r.h.ah=2; /* cursor addressing function */
  r.h.dl = y; /* column coordinate */
  r.h.dh = x; /* row coordinate */
  r.h.bh = 0; /* video page */
  int86(0x10, &r, &r);
}

/***********************************************/
/* Mouse interface functions.                */
/***********************************************/

/* Turn off the mouse cursor. */
void cursor_off()
```

```
{
  int fnum;

  fnum = 2; /* erase the cursor */
  cmouses(&fnum, &fnum, &fnum, &fnum);
}

/* Turn on the mouse cursor. */
void cursor_on()
{
  int fnum;

  fnum = 1; /* show the cursor */
  cmouses(&fnum, &fnum, &fnum, &fnum);

}


/* Return true if right button is pressed;
   false otherwise. */
rightb_pressed()
{
  int fnum, arg2, arg3, arg4;

  fnum = 3; /* get position and button status */
  cmouses(&fnum, &arg2, &arg3, &arg4);
  return arg2 & 2;
}

/* Return true if left button is pressed;
   false otherwise. */
leftb_pressed()
{
  int fnum, arg2, arg3, arg4;

  fnum = 3; /* get position and button status */
  cmouses(&fnum, &arg2, &arg3, &arg4);
  return arg2 & 1;
}

/* Set mouse cursor coordinates. */
void set_mouse_position(x, y)
int x, y;
{
  int fnum, arg2;

  fnum = 4; /* set position */
  cmouses(&fnum, &arg2, &x, &y);
}

/* Return mouse cursor coordinates. */
void mouse_position(x, y)
int *x, *y;
{
  int fnum, arg2, arg3, arg4;

  fnum = 3; /* get position and button status */
  cmouses(&fnum, &arg2, &arg3, &arg4);
  *x = arg3;
  *y = arg4;
}
```

```
/* Return the direction of travel. */
void mouse_motion(deltax, deltay)
char *deltax, *deltay;
{
  int fnum, arg2, arg3, arg4;

  fnum = 11; /* get direction of motion */
  cmouses(&fnum, &arg2, &arg3, &arg4);
  if(arg3>0) *deltax = RIGHT;
  else if(arg3<0) *deltax = LEFT;
  else *deltax = NOT_MOVED;

  if(arg4>0) *deltay = DOWN;
  else if(arg4<0) *deltay = UP;
  else *deltay = NOT_MOVED;
}

/* Reset the mouse. */
void mouse_reset()
{
  int fnum, arg2, arg3, arg4;

  fnum = 0; /* reset the mouse */
  cmouses(&fnum, &arg2, &arg3, &arg4);
  if(fnum!=-1) {
    printf("mouse hardware or software not installed");
    exit(1);
  }
  if(arg2!=2) {
    printf("two-button mouse required");
    exit(1);
  }
}
```

To use the program, specify on the command line the number of the video mode that you wish to use. The program reports the direction that the mouse travels and also reports when a button is pressed. In addition, pressing the right button shows the current X,Y position. Pressing both buttons terminates the program. You should try this program using different video modes to see the effect.

INTEGRATING MOUSE INPUT INTO THE PAINT PROGRAM

We are now ready to develop the routines that allow the mouse to control the paint program. The mouse interface will be added to the existing control routines rather than substituted for them. This means that the arrow keys will still be 100 percent functional, and the user will be able to choose the best input device for the situation.

Before the mouse can be integrated into the paint program it is necessary to develop two additional mouse-related routines. The first, **wait__on**( ), waits until the specified button is released. This is important because interrupts are continuously generated until the button is released. (It is impossible to press the button quickly enough to generate only one interrupt.) In many routines it is important to avoid this situation and make each button press generate (or rather, appear to generate) only one interrupt until it is released. To accomplish this, your routines must call **wait__on**( ), shown here, before continuing after a button press.

```
/* Return 1 when specified button released. */
void wait_on(button)
int button;
{
  if(button==LEFTB)
    while(leftb_pressed()) ;
  else
    while(rightb_pressed()) ;
}
```

The macros LEFTB and RIGHTB, shown here, should be used when calling **wait__on**( ).

```
#define LEFTB   1
#define RIGHTB  2
```

The second required routine is called **mouse__menu**( ). This routine displays a one-line menu and allows the user to make a selection by moving the mouse to the appropriate item and pressing either button. This function works only in mode 4 graphics. The function is passed a two-dimensional character array that holds the menu selections, the number of selections, and the X,Y position to display the menu. The character array allows each item in the list a maximum length of 19 characters. It returns the number of the selection beginning with 0, or −1 if no selection is made. When the function begins, it computes the length, in pixels, of each menu item and stores the pixel location of the

beginning and ending horizontal pixel position of each item in the array
len. (In mode 4 graphics, each character is 16 pixels wide and 8 pixels
high.) After this computation, the function waits until a button is
pressed and then checks to see if the mouse is pointing to a menu
selection. If it is, the number of that selection is returned to the calling
routine. The **mouse—menu( )** function is shown here.

```
/* Display a one line mouse menu and return selection. */
mouse_menu(count, item, x, y)
int count; /* number of menu items */
char item[][20]; /* menu items */
int x, y; /* display position */
{
   int i, len[MENU_MAX][2], t;
   int mousex, mousey;

   goto_xy(x, y);
   t = 0;
   for(i=0; i<count; i++) {
    printf("%s  ", item[i]);
    len[i][0] = t;
    /* each character is 16 pixels wide */
    len[i][1] = t + strlen(item[i])*16;
    t = len[i][1] + 32; /* add 2 for the spaces between items */
   }

   /* wait until user makes a selection */
   do {
     if(rightb_pressed() || leftb_pressed()) break;
   } while(!kbhit());
   /* wait until button not pressed */
   while(rightb_pressed() || leftb_pressed()) ;

   /* get the current mouse position */
   mouse_position(&mousex, &mousey);

   /* check to see if that position is on a menu selection */
   if(mousey>=0 && mousey<8) /* chars are 8 units tall */
     for(i=0; i<count; i++) {
       if(mousex>len[i][0] && mousex<len[i][1])
         return i;
     }
   return -1; /* no selection made */
}
```

The Main Loop

Although most of the original code to the paint program remains
unchanged, the **main( )** function, shown here, is significantly altered to
accommodate the mouse routines.

```
main()
{
  char done=0;

  mode(4);  /* switch to mode 4 CGA/EGA graphics */
  palette(0); /* palette 0 */
  mouse_reset(); /* initialize the mouse */

  xhairs(x, y); /* show the crosshairs */
  set_mouse_position(y*2, x); /* set initial mouse position */
  do {
    /* see if mouse has been moved */
    mouse_motion(&deltax, &deltay);
    if(deltax || deltay) read_mouse();
    /* check for button press */
    if(leftb_pressed() || rightb_pressed())
      read_mouse();
    if(kbhit()) {
      done = read_kb();
      /* reposition mouse to match new cross hairs location */
      set_mouse_position(y*2, x);
    }
  } while (!done);
  mode(2);
}
```

As you can see, except for **done**, **main( )** has no local variables.
Instead, all the control and counter variables necessary to the operation
of the program are global so that both the keyboard and mouse routines
can access them without having to pass a large number of arguments. As
you can see, the status of the mouse and the keyboard are monitored
inside the loop. Whenever the state of either device changes, the
appropriate function is called. Note that the mouse cursor is not turned
on. Instead, during the drawing part of the program, the cross hairs are
used to show the current screen position. The mouse cursor is activated
only when a menu selection is made.

The **read—kb( )** function, which processes keyboard input, is
shown here. It is basically the same as in the original program.

```
/* Read and process a keyboard command. */
read_kb()
{
  union k{
    char c[2];
    int i;
  } key;

  key.i = bioskey(0);
  xhairs(x, y);    /* erase the crosshairs */
  if(!key.c[0]) switch(key.c[1]) {
```

```
              case 75: /* left */
                if(on_flag) line(x, y, x, y-inc, cc);
                y -= inc;
                break;
              case 77: /* right */
                if(on_flag) line(x, y, x, y+inc, cc);
                y += inc;
                break;
              case 72: /* up */
                if(on_flag) line(x, y, x-inc, y, cc);
                x -= inc;
                break;
              case 80: /* down */
                if(on_flag) line(x, y, x+inc, y, cc);
                x += inc;
                break;
              case 71: /* up left */
                if(on_flag) line(x, y, x-inc, y-inc, cc);
                x -= inc; y -= inc;
                break;
              case 73: /* up right */
                if(on_flag) line(x, y, x-inc, y+inc, cc);
                x -= inc; y += inc;
                break;
              case 79: /* down left*/
                if(on_flag) line(x, y, x+inc, y-inc, cc);
                x += inc; y -= inc;
                break;
              case 81: /* down right */
                if(on_flag) line(x, y, x+inc, y+inc, cc);
                x += inc; y += inc;
                break;
              case 59: inc = 1;  /* F1 - slow speed */
                break;
              case 60: inc = 5;  /* F2 - fast speed */
                break;
            }
            else switch(tolower(key.c[0])) {
              case 'o': on_flag = !on_flag; /* toggle brush */
                break;
              case '1': cc = 1; /* color 1 */
                break;
              case '2': cc = 2; /* color 2 */
                break;
              case '3': cc = 3; /* color 3 */
                break;
              case '0': cc = 0; /* color 0 */
                break;
              case 'b': box(startx, starty, endx, endy, cc);
                break;
              case 'f': fill_box(startx, starty, endx, endy, cc);
                break;
              case 'l': line(startx, starty, endx, endy, cc);
                break;
              case 'c': circle(startx, starty, endy-starty, cc);
                break;
              case 'h': fill_circle(startx, starty, endy-starty, cc);
                break;
              case 's': save_pic();
                break;
              case 'r': load_pic();
                break;
```

```
      case 'm': /* move a region */
        move(startx, starty, endx, endy, x, y);
        break;
      case 'x': /* copy a region */
        copy(startx, starty, endx, endy, x, y);
        break;
      case 'd':  /* define an object to rotate */
        sides = define_object(object, x, y);
        break;
      case 'a': /* rotate the object */
        rotate_object(object, 0.05, x, y, sides);
          break;
      case '\r': /* set endpoints for line, circle, or box */
        if(first_point) {
          startx = x; starty = y;
        }
        else {
          endx = x; endy = y;
        }
        first_point = !first_point;
        break;
      case 'p': pal_num = pal_num==1 ? 2:1;
        palette(pal_num);
    }
    xhairs(x, y); /* redisplay the cross hairs */

    if(tolower(key.c[0])=='q') return 1;
    return 0;
}
```

The **read_mouse**( ) function, which processes mouse input, is shown here.

```
/* Read and process mouse input. */
read_mouse()
{
  int oldx, oldy;
  int choice;

  oldx = x; oldy = y;
  xhairs(x, y); /* erase from current position */

  /* press both buttons to activate mouse menu */
  if(rightb_pressed() && leftb_pressed()) {
    choice = menu(); /* get mouse menu selection */
    switch(choice) {
      case 0: box(startx, starty, endx, endy, cc);
        break;
      case 1: circle(startx, starty, endy-starty, cc);
        break;
      case 2: line(startx, starty, endx, endy, cc);
        break;
      case 3: fill_box(startx, starty, endx, endy, cc);
        break;
      case 4: fill_circle(startx, starty, endy-starty, cc);
        break;

    }
  }
```

```
/* right button defines endpoints for shapes */
else if(rightb_pressed()) {
  if(first_point) {
    startx = x; starty = y;
  }
  else {
    endx = x; endy = y;
  }
  first_point = !first_point;
  wait_on(RIGHTB); /* wait until button released */
}

if(deltax || deltay) {
  mouse_position(&y, &x);
  y = y / 2; /* normalize virtual screen coordinates */

  /* press left button to draw */
  if(leftb_pressed()) mouse_on_flag = 1;
  else mouse_on_flag = 0;
  if(mouse_on_flag) line(oldx, oldy, x, y, cc);
}
xhairs(x, y); /* redisplay cross hairs */
}
```

The **read—mouse( )** function works as follows. First it checks to see if both buttons are pressed. If they are, the mouse menu is activated by calling **menu( )**, which sets up the call to **mouse—menu( )**. If a menu selection is made, the appropriate action is taken. As currently implemented the mouse menu only allows boxes, circles, lines, and fills to be selected by the mouse. (You might also want to allow the mouse to select color and palette.)

The right button is used to define the end points of lines, boxes, and circles exactly the same as the ENTER key, which is used for the same purpose. Simply position the mouse at the first end point of the object and press the button. Next, move the mouse to the location of the second end point and press the button again.

When the left button is not pressed, the mouse can be moved about the screen without leaving a trail, that is, the default state of the mouse is pen up. To cause the mouse to write to the screen you must press the left button. While the button is pressed, the pen is down.

Finally, if the mouse has moved, the X,Y counters are updated.

The **menu( )** function, shown here, sets up a call to **mouse— menu( )**.

```
/* Display a menu. */
menu()
{
  register int i, j;
  char far *ptr = (char far *) 0xB8000000; /* pointer
                                     to CGA memory */
  char far *temp;
  unsigned char buf[14][80]; /* hold the contents of screen */
  int x, y, choice;
  char items[][20] = {
    "BOX",
    "CIRCLE",
    "LINE",
    "FILL BOX",
    "FILL CIRCLE"
  };

  temp = ptr;
  /* save the top of the current screen */
  for(i=0; i<14; i++)
    for(j=0; j<80; j+=2) {
      buf[i][j] = *temp; /* even byte */
      buf[i][j+1] = *(temp+8152); /* odd byte */
      *temp = 0; *(temp+8152) = 0;  /* clear top of screen */
      temp++;
    }

  goto_xy(0, 0);
  /* wait until last button press has cleared */
  while(rightb_pressed() || leftb_pressed()) ;

  cursor_on();

  choice = mouse_menu(5, items, 0, 0);

  cursor_off();
  temp = ptr;
  /* restore the top of the current screen */
  for(i=0; i<14; i++)
    for(j=0; j<80; j+=2) {
      *temp = buf[i][j];
      *(temp+8152) = buf[i][j+1];
      temp++;
    }
  return choice;
}
```

The function operates by first saving the top of the screen and then making sure that neither button is pressed. It then turns on the mouse cursor and calls **mouse__menu( )**. Upon return from **mouse__menu( )**, the cursor is turned off, the top of the screen is restored, and the function returns the value of the selection.

Defining Objects with the Mouse

The original paint program allows an object to be defined using the **define_object**( ) function by specifying the end points of each line segment. Once the object is defined, it can then be rotated. The version of **define_object**( ) shown here allows the mouse to select the end points of the object as well.

```
/* Define an object by specifying its endpoints using
   either the mouse or the keyboard. */
define_object(ob, x, y)
double ob[][4];
int x, y;
{

  union k{
    char c[2];
    int i;
  } key;
  register int i, j;
  char far *ptr = (char far *) 0xB8000000; /* pointer
                                              to CGA memory */
  char far *temp;
  unsigned char buf[14][80]; /* hold the contents of screen */
  int sides=0;
  int deltax, deltay, oldx, oldy;

  temp = ptr;
  /* save the top of the current screen */
  for(i=0; i<14; i++)
    for(j=0; j<80; j+=2) {
      buf[i][j] = *temp;
      buf[i][j+1] = *(temp+8152);
      *temp = 0; *(temp+8152) = 0; /* clear the top of the screen */
      temp++;
    }

  i = 0;
  key.i = 0;
  xhairs(x, y);
  do {
    goto_xy(0, 0);
    printf("Define side %d,", sides+1);
    if(i==0) printf(" enter first endpoint");
    else printf(" enter second endpoint");

    do {
      /* mouse additions ******************************/
      /* see if mouse has moved */
      mouse_motion(&deltax, &deltay);
      /* use left button to define a point */
      if(leftb_pressed()) {
        xhairs(x, y);   /* erase the crosshairs */
```

```
      /* store coordinates of the point */
      ob[sides][i++] = (double) x;
      ob[sides][i++] = (double) y;
      if(i==4) {
        i = 0;
        sides++;
      }
      break;
  }
} while(!kbhit() && !deltax && !deltay);
if(leftb_pressed()) wait_on(LEFTB);

if(deltax || deltay) {
  /* if mouse moved, update position */
  oldx = x; oldy = y;
  mouse_position(&y, &x);
  y = y / 2; /* normalize virtual screen coordinates */
  xhairs(oldx, oldy);    /* erase the crosshairs */
}
/* end of mouse code *******************************/
else if(kbhit()) {
  key.i = bioskey(0);
  xhairs(x, y);    /* plot the crosshairs */
  if(key.c[0]==13) {
    /* use RETURN to define a point */
    ob[sides][i++] = (double) x;
    ob[sides][i++] = (double) y;
    if(i==4) {
      i = 0;
      sides++;
    }
  }

  /* if arrow key, move the crosshairs */
  if(!key.c[0]) switch(key.c[1]) {
    case 75: /* left */
    y-=1;
    break;
    case 77: /* right */
    y+=1;
    break;
    case 72: /* up */
    x-=1;
    break;
    case 80: /* down */
    x+=1;
    break;
    case 71: /* up left */
    x-=1; y-=1;
    break;
    case 73: /* up right */
    x-=1; y+=1;
    break;
    case 79: /* down left*/
    x+=1;y-=1;
    break;
    case 81: /* down right */
    x+=1;y+=1;
    break;
  }
}
```

```
    if(key.c[1]!=59) xhairs(x, y);
} while(key.c[1]!=59); /* F1 to stop */

  temp = ptr;
  /* restore the top of the current screen */
  for(i=0; i<14; i++)
    for(j=0; j<80; j+=2) {
      *temp = buf[i][j];
      *(temp+8152) = buf[i][j+1];
      temp++;
    }
  return sides;
}
```

As you can see, the left button is used to select the end points. The mouse motion code is the same as in the **read_mouse()** function. Aside from the addition of the mouse input code, the function is unchanged. To define a point, move the mouse to the proper location and press the button.

The Entire Revised Paint Program

The code to the entire revised paint program is shown here.

```
/* This version of the paint program for the CGA/ECA allows
   the use of a Microsoft/IBM mouse as an alternate input
   device.
 */

#define NUM_SIDES 20 /* Number of sides an object may
                           have.  Enlarge as needed */
#define NOT_MOVED 0
#define RIGHT     1
#define LEFT      2
#define UP        3
#define DOWN      4

#define LEFTB    1
#define RIGHTB   2

#define MENU_MAX 20 /* number of mouse menu items */

#include "dos.h"
#include "stdio.h"
#include "math.h"

void mode(), line(), box(),fill_box();
void mempoint(), palette(), xhairs();
void circle(), plot_circle(), fill_circle();
```

```
void rotate_point(), rotate_object(), goto_xy();
void display_object(), copy(), move();
void save_pic(), load_pic();
void set_mouse_position(), mouse_position(), mouse_motion();
void cursor_on(), cursor_off(), wait_on(), mouse_reset();

unsigned char read_point();

/* This array will hold the coordinates of an object
   defined dynamically.
*/
double object[NUM_SIDES][4];

double asp_ratio; /* holds aspect ratio for circles */

   int x=10, y=10; /* current screen position */
   int cc=2; /* current color */
   int on_flag=1, mouse_on_flag=0; /* pen on or off */
   int pal_num=1; /* palette number */
   /* the endpoints of a defined line, circle, or box */
   int startx=0, starty=0, endx=0, endy=0, first_point=1;
   int inc=1; /* movement increment */
   int  sides=0; /* number of sides of a defined object */
   int deltax, deltay; /* mouse change in position indicators */

main()
{
   char done=0;

   mode(4);  /* switch to mode 4 CGA/EGA graphics */
   palette(0); /* palette 0 */

   mouse_reset(); /* initialize the mouse */

   xhairs(x, y); /* show the crosshairs */
   set_mouse_position(y*2, x); /* set initial mouse position */
   do {
     /* see if mouse has been moved */
     mouse_motion(&deltax, &deltay);
     if(deltax || deltay) read_mouse();
     /* check for button press */
     if(leftb_pressed() || rightb_pressed())
       read_mouse();
     if(kbhit()) {
       done = read_kb();
       /* reposition mouse to match new cross hairs location */
       set_mouse_position(y*2, x);
     }
   } while (!done);
   mode(2);
}

/* Read and process mouse input. */
read_mouse()
{
   int oldx, oldy;
   int choice;

   oldx = x; oldy = y;
   xhairs(x, y); /* erase from current position */
```

```
/* press both buttons to activate mouse menu */
if(rightb_pressed() && leftb_pressed()) {
  choice = menu(); /* get mouse menu selection */
  switch(choice) {
    case 0: box(startx, starty, endx, endy, cc);
      break;
    case 1: circle(startx, starty, endy-starty, cc);
      break;
    case 2: line(startx, starty, endx, endy, cc);
      break;
    case 3: fill_box(startx, starty, endx, endy, cc);
      break;
    case 4: fill_circle(startx, starty, endy-starty, cc);
      break;

  }
}
/* right button defines endpoints for shapes */
else if(rightb_pressed()) {
  if(first_point) {
    startx = x; starty = y;
  }
  else {
    endx = x; endy = y;
  }
  first_point = !first_point;
  wait_on(RIGHTB); /* wait until button released */
}

if(deltax || deltay) {
  mouse_position(&y, &x);
  y = y / 2; /* normalize virtual screen coordinates */

  /* press left button to draw */
  if(leftb_pressed()) mouse_on_flag = 1;
  else mouse_on_flag = 0;
  if(mouse_on_flag) line(oldx, oldy, x, y, cc);
}
xhairs(x, y); /* redisplay cross hairs */
}

/* Read and process a keyboard command. */
read_kb()
{
  union k{
    char c[2];
    int i;
  } key;

  key.i = bioskey(0);
  xhairs(x, y);     /* erase the crosshairs */
  if(!key.c[0]) switch(key.c[1]) {
    case 75: /* left */
      if(on_flag) line(x, y, x, y-inc, cc);
      y -= inc;
      break;
    case 77: /* right */
      if(on_flag) line(x, y, x, y+inc, cc);
      y += inc;
      break;
    case 72: /* up */
      if(on_flag) line(x, y, x-inc, y, cc);
      x -= inc;
      break;
```

```
        case 80: /* down */
          if(on_flag) line(x, y, x+inc, y, cc);
          x += inc;
          break;
        case 71: /* up left */
          if(on_flag) line(x, y, x-inc, y-inc, cc);
          x -= inc; y -= inc;
          break;
        case 73: /* up right */
          if(on_flag) line(x, y, x-inc, y+inc, cc);
          x -= inc; y += inc;
          break;
        case 79: /* down left*/
          if(on_flag) line(x, y, x+inc, y-inc, cc);
          x += inc; y -= inc;
          break;
        case 81: /* down right */
          if(on_flag) line(x, y, x+inc, y+inc, cc);
          x += inc; y += inc;
          break;
        case 59: inc = 1;   /* F1 - slow speed */
          break;
        case 60: inc = 5;   /* F2 - fast speed */
          break;
      }
      else switch(tolower(key.c[0])) {
        case 'o': on_flag = !on_flag; /* toggle brush */
          break;
        case '1': cc = 1; /* color 1 */
          break;
        case '2': cc = 2; /* color 2 */
          break;
        case '3': cc = 3; /* color 3 */
          break;
        case '0': cc = 0; /* color 0 */
          break;
        case 'b': box(startx, starty, endx, endy, cc);
          break;
        case 'f': fill_box(startx, starty, endx, endy, cc);
          break;
        case 'l': line(startx, starty, endx, endy, cc);
          break;
        case 'c': circle(startx, starty, endy-starty, cc);
          break;
        case 'h': fill_circle(startx, starty, endy-starty, cc);
          break;
        case 's': save_pic();
          break;
        case 'r': load_pic();
          break;
        case 'm': /* move a region */
          move(startx, starty, endx, endy, x, y);
          break;
        case 'x': /* copy a region */
          copy(startx, starty, endx, endy, x, y);
          break;
        case 'd':  /* define an object to rotate */
          sides = define_object(object, x, y);
          break;
        case 'a': /* rotate the object */
          rotate_object(object, 0.05, x, y, sides);
            break;
        case '\r': /* set endpoints for line, circle, or box */
          if(first_point) {
```

```
          startx = x; starty = y;
        }
        else {
          endx = x; endy = y;
        }
        first_point = !first_point;
        break;
      case 'p': pal_num = pal_num==1 ? 2:1;
        palette(pal_num);
    }
    xhairs(x, y); /* redisplay the cross hairs */

    if(tolower(key.c[0])=='q') return 1;
    return 0;
}

/* Set the palette. */
void palette(pnum)
int pnum;
{
  union REGS r;

  r.h.bh = 1;    /* code for mode 4 graphics */
  r.h.bl = pnum;
  r.h.ah = 11;   /* set palette function */
  int86(0x10, &r, &r);
}

/* Set the video mode. */
void mode(mode_code)
int mode_code;
{
  union REGS r;

  r.h.al = mode_code;
  r.h.ah = 0;
  int86(0x10, &r, &r);
}


/* Draw a box. */
void box(startx, starty, endx, endy, color_code)
int startx, starty, endx, endy, color_code;
{
  line(startx, starty, endx, starty, color_code);
  line(startx, starty, startx, endy, color_code);
  line(startx, endy, endx, endy, color_code);
  line(endx, starty, endx, endy, color_code);
}


/* Draw a line in specified color
   using Bresenham's integer based algorithm.
*/
void line(startx, starty, endx, endy, color)
int startx, starty, endx, endy, color;
{
  register int t, distance;
  int x=0, y=0, delta_x, delta_y;
  int incx, incy;
```

```
        /* compute the distances in both directions */
        delta_x = endx-startx;
        delta_y = endy-starty;

        /* Compute the direction of the increment,
           an increment of 0 means either a vertical or horizontal
           line.
        */
        if(delta_x>0) incx = 1;
        else if(delta_x==0) incx = 0;
        else incx=-1;

        if(delta_y>0) incy = 1;
        else if(delta_y==0) incy = 0;
        else incy = -1;

        /* cetermine which distance is greater */
        delta_x = abs(delta_x);
        delta_y = abs(delta_y);
        if(delta_x>delta_y) distance = delta_x;
        else distance = delta_y;

        /* draw the line */
        for(t=0; t<=distance+1; t++) {
          mempoint(startx, starty, color);
          x+=delta_x;
          y+=delta_y;
          if(x>distance) {
            x-=distance;
            startx+=incx;
          }
          if(y>distance) {
            y-=distance;
            starty+=incy;
          }
        }
    }

/* Fill box with specified color. */
void fill_box(startx, starty, endx, endy, color_code)
int startx, starty, endx, endy, color_code;
{
   register int i, begin, end;

   begin = startx<endx ? startx : endx;
   end = startx>endx ? startx : endx;

   for(i=begin; i<=end;i++)
     line(i, starty, i, endy, color_code);

}

/* Draw a circle using Bresenham's integer based Algorithm. */
void circle(x_center, y_center, radius,  color_code)
int x_center, y_center, radius, color_code;
{
   register int x, y, delta;

   asp_ratio = 1.0;  /* for different aspect ratios, alter
                        this number */
```

```
      y = radius;
      delta = 3 - 2 * radius;

      for(x=0; x<y; ) {
        plot_circle(x, y, x_center, y_center, color_code);

        if (delta < 0)
          delta += 4*x+6;
        else {
          delta += 4*(x-y)+10;
          y--;
        }
        x++;
      }
      x = y;
      if(y) plot_circle(x, y, x_center, y_center, color_code);
    }

    /* Plot_circle actually prints the points that
       define the circle. */
    void plot_circle(x, y, x_center, y_center, color_code)
    int x, y, x_center, y_center, color_code;
    {
      int startx, endx, x1, starty, endy, y1;

      starty = y*asp_ratio;
      endy = (y+1)*asp_ratio;
      startx = x*asp_ratio;
      endx = (x+1)*asp_ratio;

      for (x1=startx; x1<endx; ++x1)  {
        mempoint(x1+x_center, y+y_center, color_code);
        mempoint(x1+x_center, y_center-y, color_code);
        mempoint(x_center-x1, y_center-y, color_code);
        mempoint(x_center-x1, y+y_center, color_code);
      }

      for (y1=starty; y1<endy; ++y1) {
        mempoint(y1+x_center, x+y_center, color_code);
        mempoint(y1+x_center, y_center-x, color_code);
        mempoint(x_center-y1, y_center-x, color_code);
        mempoint(x_center-y1, x+y_center, color_code);
      }
    }

    /* Fill a circle by repeatedly calling circle()
       with smaller radius.
    */
    void fill_circle(x, y, r, c)
    int x, y, r, c;
    {
      while(r) {
        circle(x, y, r, c);
        r--;
      }
    }

    /* Display crosshair locator. */
    void xhairs(x,y)
    int x, y;
    {
      line(x-4, y, x+5, y, 1 | 128);
      line(x, y+4, x, y-3, 1 | 128);
    }
```

```
/* Write a point directly to the CGA/EGA */
void mempoint(x, y, color_code)
int x, y, color_code;
{
  union mask {
    char c[2];
    int i;
  } bit_mask;
  int i, index, bit_position;
  unsigned char t;
  char xor; /* xor color in or overwrite */
  char far *ptr = (char far *) 0xB8000000; /* pointer
                                              to CGA memory */

  bit_mask.i=0xFF3F;     /* 11111111 00111111 in binary */

  /* check range for mode 4 */
  if(x<0 || x>199 || y<0 || y>319) return;

  xor=color_code & 128; /* see if xor mode is set */
  color_code = color_code & 127; /* mask off high bit */

  /* set bit_mask and color_code bits to the right location */
  bit_position = y%4;
  color_code<<=2*(3-bit_position);
  bit_mask.i>>=2*bit_position;


  /* find the correct byte in screen memory */
  index = x*40 +(y >> 2);
  if(x % 2) index += 8152; /* if odd use 2nd bank */

  /* write the color */
  if(!xor) { /* overwrite mode */
    t = *(ptr+index) & bit_mask.c[0];
    *(ptr+index) = t | color_code;
  }
  else { /* xor mode */
    t = *(ptr+index) | (char)0;
    *(ptr+index) = t ^ color_code;
  }
}

/* Read byte directly from the CGA/EGA in mode 4. */
unsigned char read_point(x, y)
int x, y;
{
  union mask {
    char c[2];
    int i;
  } bit_mask;
  int i, index, bit_position;
  unsigned char t;
  char xor; /* xor color in or overwrite */
  char far *ptr = (char far *) 0xB8000000; /* pointer
                                              to CGA memory */

  bit_mask.i=3; /* 11111111 00111111 in binary */

  /* check range for mode 4 */
  if(x<0 || x>199 || y<0 || y>319) return 0;

  /* set bit_mask and color_code bits to the right location */
```

```
    bit_position = y%4;
    bit_mask.i<<=2*(3-bit_position);
    /* find the correct byte in screen memory */
    index = x*40 +(y >> 2);
    if(x % 2) index += 8152; /* if odd use 2nd bank */

    /* read the color */
    t = *(ptr+index) & bit_mask.c[0];
    t >>=2*(3-bit_position);
    return t;
}

/* save the video graphics display */
void save_pic()
{
    char fname[80];
    FILE *fp;
    register int i, j;
    char far *ptr = (char far *) 0xB8000000; /* pointer
                                             to CGA memory */
    char far *temp;
    unsigned char buf[14][80]; /* hold the contents of screen */

    temp = ptr;
    /* save the top of the current screen */
    for(i=0; i<14; i++)
      for(j=0; j<80; j+=2) {
        buf[i][j] = *temp; /* even byte */
        buf[i][j+1] = *(temp+8152); /* odd byte */
        *temp = 0; *(temp+8152) = 0;  /* clear top of screen */
        temp++;
      }

    goto_xy(0, 0);
    printf("Filename: ");
    gets(fname);
    if(!(fp=fopen(fname, "wb"))) {
      printf("cannot open file\n");
      return;
    }

    temp = ptr;
    /* restore the top of the current screen */
    for(i=0; i<14; i++)
      for(j=0; j<80; j+=2) {
        *temp = buf[i][j];
        *(temp+8152) = buf[i][j+1];
        temp++;
      }

    /* save image to file */
    for(i=0; i<8152; i++) {
      putc(*ptr, fp); /* even byte */
      putc(*(ptr+8152), fp); /* odd byte */
      ptr++;
    }

    fclose(fp);
}
```

```c
/* load the video graphics display */
void load_pic()
{
  char fname[80];
  FILE *fp;
  register int i, j;
  char far *ptr = (char far *) 0xB8000000; /* pointer
                                              to CGA memory */
  char far *temp;
  unsigned char buf[14][80]; /* hold the contents of screen */

  temp = ptr;
  /* save the top of the current screen */
  for(i=0; i<14; i++)
    for(j=0; j<80; j+=2) {
      buf[i][j] = *temp;
      buf[i][j+1] = *(temp+8152);
      *temp = 0; *(temp+8152) = 0; /* clear the top of the screen */
      temp++;
    }

  goto_xy(0, 0);
  printf("Filename: ");
  gets(fname);
  if(!(fp=fopen(fname, "rb"))) {
    goto_xy(0, 0);
    printf("cannot open file\n");
    temp = ptr;
    /* restore the top of the current screen */
    for(i=0; i<14; i++)
      for(j=0; j<80; j+=2) {
        *temp = buf[i][j];
        *(temp+8152) = buf[i][j+1];
        temp++;
      }
    return;
  }

  /* load image from file */
  for(i=0; i<8152; i++) {
    *ptr = getc(fp); /* even byte */
    *(ptr+8152) = getc(fp); /* odd byte */
    ptr++;
  }

  fclose(fp);
}

/* Send the cursor to the specified X,Y position. */
void goto_xy(x, y)
int x, y;
{
  union REGS r;

  r.h.ah=2; /* cursor addressing function */
  r.h.dl = y; /* column coordinate */
  r.h.dh = x; /* row coordinate */
  r.h.bh = 0; /* video page */
  int86(0x10, &r, &r);
}
```

```
/* Move one region to another location. */
void move(startx, starty, endx, endy, x, y)
int startx, starty; /* upper left coordinate */
int endx, endy; /* lower right coordinate of region to move */
int x, y; /* upper left of region receiving the image */
{
  int i, j;
  unsigned char c;

  for(; startx<=endx; startx++, x++)
    for(i=starty, j=y; i<=endy; i++, j++) {
      c = read_point(startx, i); /* read point */
      mempoint(startx, i, 0); /* erase old image */
      mempoint(x, j, c); /* write it to new location */
    }
}

/* Copy one region to another location. */
void copy(startx, starty, endx, endy, x, y)
int startx, starty; /* upper left coordinate */
int endx, endy; /* lower right coordinate of region to copy */
int x, y; /* upper left of region receiving the image */
{
  int i, j;
  unsigned char c;

  for(; startx<=endx; startx++, x++)
    for(i=starty, j=y; i<=endy; i++, j++) {
      c = read_point(startx, i); /* read point */
      mempoint(x, j, c); /* write it to new location */
    }
}


/* Rotate a point around the origin, specified by
   x_org and y_org,  by angle theta. */
void rotate_point(theta, x, y, x_org, y_org)
double theta, *x, *y;
int x_org, y_org;
{
  double tx, ty;

  /* normalize x and y to origin */
  tx = *x - x_org;
  ty = *y - y_org;

  /* rotate */
  *x = tx * cos(theta) - ty * sin(theta);
  *y = tx * sin(theta) + ty * cos(theta);

  /* return to PC coordinate values */
  *x += x_org;
  *y += y_org;

}

/* Rotate the specified object. */
void rotate_object(ob, theta, x, y, sides)
double ob[][4]; /* object definition */
double theta; /* angle of rotation in radians */
int x, y; /* location of origin */
int sides;
```

```
{
  register int i, j;
  double tempx, tempy;  /* these help with the type conversions */
  char ch;

  for(;;) {
    ch = getch(); /* see which direction to rotate */
    switch(tolower(ch)) {
      case 'l': /* rotate counterclockwise */
        theta = theta < 0 ? -theta : theta;
        break;
      case 'r': /* rotate clockwise */
        theta = theta > 0 ? -theta : theta;
        break;
      default: return;
    }

    for(j=0; j<sides; j++) {
      /* erase old line */
      line((int) ob[j][0], (int) ob[j][1],
        (int) ob[j][2], (int) ob[j][3], 0);

      rotate_point(theta, &ob[j][0],
        &ob[j][1], x, y);

      rotate_point(theta, &ob[j][2],
        &ob[j][3], x, y);

      line((int)ob[j][0], (int) ob[j][1],
        (int) ob[j][2], (int) ob[j][3], 2);
    }
  }
}

/* Display an object. */
void display_object(ob, sides)
double ob[][4];
int sides;
{
  register int i;

  for(i=0; i<sides; i++)
    line((int) ob[i][0], (int) ob[i][1],
      (int) ob[i][2], (int) ob[i][3], 2);
}

/* Define an object by specifying its endpoints using
   either the mouse or the keyboard. */
define_object(ob, x, y)
double ob[][4];
int x, y;
{

  union k{
    char c[2];
    int i;
  } key;
  register int i, j;
  char far *ptr = (char far *) 0xB8000000; /* pointer
                                              to CGA memory */
  char far *temp;
  unsigned char buf[14][80]; /* hold the contents of screen */
```

```
int sides=0;
int deltax, deltay, oldx, oldy;

temp = ptr;
/* save the top of the current screen */
for(i=0; i<14; i++)
  for(j=0; j<80; j+=2) {
    buf[i][j] = *temp;
    buf[i][j+1] = *(temp+8152);
    *temp = 0; *(temp+8152) = 0; /* clear the top of the screen */
    temp++;
  }

i = 0;
key.i = 0;
xhairs(x, y);
do {
  goto_xy(0, 0);
  printf("Define side %d,", sides+1);
  if(i==0) printf(" enter first endpoint");
  else printf(" enter second endpoint");

  do {
    /* mouse additions ******************************/
    /* see if mouse has moved */
    mouse_motion(&deltax, &deltay);
    /* use left button to define a point */
    if(leftb_pressed()) {
      xhairs(x, y);    /* erase the crosshairs */
      /* store coordinates of the point */
      ob[sides][i++] = (double) x;
      ob[sides][i++] = (double) y;
      if(i==4) {
        i = 0;
        sides++;
      }
      break;
    }
  } while(!kbhit() && !deltax && !deltay);
  if(leftb_pressed()) wait_on(LEFTB);

  if(deltax || deltay) {
    /* if mouse moved, update position */
    oldx = x; oldy = y;
    mouse_position(&y, &x);
    y = y / 2; /* normalize virtual screen coordinates */
    xhairs(oldx, oldy);    /* erase the crosshairs */
  }
  /* end of mouse code ******************************/
  else if(kbhit()) {
    key.i = bioskey(0);
    xhairs(x, y);    /* plot the crosshairs */
    if(key.c[0]==13) {
      /* use RETURN to define a point */
      ob[sides][i++] = (double) x;
      ob[sides][i++] = (double) y;
      if(i==4) {
        i = 0;
        sides++;
      }
    }
  }
```

```
        /* if arrow key, move the crosshairs */
        if(!key.c[0]) switch(key.c[1]) {
          case 75: /* left */
            y-=1;
            break;
          case 77: /* right */
            y+=1;
            break;
          case 72: /* up */
            x-=1;
            break;
          case 80: /* down */
            x+=1;
            break;
          case 71: /* up left */
            x-=1; y-=1;
            break;
          case 73: /* up right */
            x-=1; y+=1;
            break;
          case 79: /* down left*/
            x+=1;y-=1;
            break;
          case 81: /* down right */
            x+=1;y+=1;
            break;
        }
      }
    if(key.c[1]!=59) xhairs(x, y);
  } while(key.c[1]!=59); /* F1 to stop */

  temp = ptr;
  /* restore the top of the current screen */
  for(i=0; i<14; i++)
    for(j=0; j<80; j+=2) {
      *temp = buf[i][j];
      *(temp+8152) = buf[i][j+1];
      temp++;
    }
  return sides;
}

/* Display a menu. */
menu()
{
  register int i, j;
  char far *ptr = (char far *) 0xB8000000; /* pointer
                                         to CGA memory */
  char far *temp;
  unsigned char buf[14][80]; /* hold the contents of screen */
  int x, y, choice;
  char items[][20] = {
    "BOX",
    "CIRCLE",
    "LINE",
    "FILL BOX",
    "FILL CIRCLE"
  };

  temp = ptr;
  /* save the top of the current screen */
```

```
      for(i=0; i<14; i++)
        for(j=0; j<80; j+=2) {
          buf[i][j] = *temp; /* even byte */
          buf[i][j+1] = *(temp+8152); /* odd byte */
          *temp = 0; *(temp+8152) = 0;  /* clear top of screen */
          temp++;
        }

      goto_xy(0, 0);
      /* wait until last button press has cleared */
      while(rightb_pressed() || leftb_pressed()) ;
      cursor_on();

      choice = mouse_menu(5, items, 0, 0);

      cursor_off();
      temp = ptr;
      /* restore the top of the current screen */
      for(i=0; i<14; i++)
        for(j=0; j<80; j+=2) {
          *temp = buf[i][j];
          *(temp+8152) = buf[i][j+1];
          temp++;
        }
      return choice;
}

/**************************************************/
/* Mouse interface functions.                   */
/**************************************************/

/* Turn off the mouse cursor. */
void cursor_off()
{
  int fnum;

  fnum = 2; /* erase the cursor */
  cmouses(&fnum, &fnum, &fnum, &fnum);
}

/* Turn on the mouse cursor. */
void cursor_on()
{
  int fnum;

  fnum = 1; /* show the cursor */
  cmouses(&fnum, &fnum, &fnum, &fnum);
}


/* Return true if right button is pressed;
   false otherwise. */
rightb_pressed()
{
  int fnum, arg2, arg3, arg4;

  fnum = 3; /* get position and button status */
  cmouses(&fnum, &arg2, &arg3, &arg4);
  return arg2 & 2;
}
```

```
/* Return true if left button is pressed;
   false otherwise. */
leftb_pressed()
{
  int fnum, arg2, arg3, arg4;

  fnum = 3; /* get position and button status */
  cmouses(&fnum, &arg2, &arg3, &arg4);
  return arg2 & 1;
}

/* Set mouse cursor coordinates. */
void set_mouse_position(x, y)
int x, y;
{
  int fnum, arg2;

  fnum = 4; /* set position */
  cmouses(&fnum, &arg2, &x, &y);
}

/* Return mouse cursor coordinates. */
void mouse_position(x, y)
int *x, *y;
{
  int fnum, arg2, arg3, arg4;

  fnum = 3; /* get position and button status */
  cmouses(&fnum, &arg2, &arg3, &arg4);
  *x = arg3;
  *y = arg4;
}

/* Return the direction of travel. */
void mouse_motion(deltax, deltay)
char *deltax, *deltay;
{
  int fnum, arg2, arg3, arg4;

  fnum = 11; /* get direction of motion */
  cmouses(&fnum, &arg2, &arg3, &arg4);
  if(arg3>0) *deltax = RIGHT;
  else if(arg3<0) *deltax = LEFT;
  else *deltax = NOT_MOVED;

  if(arg4>0) *deltay = DOWN;
  else if(arg4<0) *deltay = UP;
  else *deltay = NOT_MOVED;
}

/* Display a one line mouse menu and return selection. */
mouse_menu(count, item, x, y)
int count; /* number of menu items */
char item[][20]; /* menu items */
int x, y; /* display position */
{
  int i, len[MENU_MAX][2], t;
  int mousex, mousey;

  goto_xy(x, y);
  t = 0;
```

```
  for(i=0; i<count; i++) {
   printf("%s  ", item[i]);
   len[i][0] = t;
   len[i][1] = t + strlen(item[i])*16;
   t = len[i][1] + 32;
  }

  do {
    if(rightb_pressed() || leftb_pressed()) break;
  } while(!kbhit());
  /* wait until button not pressed */
  while(rightb_pressed() || leftb_pressed()) ;

  mouse_position(&mousex, &mousey);

  if(mousey>=0 && mousey<8)
    for(i=0; i<count; i++) {
      if(mousex>len[i][0] && mousex<len[i][1])
        return i;
    }
  return -1; /* no selection made */
}

/* Return 1 when specified button released. */
void wait_on(button)
int button;
{
  if(button==LEFTB)
    while(leftb_pressed()) ;
  else
    while(rightb_pressed()) ;

}

/* Reset the mouse. */
void mouse_reset()
{
  int fnum, arg2, arg3, arg4;

  fnum = 0; /* reset the mouse */
  cmouse(&fnum, &arg2, &arg3, &arg4);
  if(fnum!=-1) {
    printf("mouse hardware or software not installed");
    exit(1);
  }
  if(arg2!=2) {
   printf("two-button mouse required");
    exit(1);
  }
}
```

The paint program is now much more exciting to use because you can draw "free hand" curves instead of just straight lines. For example, the picture shown in Figure 9-1 was created in just a few minutes time. The picture presented in Figure 9-2 shows the mouse menu and the default graphics mouse cursor.

Figure 9-1.

Sample output from the paint program,
Mountain with Tower at Sunrise

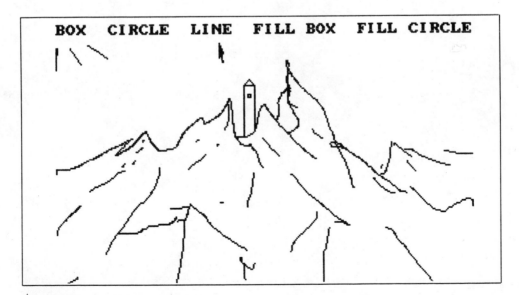

Figure 9-2.

Example of a mouse menu

SOME ADDITIONAL ENHANCEMENTS

First, you might want to expand the **mouse_menu( )** function so that more than one line of selections can be displayed. In fact, with careful thought, you can integrate the mouse into the pop-up and pull-down window routines developed in Chapter 1. If you enjoy using icons, you might want to change the menu function so that icons rather than words are displayed. Another enhancement is to create a routine that allows the mouse to "drag" a part of the screen from one place to another.

10: Creating Business Bar Graphs

In this chapter we develop routines that can be used to create one of the most common types of business graphs—the bar graph. The ability to display numeric data in visual form is very useful in many situations. As you will see, it is not as difficult to create bar graphs as you might think.

The chapter begins by developing a small toolbox of business-related graphics functions. The second half of the chapter explains how these toolbox routines can be used to create a simple, but useful, general-purpose bar graph program that allows up to three sets of information to be plotted on the screen at the same time. This chapter also develops a no-frills "slide-show" presentation program that displays graphs easily.

The examples in this chapter require a PC-type computer with a color graphics adapter. Video mode 4 is used because it works with all the color adapters. However, you can easily change the functions to work with other adapters.

NORMALIZING THE DATA

Before developing routines that plot data on the screen, you must understand how these values are translated into the appropriate screen coordinates. As you probably recall, the dimensions of the screen in video mode 4 are 320 × 200, with 320 being the horizontal dimension and 200 the vertical dimension. Assuming that the bar graph is displayed with the bars running vertically, the values of the information must be converted in such a way that they fit in the range 0 through 199. This conversion process is known as *normalization*.

To normalize a value you must multiply it by some ratio that guarantees the result will be within the range of the screen. In order to accomplish this, the minimum and maximum values of the data to be plotted must be known. To compute the proper ratio, first subtract the minimum value from the maximum value. Then divide the maximum value of the range you wish to normalize to by this result. This ratio is then used to adjust each item of data. Assuming that the entire vertical range of the screen in video mode 4 is used, the ratio is computed using this formula:

normalization __ factor = 200 / (max—min)

Therefore, each item of data is normalized by this formula:

normalized __ data = raw __ data * normalization __ factor

DEVELOPING THE BAR GRAPH FUNCTION

Before developing the function that actually draws the bar graph on the screen, it is necessary to define exactly what it will do. First, it must accomplish its primary purpose of displaying the data in the form of a bar graph. The function will accept as input an array of floating point values and transform them into their normalized integer equivalents.

The function must be capable of being called repeatedly with different sets of data so that several sets can be displayed at the same time. To do this, the function must accept an argument that determines the spacing between the bars when two or more sets of data are plotted. The function must also plot each set of data in a different color. Finally, it must allow the thickness of the bars to be specified. The function **bargraph( )**, shown here, accomplishes these goals.

```
/* Display a bar chart. */
void bargraph(data, num, offset, min, max, width)
double *data; /* array of data */
int num; /* number of elements in array */
int offset; /* determine spacing between sets of data */
int min, max; /* minimum and maximum values to be plotted */
int width; /* thickness of the lines */
{
  int y, t, incr;
  double norm_data, norm_ratio, spread;
  char s[80];
  static int color=0;
  int tempwidth;

  /* always use a different color */
  color++;
  if(color>3) color=1;

  /* determine normalization factor */
  spread = (double) max-min;
  norm_ratio = 180/spread;

  incr = 280/num; /* determine spacing between values */
  tempwidth = width;
  for(t=0; t<num; ++t) {
    norm_data = data[t];

    /* adjust for negative values */
    norm_data = norm_data-(double) min;

    norm_data *= norm_ratio; /* normalize */
    y = (int) norm_data; /* type conversion */
    do {
      line(179, ((t*incr)+20+offset+width), 179-y,
        ((t*incr)+20+offset+width), color);
      width--;
    } while (width);
    width = tempwidth;
  }
}
```

Let's look closely at this function. The function is passed the array of data, the number of elements in the array, the spacing between the bars when multiple data sets are plotted, the minimum and maximum values of the data, and the width, in pixels, of the bars. The **static** variable **color** is used to insure that each time **bargraph( )** is called a new color is used. In this way multiple sets of data can be distinguished by the color with which they are plotted. Next, the normalization factor is computed. The value of 180 rather than 200 is used as the maximum screen height so that two lines of text information can be shown at the bottom of the graph. Although not necessary, it is usually more pleasing when a bar graph fills the entire display regardless of how many values are being plotted; a bar graph of a small number of values, for example, looks more appealing if the bars are spread out rather than bunched up at one end of the display. To accomplish this, the width of the screen (less some room for range labels) is divided by the number of values to be displayed. This value is then used to determine the horizontal position of the bars. Finally, the loop normalizes each value and plots a line of the specified thickness beginning at the specified offset.

The **bargraph( )** function is the key routine, but is only one of several tools that allow you to create almost any type of bar graph. You'll learn about the rest of these bar graph toolbox functions in the discussion that follows.

Drawing a Grid

Along the lower edge of the bars, you will probably want to provide a baseline. The function **grid( )**, shown here, does just that.

```
/* Draw the chart grid. */
void grid(min, max)
int min, max;
{
  register int t;

  goto_xy(22, 0); printf("%d", min);
  goto_xy(0, 0); printf("%d", max);
  line(180, 10, 180, 300, 1);
}
```

As you can see, like **bargraph( )**, this function leaves the bottom two lines of the display untouched. These bottom lines allow labeling and other information.

Labeling the Values

It is very common to label the values plotted on the screen. For example, if a bar chart shows five years of corporate profits, you will probably want to label each year. Although you can do this manually using the **goto___xy( )** and **printf( )** functions, the **label( )** function, shown here, automatically places a label under each value. It accepts as input an array of strings (labels) and the number of entries. Each label is restricted to a length of 20 characters (including the null terminator), but this is not a severe restriction because in video mode 4 only 40 characters can be displayed on one line making short labels desirable.

```
/* Display labels on the screen. */
void label(str, num)
char str[][20]; /* strings to display */
int num; /* number of labels */
{
  int i, j, inc;

  inc = 38 / num;
  i = 2; /* initial horizontal starting point */
  for(j=0; j<num; j++) {
    goto_xy(23, i);
    printf(str[j]);
    i += inc;
  }
}
```

Drawing Reference Lines

In some situations, it is helpful to add horizontal lines at consistent intervals to aid in comparing widely separated bars. Generally, you will not want to use solid reference lines because they are too distracting. Instead, dotted lines are drawn. The function **hashlines( )**, shown here, draws these dotted reference lines.

```
/* Draw dotted reference lines across the screen. */
void hashlines()
{
  int i, j;

  for(i=10; i<180; i+=10) {
    for(j=10; j<300; j+=5)
      mempoint(i, j, 3); /* one point every 5 pixels */
  }
}
```

Displaying a Legend

When multiple sets of data are plotted, it is a good idea to identify the color of the bar that goes with each set. One way to do this is to show a legend that contains the name of each set of data and the color used to display it. The function **legend**( ), shown here, draws this legend. It takes as arguments a list of names and the number of names. It displays the name and a box filled with the color associated with that name across the bottom row of the screen. It uses the **fill_box**( ) function developed earlier in this book to draw the colored box.

```
/* Show a legend. */
void legend(names, num)
char names[][20];
int num; /* number of names */
{
  int color=1, i, j;

  goto_xy(24, 0); /* legend goes on bottom line */
  j = 0;
  for(i=0; i<num; i++) {
    /* print the label */
    printf("%s    ", names[i]);
    /* Compute where colored box goes by
       converting cursor location into graphics
       coordinates.  Each character is 8 pixels wide in
       mode 4 graphics.
    */
    j += strlen(names[i])*8+4;
    fill_box(192, j, 198, j+12, color);
    j += 28;  /* advance to next field */
    color++;
    if(color>3) color = 1;
  }
}
```

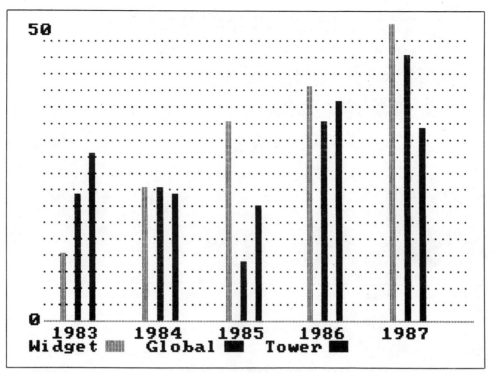

Figure 10-1.

Output from the bar graph
demonstration program

A Simple Demonstration Program

The following program shows all the bar graph toolbox routines in
action. It produces the output shown in Figure 10-1. The program
shows the average price per share of three imaginary companies over
five years.

```
/* A bar graph demonstration program. */
#include "dos.h"

void bargraph(), mode(), mempoint();
void line(), goto_xy(), grid(), label();
```

```
void hashlines(), legend(), read_cursor_xy();
void palette(), color_puts(), fill_box();

main()
{
  double widget[]={
    10.1, 20, 30, 35.34, 50
  };
  double global[]={
    19, 20, 8.8, 30, 40
  };
  double tower[]={
    25.25, 19, 17.4, 33, 29
  };
  int min, max;

  char n[][20]={
    "Widget",
    "Global",
    "Tower"
  };
  char lab[][20]={
    "1983",
    "1984",
    "1985",
    "1986",
    "1987"
  };

  mode(4); /* 320x200  graphics mode */
  palette(0);


  grid(0, 50); /* display the grid */
  hashlines(); /* display dotted reference lines */
  label(lab, 5); /* label the graph */
  legend(n, 3); /* show the legend */

  /* plot the stock prices of the three companies */
  bargraph(widget, 5, 0, 0, 50, 4);
  bargraph(global, 5, 10, 0, 50, 4);
  bargraph(tower, 5, 20, 0, 50, 4);

  getch();
  mode(3);
}

/* Draw the chart grid. */
void grid(min, max)
int min, max;
{
  register int t;

  goto_xy(22, 0); printf("%d", min);
  goto_xy(0, 0); printf("%d", max);
  line(180, 10, 180, 300, 1);
}

/* Display labels on the screen. */
void label(str, num)
char str[][20]; /* strings to display */
int num; /* number of labels */
```

```
{
  int i, j, inc;

  inc = 38 / num;
  i = 2; /* initial horizontal starting point */
  for(j=0; j<num; j++) {
    goto_xy(23, i);
    printf(str[j]);
    i += inc;
  }
}

/* Draw dotted reference lines across the screen. */
void hashlines()
{
  int i, j;

  for(i=10; i<180; i+=10) {
    for(j=10; j<300; j+=5)
      mempoint(i, j, 3); /* one point every 5 pixels */
  }
}

/* Show a legend. */
void legend(names, num)
char names[][20];
int num; /* number of names */
{
  int color=1, i, j;

  goto_xy(24, 0); /* legend goes on bottom line */
  j = 0;
  for(i=0; i<num; i++) {
    /* print the label */
    printf("%s    ", names[i]);
    /* Compute where colored box goes by
       converting cursor location into graphics
       coordinates.  Each character is 8 pixels wide in
       mode 4 graphics.
    */
    j += strlen(names[i])*8+4;
    fill_box(192, j, 198, j+12, color);
    j += 28;   /* advance to next field */
    color++;
    if(color>3) color = 1;
  }
}

/* Display a bar chart. */
void bargraph(data, num, offset, min, max, width)
double *data; /* array of data */
int num; /* number of elements in array */
int offset; /* determine exact screen position */
int min, max; /* minimum and maximum values to be plotted */
int width; /* thickness of the lines */
{
  int y, t, incr;
  double norm_data, norm_ratio, spread;
  char s[80];
  static int color=0;
  int tempwidth;
```

```
/* always use a different color */
color++;
if(color>3) color=1;

/* determine normalization factor */
spread = (double) max-min;
norm_ratio = 180/spread;

incr = 280/num; /* determine spacing between lines */
tempwidth = width;
for(t=0; t<num; ++t) {
  norm_data = data[t];

  /* adjust for negative values */
  norm_data = norm_data-(double) min;

  norm_data *= norm_ratio; /* normalize */
  y = (int) norm_data; /* type conversion */
  do {
    line(179, ((t*incr)+20+offset+width), 179-y,
      ((t*incr)+20+offset+width), color);
    width--;
  } while (width);
  width = tempwidth;
  }
}

/* Draw a line in specified color
   using Bresenham's integer based algorithm.
*/
void line(startx, starty, endx, endy, color)
int startx, starty, endx, endy, color;
{
  register int t, distance;
  int x=0, y=0, delta_x, delta_y;
  int incx, incy;

  /* compute the distances in both directions */
  delta_x = endx-startx;
  delta_y = endy-starty;

  /* Compute the direction of the increment,
     an increment of 0 means either a vertical or horizontal
     line.
  */
  if(delta_x>0) incx = 1;
  else if(delta_x==0) incx = 0;
  else incx=-1;

  if(delta_y>0) incy = 1;
  else if(delta_y==0) incy = 0;
  else incy = -1;

  /* determine which distance is greater */
  delta_x = abs(delta_x);
  delta_y = abs(delta_y);
  if(delta_x>delta_y) distance = delta_x;
  else distance = delta_y;

  /* draw the line */
  for(t=0; t<=distance+1; t++) {
    mempoint(startx, starty, color);
```

```
    x+=delta_x;
    y+=delta_y;
    if(x>distance) {
      x-=distance;
      startx+=incx;
    }
    if(y>distance) {
      y-=distance;
      starty+=incy;
    }
  }
}


/* Fill box with specified color. */
void fill_box(startx, starty, endx, endy, color_code)
int startx, starty, endx, endy, color_code;
{
  register int i, begin, end;

  begin = startx<endx ? startx : endx;
  end = startx>endx ? startx : endx;

  for(i=begin; i<=end;i++)
    line(i, starty, i, endy, color_code);
}


/* Write a point directly to the CGA/EGA */
void mempoint(x, y, color_code)
int x, y, color_code;
{
  union mask {
    char c[2];
    int i;
  } bit_mask;
  int i, index, bit_position;
  unsigned char t;
  char xor; /* xor color in or overwrite */
  char far *ptr = (char far *) 0xB8000000; /* pointer
                                              to CGA memory */

  bit_mask.i=0xFF3F;     /* 11111111 00111111 in binary */

  /* check range for mode 4 */
  if(x<0 || x>199 || y<0 || y>319) return;

  xor=color_code & 128; /* see if xor mode is set */
  color_code = color_code & 127; /* mask off high bit */


  /* set bit_mask and color_code bits to the right location */
  bit_position = y%4;
  color_code<<=2*(3-bit_position);
  bit_mask.i>>=2*bit_position;


  /* find the correct byte in screen memory */
  index = x*40 +(y >> 2);
  if(x % 2) index += 8152; /* if odd use 2nd bank */

  /* write the color */
  if(!xor) { /* overwrite mode */
    t = *(ptr+index) & bit_mask.c[0];
```

```
      *(ptr+index) = t | color_code;
  }
  else { /* xor mode */
    t = *(ptr+index) | (char)0;
    *(ptr+index) = t ^ color_code;
  }
}


/* Set the video mode. */
void mode(mode_code)
int mode_code;
{
  union REGS r;

  r.h.al = mode_code;
  r.h.ah = 0;
  int86(0x10, &r, &r);
}

/* send the cursor to x,y */
void goto_xy(x, y)
int x, y;
{
  union REGS r;

  r.h.ah = 2; /* cursor addressing function */
  r.h.dl = y; /* column coordinate */
  r.h.dh = x; /* row coordinate */
  r.h.bh = 0; /* video page */
  int86(0x10, &r, &r);
}

/* Set the palette. */
void palette(pnum)
int pnum;
{
  union REGS r;

  r.h.bh = 1;   /* code for mode 4 graphics */
  r.h.bl = pnum;
  r.h.ah = 11;  /* set palette function */
  int86(0x10, &r, &r);
}
```

A GRAPHING PROGRAM

You can use the bar graph toolbox functions to construct a program that
allows the creation of bar charts. The program lets you enter the number
of sets of data, the number of entries per set, the names and the labels
associated with the data, and the thickness and spacing of the bars. Once

the information has been specified, the program automatically draws
the bar graph. You can also instruct the program to save the graph to a
disk file for later presentation.

The main( ) Function

The operation of the graph program is outlined in the code to the
main( ) function, shown here along with some macros.

```
#define MAX_SETS 3
#define MAX_ENTRIES 50
#define MAX_LABELS 20
#define MAX_NAMES 20

main()
{
  double v[MAX_SETS][MAX_ENTRIES]; /* holds the data */
  int num_entries;
  int num_sets;
  int min, max, i;
  int lines, offset;
  char save=0; /* save graph? */
  char names[MAX_NAMES][20];
  char lab[MAX_LABELS][20];

  /* read in the information */
  enter(v, &num_entries, &num_sets);

  /* find minimum and maximum values */
  min_max(v, num_entries, num_sets, &min, &max);

  /* get the names of what is being graphed */
  get_names(names, num_sets);

  /* get the labels for the graph */
  get_labels(lab, num_entries);

  /* get line thickness */
  lines = get_line_size();

  /* get the spacing between sets of data */
  offset = get_offset();

  /* save to disk file ? */
  printf("save the graph to disk file? (Y/N) ");
  if(tolower(getche())=='y') save = 1;

  mode(4); /* 320x200  graphics mode */
  palette(0);

  grid(min, max); /* display the grid */
  hashlines(); /* display dotted reference lines */
```

```
      label(lab, num_entries); /* label the graph */
      legend(names, num_sets); /* show the legend */

      /* plot the values */
      for(i=0; i<num_sets; i++)
        bargraph(v[i], num_entries, i*offset, min, max, lines);

      if(save) save_pic();
      getch();
      mode(3);
}
```

As you can see, **main( )** begins by declaring a number of variables that will have their values set by the user. The array **v** is defined to be large enough to hold three sets of data with up to 50 values per set. (These dimensions are arbitrary and you may change them if you like.) The function then reads in the data to display. Next, the minimum and maximum values to that data are found. After that, the grid, reference lines, names, and legend are displayed. Finally, the bars are plotted. Before exiting, the screen can be saved using the **save—pic( )** function developed for the paint program if desired. Let's look at some of the functions used by the program that are not part of the bar graph toolbox already developed.

The enter( ) Function

The **enter( )** function, shown here, is called with the address of the array that will receive the data and with the addresses of the variables that will receive the number of entries and the number of sets. The function begins by prompting the user for the number of sets followed by the number of entries. It then reads in the information for each set.

```
/* Enter values to be plotted */
enter(v, entries, sets)
double v[][MAX_ENTRIES]; /* data array */
int *entries; /* number of entries in each set of data */
int *sets; /* number of sets of data */
{
  int i, j, count, num;
  char s[80];

  printf("How many sets of data? (1 to %d) ", MAX_SETS);
  scanf("%d%c", &count, &j);
  if(count>MAX_SETS) count = MAX_SETS; /* prevent array overrun */
  *sets = count;
```

```
printf("How many entries? (1 to %d) ", MAX_ENTRIES);
scanf("%d%c", &num, &j);
if(num>MAX_SETS) num = MAX_ENTRIES; /* prevent array overrun */
*entries = num;

j = 0;

/* read in the values */
while((j<count)) {
  printf("Data set %d\n", j+1);
  for(i=0; i<num; i++) {
    printf("%d: ", i+1);
    gets(s);
    sscanf(s,"%lf", &v[j][i]);
  }
  j++;
}
return count;
}
```

The min—max( ) Function

Since the **bargraph**( ) function needs to know the minimum and maximum values of the data to be displayed, a function that determines these values is required. Because multiple sets of data may be plotted on the same grid, it is necessary to check each set of data in order to insure that the smallest minimum and the greatest maximum values are used. The min—max( ) function shown here along with its two support functions, accomplishes this task.

```
/* Find the smallest minimum and greatest maximum values
   among all the sets of data.
*/
void min_max(v, entries, sets, min, max)
double v[][MAX_ENTRIES]; /* values */
int entries; /* number of entries */
int sets; /* number of sets */
int *min, *max; /* return minimum and maximum values */
{
  int i, j;
  int tmin, tmax;

  *min = *max = 0;

  for(i=0; i<sets; i++) {
    tmax = getmax(v[i], entries);
    tmin = getmin(v[i], entries);
    if(tmax > *max) *max = tmax;
    if(tmin < *min) *min = tmin;
  }
}
```

```
/* Returns the maximum value of the data. */
getmax(data, num)
double *data;
int num;
{
  int t, max;

  max = (int) data[0];
  for(t=1; t<num; ++t)
    if(data[t]>max) max = (int) data[t];
  return max;
}

/* Returns the minimum value of the data. */
getmin(data, num)
double *data;
int num;
{
  int t, min;

  min = (int) data[0];
  for(t=1; t<num; ++t)
    if(data[t]<min) min = (int) data[t];
  return min;
}
```

The Entire Bar Graph Program

The entire bar graph program is shown here.

```
/* A bar graph generator program. */
#include "dos.h"

#include "stdio.h"

#define MAX_SETS 3
#define MAX_ENTRIES 50
#define MAX_LABELS 20
#define MAX_NAMES 20

void bargraph(), mode(), mempoint();
void line(), goto_xy(), grid(), label();
void hashlines(), legend(), read_cursor_xy();
void palette(), color_puts(), fill_box();
void get_labels(), get_names(), min_max();
void save_pic();

main()
{
  double v[MAX_SETS][MAX_ENTRIES]; /* holds the data */
  int num_entries;
  int num_sets;
  int min, max, i;
  int lines, offset;
```

```
      char save=0; /* save graph? */
      char names[MAX_NAMES][20];
      char lab[MAX_LABELS][20];

      /* read in the information */
      enter(v, &num_entries, &num_sets);

      /* find minimum and maximum values */
      min_max(v, num_entries, num_sets, &min, &max);

      /* get the names of what is being graphed */
      get_names(names, num_sets);

      /* get the labels for the graph */
      get_labels(lab, num_entries);

      /* get line thickness */
      lines = get_line_size();

      /* get the spacing between sets of data */
      offset = get_offset();

      /* save to disk file ? */
      printf("save the graph to disk file? (Y/N) ");
      if(tolower(getche())=='y') save = 1;
      mode(4); /* 320x200  graphics mode */
      palette(0);

      grid(min, max); /* display the grid */
      hashlines(); /* display dotted reference lines */
      label(lab, num_entries); /* label the graph */
      legend(names, num_sets); /* show the legend */

      /* plot the values */
      for(i=0; i<num_sets; i++)
        bargraph(v[i], num_entries, i*offset, min, max, lines);

      if(save) save_pic();
      getch();
      mode(3);
}

/* Enter values to be plotted */
enter(v, entries, sets)
double v[][MAX_ENTRIES]; /* data array */
int *entries; /* number of entries in each set of data */
int *sets; /* number of sets of data */
{
      int i, j, count, num;
      char s[80];

      printf("How many sets of data? (1 to %d) ", MAX_SETS);
      scanf("%d%c", &count, &j);
      if(count>MAX_SETS) count = MAX_SETS; /* prevent array overrun */
      *sets = count;

      printf("How many entries? (1 to %d) ", MAX_ENTRIES);
      scanf("%d%c", &num, &j);
      if(num>MAX_SETS) num = MAX_ENTRIES; /* prevent array overrun */
      *entries = num;

      j = 0;
```

```
      /* read in the values */
      while((j<count)) {
        printf("Data set %d\n", j+1);
        for(i=0; i<num; i++) {
          printf("%d: ", i+1);
          gets(s);
          sscanf(s,"%lf", &v[j][i]);
        }
        j++;
      }
      return count;
}

/* Input the names of the sets. */
void get_names(n, num)
char n[][20]; /* array for the names */
int num;   /* number of sets */
{
  int i;

  for(i=0; i<num; i++) {
    printf("Enter name: ");
    gets(n[i]);
  }
}

/* Input the label of each entry. */
void get_labels(l, num)
char l[][20]; /* array for the labels */
int num;   /* number of entries */
{
  int i;

  for(i=0; i<num; i++) {
    printf("Enter label: ");
    gets(l[i]);
  }
}

/* Input distance between bars in pixels */
get_offset()
{
  int i;

  printf("Enter distance between bars in pixels: ");
  scanf("%d%*c", &i);
  return i;
}

/* Input bar thickness in pixels */
get_line_size()
{
  int i;

  printf("Enter thickness of bars in pixels: ");
  scanf("%d", &i);
  return i;
}
```

```
/* Draw the chart grid. */
void grid(min, max)
int min, max;
{
  register int t;

  goto_xy(22, 0); printf("%d", min);
  goto_xy(0, 0); printf("%d", max);
  line(180, 10, 180, 300, 1);
}

/* Display labels on the screen. */
void label(str, num)
char str[][20]; /* strings to display */
int num; /* number of labels */
{
  int i, j, inc;

  inc = 38 / num;
  i = 2; /* initial horizontal starting point */
  for(j=0; j<num; j++) {
    goto_xy(23, i);
    printf(str[j]);
    i += inc;
  }
}

/* Draw dotted reference lines across the screen. */
void hashlines()
{
  int i, j;

  for(i=10; i<180; i+=10) {
    for(j=10; j<300; j+=5)
      mempoint(i, j, 3); /* one point every 5 pixels */
  }
}

/* Show a legend. */
void legend(names, num)
char names[][20];
int num; /* number of names */
{
  int color=1, i, j;

  goto_xy(24, 0); /* legend goes on bottom line */
  j = 0;
  for(i=0; i<num; i++) {
    /* print the label */
    printf("%s    ", names[i]);
    /* Compute where colored box goes by
       converting cursor location into graphics
       coordinates.  Each character is 8 pixels wide in
       mode 4 graphics.
    */
    j += strlen(names[i])*8+4;
    fill_box(192, j, 198, j+12, color);
    j += 28;  /* advance to next field */
```

```
      color++;
      if(color>3) color = 1;
   }
}

/* Display a bar chart. */
void bargraph(data, num, offset, min, max, width)
double *data; /* array of data */
int num; /* number of elements in array */
int offset; /* determine exact screen position */
int min, max; /* minimum and maximum values to be plotted */
int width; /* thickness of the lines */
{
  int y, t, incr;
  double norm_data, norm_ratio, spread;
  char s[80];
  static int color=0;
  int tempwidth;

  /* always use a different color */
  color++;
  if(color>3) color=1;

  /* determine normalization factor */
  spread = (double) max-min;
  norm_ratio = 180/spread;

  incr = 280/num; /* determine spacing between lines */
  tempwidth = width;
  for(t=0; t<num; ++t) {
    norm_data = data[t];

    /* adjust for negative values */
    norm_data = norm_data-(double) min;

    norm_data *= norm_ratio; /* normalize */
    y = (int) norm_data; /* type conversion */
    do {
      line(179, ((t*incr)+20+offset+width), 179-y,
        ((t*incr)+20+offset+width), color);
      width--;
    } while (width);
    width = tempwidth;
  }
}

/* Find the smallest minimum and greatest maximum values
   among all the sets of data.
*/
void min_max(v, entries, sets, min, max)
double v[][MAX_ENTRIES]; /* values */
int entries; /* number of entries */
int sets; /* number of sets */
int *min, *max; /* return minimum and maximum values */
{
  int i, j;
  int tmin, tmax;

  *min = *max = 0;
```

```
    for(i=0; i<sets; i++) {
        tmax = getmax(v[i], entries);
        tmin = getmin(v[i], entries);
        if(tmax > *max) *max = tmax;
        if(tmin < *min) *min = tmin;
    }
}


/* Returns the maximum value of the data. */
getmax(data, num)
double *data;
int num;
{
    int t, max;

    max = (int) data[0];
    for(t=1; t<num; ++t)
        if(data[t]>max) max = (int) data[t];
    return max;
}

/* Returns the minimum value of the data. */
getmin(data, num)
double *data;
int num;
{
    int t, min;

    min = (int) data[0];
    for(t=1; t<num; ++t)
        if(data[t]<min) min = (int) data[t];
    return min;
}

/* Draw a line in specified color
    using Bresenham's integer based algorithm.
*/
void line(startx, starty, endx, endy, color)
int startx, starty, endx, endy, color;
{
    register int t, distance;
    int x=0, y=0, delta_x, delta_y;
    int incx, incy;

    /* compute the distances in both directions */
    delta_x = endx-startx;
    delta_y = endy-starty;

    /* Compute the direction of the increment,
        an increment of 0 means either a vertical or horizontal
        line.
    */
    if(delta_x>0) incx = 1;
    else if(delta_x==0) incx = 0;
    else incx=-1;

    if(delta_y>0) incy = 1;
    else if(delta_y==0) incy = 0;
```

```
        else incy = -1;

        /* determine which distance is greater */
        delta_x = abs(delta_x);
        delta_y = abs(delta_y);
        if(delta_x>delta_y) distance = delta_x;
        else distance = delta_y;

        /* draw the line */
        for(t=0; t<=distance+1; t++) {
          mempoint(startx, starty, color);
          x+=delta_x;
          y+=delta_y;
          if(x>distance) {
            x-=distance;
            startx+=incx;
          }
          if(y>distance) {
            y-=distance;
            starty+=incy;
          }
        }
      }

/* Fill box with specified color. */
void fill_box(startx, starty, endx, endy, color_code)
int startx, starty, endx, endy, color_code;
{
  register int i, begin, end;

  begin = startx<endx ? startx : endx;
  end = startx>endx ? startx : endx;

  for(i=begin; i<=end;i++)
    line(i, starty, i, endy, color_code);
}


/* Write a point directly to the CGA/EGA */
void mempoint(x, y, color_code)
int x, y, color_code;
{
  union mask {
    char c[2];
    int i;
  } bit_mask;
  int i, index, bit_position;
  unsigned char t;
  char xor; /* xor color in or overwrite */
  char far *ptr = (char far *) 0xB8000000; /* pointer
                                              to CGA memory */

  bit_mask.i=0xFF3F;      /* 11111111 00111111 in binary */

  /* check range for mode 4 */
  if(x<0 || x>199 || y<0 || y>319) return;

  xor=color_code & 128; /* see if xor mode is set */
  color_code = color_code & 127; /* mask off high bit */
```

```c
  /* set bit_mask and color_code bits to the right location */
  bit_position = y%4;
  color_code<<=2*(3-bit_position);
  bit_mask.i>>=2*bit_position;


  /* find the correct byte in screen memory */
  index = x*40 +(y >> 2);
  if(x % 2) index += 8152; /* if odd use 2nd bank */

  /* write the color */
  if(!xor) { /* overwrite mode */
    t = *(ptr+index) & bit_mask.c[0];
    *(ptr+index) = t | color_code;
  }
  else { /* xor mode */
    t = *(ptr+index) | (char)0;
    *(ptr+index) = t ^ color_code;
  }
}


/* Set the video mode. */
void mode(mode_code)
int mode_code;
{
  union REGS r;

  r.h.al = mode_code;
  r.h.ah = 0;
  int86(0x10, &r, &r);
}

/* send the cursor to x,y */
void goto_xy(x, y)
int x, y;
{
  union REGS r;

  r.h.ah = 2; /* cursor addressing function */
  r.h.dl = y; /* column coordinate */
  r.h.dh = x; /* row coordinate */
  r.h.bh = 0; /* video page */
  int86(0x10, &r, &r);
}

/* Set the palette. */
void palette(pnum)
int pnum;
{
  union REGS r;

  r.h.bh = 1;   /* code for mode 4 graphics */
  r.h.bl = pnum;
  r.h.ah = 11; /* set palette function */
  int86(0x10, &r, &r);
}

/* save the video graphics display */
```

```
void save_pic()
{
  char fname[80];
  FILE *fp;
  register int i, j;
  char far *ptr = (char far *) 0xB8000000; /* pointer
                                              to CGA memory */
  char far *temp;
  unsigned char buf[14][80]; /* hold the contents of screen */

  temp = ptr;
  /* save the top of the current screen */
  for(i=0; i<14; i++)
    for(j=0; j<80; j+=2) {
      buf[i][j] = *temp; /* even byte */
      buf[i][j+1] = *(temp+8152); /* odd byte */
      *temp = 0; *(temp+8152) = 0;  /* clear top of screen */
      temp++;
    }

  goto_xy(0, 0);
  printf("Filename: ");
  gets(fname);
  if(!(fp=fopen(fname, "wb"))) {
    printf("cannot open file\n");
    return;
  }

  temp = ptr;
  /* restore the top of the current screen */
  for(i=0; i<14; i++)
    for(j=0; j<80; j+=2) {
      *temp = buf[i][j];
      *(temp+8152) = buf[i][j+1];
      temp++;
    }

/* save image to file */
for(i=0; i<8152; i++) {
   putc(*ptr, fp); /* even byte */
   putc(*(ptr+8152), fp); /* odd byte */
   ptr++;
}

  fclose(fp);
}
```

DISPLAYING GRAPHS

If you request that the bar graph program save the graph to a disk file, you can redisplay it using the short program, called SHOW, developed in this section. The program displays the graph whose file name is specified as a command line argument. For example, to display a graph called

BACKLOG, you would use this command:

SHOW BACKLOG

The program uses the **load_pic**( ) function developed for the paint program to display a graph on the screen. (You can also use this program to display graphics images created and saved by the paint program.)

```c
/* A simple graphics presentation program. */

#include "stdio.h"
#include "dos.h"

void load_pic(), mode(), palette(), goto_xy();

main(argc, argv)
int argc;
char *argv[];
{
  if(argc!=2) {
    printf("usage: show <filename>");
    exit(1);
  }
  mode(4);
  palette(0);
  load_pic(argv[1]);
  getch();
  mode(3);
}

/* load the video graphics display */
void load_pic(fname)
char *fname;
{
  FILE *fp;
  register int i, j;
  char far *ptr = (char far *) 0xB8000000; /* pointer
                                              to CGA memory */
  char far *temp;
  unsigned char buf[14][80]; /* hold the contents of screen */

  if(!(fp=fopen(fname, "rb"))) {
    goto_xy(0, 0);
    printf("cannot open file\n");
    return;
  }

  /* load image from file */
  for(i=0; i<8152; i++) {
    *ptr = getc(fp); /* even byte */
    *(ptr+8152) = getc(fp); /* odd byte */
    ptr++;
  }
```

```
        fclose(fp);
}

/* Set the video mode. */
void mode(mode_code)
int mode_code;
{
   union REGS r;

   r.h.al = mode_code;
   r.h.ah = 0;
   int86(0x10, &r, &r);
}

/* Set the palette. */
void palette(pnum)
int pnum;
{
   union REGS r;

   r.h.bh = 1;    /* code for mode 4 graphics */
   r.h.bl = pnum;
   r.h.ah = 11;   /* set palette function */
   int86(0x10, &r, &r);
}

/* send the cursor to x,y */
void goto_xy(x, y)
int x, y;
{
   union REGS r;

   r.h.ah = 2; /* cursor addressing function */
   r.h.dl = y; /* column coordinate */
   r.h.dh = x; /* row coordinate */
   r.h.bh = 0; /* video page */
   int86(0x10, &r, &r);
}
```

SOME INTERESTING EXPERIMENTS

The value of the bar graph functions can be enhanced by parameterizing the dimensions and location of the graph so that graphs of different sizes and locations can be created. For example, it might be useful to create four small graphs, each using its own quadrant of the screen, as a way to display four sets of related information. You might also want to make the routines work with the higher resolution graphics modes. Finally, you may wish to add scatter and pie graph capabilities.

Trademarks

AT®	International Business Machines Corporation
IBM®	International Business Machines Corporation
Microsoft®	Microsoft Corporation
PS/2™	International Business Machines Corporation
Turbo C®	Borland International, Inc.

Index

The manuscript for this book was prepared and submitted to Osborne/McGraw-Hill in electronic form.

The acquisitions editor for this project was Jeffrey Pepper. The technical reviewer was Werner Feibel. Lyn Cordell was the project editor.

Text design is by Judy Wohlfrom using Garamond for both text and display.

Cover art is by Bay Graphics Design Associates. Cover supplier is Phoenix Color Corporation. This book was printed and bound by R.R. Donnelley & Sons Company, Crawfordsville, Indiana.

Other related Osborne/McGraw-Hill titles include:

Artificial Intelligence Using C
by Herb Schildt

With Herb Schildt's newest book, you can add a powerful dimension to your C programs—artificial intelligence. Schildt, a programming expert and author of seven Osborne books, shows C programmers how to use AI techniques that have traditionally been implemented with Prolog and LISP. You'll utilize AI for vision, pattern recognition, robotics, machine learning, logic, problem solving, and natural language processing. Each chapter develops practical examples that can be used in the construction of artificial intelligence applications. If you are building expert systems in C, this book contains a complete expert system that can easily be adapted to your needs. Schildt provides valuable insights that allow even greater command of the systems you create.

$21.95 p
0-07-881255-0, 360 pp., 7⅜ x 9¼

Advanced Graphics in C:
Programming and Techniques
by Nelson Johnson

Add graphics to your C programs, and you'll add significantly to your programming skills and to the effectiveness of your software. With *Advanced Graphics in C* you'll write graphics program for the IBM® EGA (enhanced graphics adapter). This guide offers a complete toolkit of all the routines you'll need for such graphics operations as drawing a line, an arc, or a circle; plotting; and filling in shapes. A complete sample graphics program with a rotatable and scalable character set is included. All the code is provided so that you can easily create the graphics you need. Johnson also includes instructions for interrupt-driven serial and parallel interfacing to mice, light pens, and digitizers. You'll learn state-of-the-art techniques from Johnson, a software developer, author, and worldwide lecturer.

$22.95 p
0-07-881257-7, 430 pp., 7⅜ x 9¼

Using Turbo C®
by Herbert Schildt

Here's the official book on Borland's tremendous new C compiler. *Using Turbo C®* is for all C programmers, from beginners to seasoned pros. Master programmer Herb Schildt devotes the first part of the book to helping you get started in Turbo C. If you've been programming in Turbo Pascal® or another language, this orientation will lead you right into Turbo C fundamentals. Schildt's emphasis on good programming structure will start you out designing programs for greater efficiency. With these basics, you'll move on to more advanced concepts such as pointers and dynamic allocation, compiler directives, unions, bitfields, and enumerations, and you'll learn about Turbo C graphics. When you've finished *Using Turbo C®*, you'll be writing full-fledged programs that get professional results.

$19.95 p
0-07-881279-8, 350 pp., 7⅜ x 9¼
The Borland-Osborne/McGraw-Hill
Programming Series

Advanced Turbo C®
by Herbert Schildt

Ready for power programming with Turbo C®? You'll find the expertise you need in *Advanced Turbo C®*, the Borland/Osborne book with the inside edge. In this instruction guide and lasting reference, Herb Schildt, the author of five acclaimed books on C, takes you the final step on the way to Turbo C mastery. Each stand-alone chapter presents a complete discussion of a Turbo C programming topic so you can pinpoint the information you need immediately. *Advanced Turbo C®* thoroughly covers sorting and searching; stacks, queues, linked lists, and binary trees; operating system interfacing; statistics; encryption and compressed data formats; random numbers and simulations; and expression parsers. In addition, you'll learn about converting Turbo Pascal® to Turbo C and using Turbo C graphics. *Advanced Turbo C®* shows you how to put the amazing compilation speed of Turbo C into action on your programs.

$22.95 p
0-07-881280-1, 325 pp., 7⅜ x 9¼
The Borland-Osborne/McGraw-Hill
Programming Series

Using Turbo Pascal®

by Steve Wood

Using Turbo Pascal® gives you a head start with Borland's acclaimed compiler, which has become a worldwide standard. Programmer Steve Wood has completely rewritten the text and now provides programming examples that run under MS-DOS®, as well as new information on memory resident applications, in-line code, interrupts, and DOS functions. If you're already programming in Pascal or any other high-level language, you'll be able to write programs that are more efficient than ever. *Using Turbo Pascal®* discusses program design and Pascal's syntax requirements, and thoroughly explores Turbo Pascal's features. Then Wood develops useful applications and gives you an overview of some of the advanced utilities and features available with Turbo Pascal. *Using Turbo Pascal®* gives you the skills to become a productive programmer—and when you're ready for more, you're ready for *Advanced Turbo Pascal®*.

$19.95 p
0-07-881284-4, 350 pp., 7⅜ x 9¼
The Borland-Osborne/McGraw-Hill Programming Series

Advanced Turbo Prolog™ Version 1.1

by Herbert Schildt

Herb Schildt now applies his expertise to Borland's remarkable Turbo Prolog™ language development system, specifically designed for fifth-generation language programming and the creation of artificial intelligence on your IBM® PC. *Advanced Turbo Prolog™* has been extensively revised to include Turbo Prolog version 1.1. The new Turbo Prolog Toolbox™, which offers more than 80 tools and 8,000 lines of source code, is also described in detail. Schildt focuses on helping you progress from intermediate to advanced techniques by considering typical AI problems and their solutions. Numerous sample programs and graphics are used throughout the text to sharpen your skills and enhance your understanding of the central issues involved in AI. Expert systems, problem solving, natural language processing, vision and pattern recognition, robotics, and logic are some of the applications that Schildt explains as he leads you to Turbo Prolog mastery.

$21.95 p
0-07-881285-2, 350 pp., 7⅜ x 9¼
The Borland-Osborne/McGraw-Hill Programming Series

Advanced Turbo Pascal®

by Herbert Schildt

Advanced Turbo Pascal® is the book you need to learn superior programming skills for the leading Pascal language development system. Revised and expanded, *Advanced Turbo Pascal®* now covers Borland's newly released Turbo Database Toolbox®, which speeds up database searching and sorting, and the Turbo Graphix Toolbox®, which lets you easily create high-resolution graphics. And, *Advanced Turbo Pascal®* includes techniques for converting Turbo Pascal for use with Borland's hot new compiler, Turbo C®. Schildt provides many programming tips to take you on your way to high performance with Turbo Pascal. You'll refine your skills with techniques for sorting and searching; stacks, queues, linked lists and binary trees; dynamic allocations; expression parsing; simulation; interfacing to assembly language routines; and efficiency, porting, and debugging. For instruction and reference, *Advanced Turbo Pascal®* is the best single resource for serious programmers.

$21.95 p
0-07-881283-6, 350 pp., 7⅜ x 9¼
The Borland-Osborne/McGraw-Hill Programming Series

Using Turbo BASIC®

by Frederick E. Mosher and David I. Schneider

Using Turbo BASIC® is your authoritative guide to Borland's incredible new compiler that offers faster compilation speeds than any other product on the market. *Using Turbo BASIC®* is packed with information for everyone from novices to seasoned programmers. Authors Mosher and Schneider, two accomplished programmers, introduce you to the Turbo BASIC® operating environment on the IBM® PC and PC-compatibles, and discuss the interactive editor and the BASIC language itself. You'll learn about recursion, math functions, graphics and sound functions, and conversions from IBM BASICA to Turbo BASIC. With this excellent step-by-step guide to Borland's new compiler, you'll have the extraordinary power of Turbo BASIC at your fingertips.

$19.95 p
0-07-881282-8, 350 pp., 7⅜ x 9¼
The Borland-Osborne/McGraw-Hill Programming Series

C: The Complete Reference
by Herbert Schildt

Once again Osborne's master C programmer and author Herb Schildt, shares his insight and expertise with all C programmers in his latest book, *C: The Complete Reference*. Designed for both beginning and advanced C programmers, this is an encyclopedia for C terms, functions, codes, applications, and more. *C: The Complete Reference* is divided into five parts, each covering an important aspect of C. Part one covers review material and discusses key words in C. Part two presents an extensive summary of C libraries by category. Part three concentrates on various algorithms and C applications and includes information on random number generators as well as artificial intelligence and graphics. Part four addresses interfacing efficiency, porting, and debugging. Finally, part five is for serious programmers who are interested in C++, C's latest direction. The book also includes complete information on the proposed ANSI standard

$27.95 p, Hardcover Edition
0-07-881313-1, 740 pp., 7³⁄₈ x 9¹⁄₄

$24.95 p, Paperback Edition
0-07-881263-1, 740 pp., 7³⁄₈ x 9¹⁄₄

1-2-3®: The Complete Reference
by Mary Campbell

1-2-3®: The Complete Reference is the authoritative desktop companion for every Lotus® 1-2-3® user. All commands, functions, and procedures are explained in detail and are demonstrated in practical "real-world" business applications. Conventionally organized according to task, this essential reference makes it easy to locate information on topics such as printing, macros, graphics production, and data mangement. Each chapter thoroughly describes a 1-2-3 task and all the procedures it requires, followed by an alphabetical listing of every command or function applied. Special emphasis is placed on compatible software packages, including Report Writer™, Reflex™ and others, that you can use to extend 1-2-3's capabilities. Campbell, a consultant and writer whose magazine columns appear monthly in *IBM PC UPDATE*, *Absolute Reference*, and *CPA Journal*, draws on her years of 1-2-3 expertise to provide you with this outstanding, comprehensive resource.

$25.95 p, Hardcover Edition
0-07-881288-7, 928 pp., 7³⁄₈ x 9¹⁄₄

$22.95 p, Paperback Edition
0-07-881005-1, 928 pp., 7³⁄₈ x 9¹⁄₄

Available at fine bookstores and computer stores everywhere.

For a complimentary catalog of all our current publications contact:
Osborne/McGraw-Hill, 2600 Tenth Street, Berkeley, CA 94710

Phone inquiries may be made using our toll-free number.
Call 800-227-0900 or 800-772-2531 (in California). TWX 910-366-7277.

Prices subject to change without notice.